CONDOR BLUES

CONDOR BLUES

British Soldiers at War

Mark Nicol

MAINSTREAM
PUBLISHING

EDINBURGH AND LONDON

Copyright © Mark Nicol, 2007
All rights reserved
The moral right of the author has been asserted

First published in Great Britain in 2007 by
MAINSTREAM PUBLISHING COMPANY (EDINBURGH) LTD
7 Albany Street
Edinburgh EH1 3UG

ISBN 9781845962333

A catalogue record for this book is
available from the British Library

Typeset in Stone Serif and Univers

Printed in Great Britain by
William Clowes Ltd, Beccles, Suffolk

NO THANKS GIVEN

I am he whom others do not want to be and I go where
    others fear to go.
I do what others have failed to do and I ask nothing
    from those who give nothing.
I accept, reluctantly, the thought of eternal loneliness
    should I fail.

I have seen the face of terror.

I have felt the stinging cold of fear and enjoyed the
    sweet taste of a moment's love.

I have cried, pained and hoped.
But most of all I have lived times others would say were
    best forgotten.

This day, I am proud of who I am.

I am an infantry soldier.

This poem was pinned to the wall at Camp Condor.
The identity of its author is unknown

Contents

Author's Note

All the material in this book not derived from documentary evidence is the result of numerous interviews with the characters from October 2005 to December 2006. Those protagonists I was unable to communicate with directly were described in detail by their colleagues and friends. I spent time in Maysan Province, Iraq, in June 2004, researching *Last Round*, my account of the deaths of the six Red Caps in Majar al-Kabir. This tragedy occurred in June 2003. The action in *Condor Blues* begins early the following year only a few kilometres from that town. While I have sought to create an evocative, lyrical narrative, I have also stayed true to the facts. Thus, *Condor Blues* is a work of non-fiction.

Preface

In October 2006 rival militias fought running battles for control of Al Amarah, Iraq, following the withdrawal of the British battlegroup from just outside the city. In the face of intense fighting between the Mahdi Army and Badr Brigades local police withdrew, and for the first time the militias threatened to bring anarchy to the capital of Maysan Province. The only option besides British forces storming Al Amarah in tanks was to deploy the Iraqi National Guard. The 605th and 606th Battalions confronted hundreds of gunmen, and after a series of skirmishes, order was restored. They had passed the most demanding test of their short history.

The process of training the Iraqi National Guard, originally known as the Iraqi Civil Defence Corps (ICDC), had really got going two and a half years previously, in the spring and summer of 2004, when platoons from the 1st Battalion, the Argyll and Sutherland Highlanders, embedded with recruits at the isolated Camp Condor.

This is the time and setting for *Condor Blues*. The characters are working-class junior soldiers, their 'Angry Dad' sergeant and a clique of well-heeled officers. The ICDC were a fledgling organisation drawn from a corrupt, tribally divided society; the Argylls were thrown into the most absurd and dangerous of situations. This is an uncensored account of self-discovery, courage and fear. Some of their behaviour was regrettable. I ask the reader not to judge individuals harshly. This was the land dubbed 'Hell with flies'.

Condor Blues includes criticisms by senior officers of how the British Army responded to the Shia uprisings of 2004 with too much 'heavy metal' and insufficient dialogue and empathy. Such tactics dismayed the likes of Lieutenant Colonel Jonny Gray, the commanding officer of the Argylls. The British Army prides itself on its intelligent approach to conflict, yet hundreds of the very people whose hearts and minds commanders were seeking to win were killed. This was to the dismay of the Argylls' hierarchy, as one of its senior officers remarked: 'We were there to encourage peace, not to start another war. It was about understanding the culture, people and customs, not trying to conquer. A different approach to dealing with the insurgents and their leadership could have produced different results.'

There has been little objective analysis of British operations in the post-invasion period, while the two major book titles covering this era, Richard Holmes's *Dusty Warriors* and Private Johnson Beharry VC's *Barefoot Soldier*, were both Ministry-of-Defence-vetted projects.

Mark Nicol
London, January 2007

1

A Recce for the Knife

One of the challenges of setting up a five-thousand-strong army from scratch within six months was to understand what we were creating. Our understanding of the cultural, tribal, religious and social issues prevailing in southern Iraq was rather superficial. This was a volume business, and we needed to recruit thousands of people. I took time to select a brigade commander, his deputy and the battalion COs [commanding officers]. I felt if we got these appointments right, then they would help us create an army whose first loyalty was to the new Iraq. I interviewed a wide range of candidates, some proffered by local dignitaries with their own agendas. We were able to rule a number of people out. This process seemed to work, but I became aware that all these officers were playing the long game. I never fully understood their long-term agendas and loyalties.

Lieutenant Colonel J.D. Gray

Friday, 5 March 2004

'Why the hell are you pointing a loaded weapon at them?' asked Sergeant Paul Kelly, his eyes bulging. 'What's your problem?'

'This bloke tried to leave the pen and go and talk to his friend,' replied Private Elliott, keeping his rifle and eyes trained on the recruits.

'Lower your weapon, now.' When Elliott failed to respond, Kelly grabbed his rifle with one hand and his throat with the other. It had taken four hours to place the correct number of volunteers for the Iraqi Civil Defence Corps (ICDC) into pens marked out on the ground with white tape. It was now noon, and the sun was very hot above them. 'Do you realise what you are doing here? They're getting pretty pissed off, and there's a lot more of them than us.'

The 606th ICDC Battalion recruits spilled out of their squares and pushed each other. Adrenalin surged inside Elliott, and he gripped his gun like it was something precious. 'Let me go,' he replied, wanting no part of a truce.

'Do you understand?'

'Let me go!'

Kelly's fingers tightened to squeeze the petulance from Elliott's voice. Feeling his sergeant's violent grip, the private realised this was a contest he could not win.

'I'll have to deal with you later,' Kelly said, relaxing his hand. 'Corporal.' He signalled to one of his junior non-commissioned officers. 'Take him back to Camp Condor.' Kelly fired Elliott a disdainful look as he was dragged away.

'Safar, Safar,' Kelly bellowed. The interpreter approached with hunched shoulders. 'Tell them that we appreciate the fact they're tired. But can they please just put up with it for a bit longer? Then they'll be paid.'

Former Iraqi Army soldiers among the volunteers had been evenly distributed between platoons. This had caused disruption, as it ran contrary to tribal and family allegiances. The recruits had, meanwhile, taken full advantage of the commotion. Their displeasure had been a constant that morning; now they walked freely between pens.

'We're almost finished,' Kelly told Major Sabeer, the intimidating ICDC company commander. Sabeer's dark eyebrows lifted in acknowledgement. 'I will see this doesn't happen again. We're on the same side, Major Sabeer. Please tell them to sit back in their squares.'

'Very well, Sergeant Kelly.'

Although his uniform stank of cigarettes and sweat, there was a well-worn dignity about Sabeer, abetted by his heavy moustache. Whether he addressed the ICDC or British officers, he spoke with the authority of a leading actor whose every word was mined from deep within. Kelly respected him as a man not dissimilar to himself.

Sabeer was said to have had an impressive career in the Iraqi Army – a little too impressive, perhaps – and Saddam Hussein, to whom he bore a resemblance, had rewarded his gallantry during the Iran–Iraq War with a gleaming Cadillac. Sabeer had later dissented from the Ba'athist regime, was imprisoned and tortured. His forearms were as thick as a galley slave's, his skin tarnished with burns. The Condorites reckoned he looked like a man who had suffered psychological as well as physical traumas. They were undecided as to whether he thought himself immortal or had a death wish. Whichever, he raised two fingers to danger. Yet his listless charges seemed incapable of conducting effective military tasks. Did they not understand his commands, Sabeer wondered? They nodded like village idiots when he briefed them. Was there a breakdown in communication between their minds and bodies? Whatever the explanation, their performance thus far disappointed.

There was a life study to be made of the ICDC, with their affectionate greetings and easy duplicity. Those waving their arms about and refusing to return to where they had been seated were the elite. Among those who had attended the initial recruitment day were a one-legged man and another who had defecated while standing in the enlistment queue. ICDC recruiting was a job-creation scheme. Most of the officers and senior non-commissioned officers were former members of the disbanded Iraqi armed forces, but they could not all have belonged to Special Forces, as so many claimed. The ICDC selection criteria were basic: so long as the recruit was medically fit, could jog 100 metres (and this was a great struggle for many) and write his name, he was selected. If the applicant said he had been a corporal in the Iraqi Army and there was no obvious reason why this could not have been the case, he was accepted at his word. The fact that some recruits had no military experience brought ignorance but also a freshness and enthusiasm to the ranks of the ICDC. The edict issued by the Coalition Provisional Authority that 10 per cent of the candidates should be women was rejected as unworkable.

The relationship between the ICDC and their mentors had developed into one of mutual suspicion. It was too dangerous to issue live rounds to Sabeer's men; friend could not be told from foe and the safety catch on Kelly's rifle was permanently off. Today was the first time he had seen Sabeer's 7.62 mm pistol slung low around his rotund frame. He recognised it as a prop of power. Such a big iron said 'Don't fuck with me'.

A Land-Rover drove into the camp, coming to a standstill next to Kelly, its engine panting like an exhausted dog. Tommo was behind the wheel. 'Hello, mate,' Kelly barked. 'How's it going?'

'Listen, Major Faux's in a bit of bother in Qalat Salih,' Private Ben 'Tommo' Thomas replied.

'Yeah?'

'He's got the quick-reaction force called out from Abu Naji. We could supply a couple of teams from here as well?'

The thought of an afternoon away from the ICDC cheered Kelly. This was in spite of the fact that Qalat Salih was one of the most dangerous towns in Maysan Province. 'Definitely. Let me warn off Lieutenant Passmore and we'll head down.'

Tommo's co-driver joined the conversation. 'Hello, Paul. The Light Infantry were on a mobile patrol and came under fire from the police station or somewhere nearby. They caught the one who opened up on them, and it was a local policeman!'

'Typical.'

'They've arrested him, and he's in the Badr building. It's getting more hostile down there – crowd developing, and that.'

'OK,' said Kelly, 'get back on the radio and tell Major Faux we'll be down shortly.'

'Slim pickings,' he thought. Kelly wanted two fire teams of five men, but as most of his soldiers were on ICDC duty he was shorthanded. 'Loz, get your kit. Tommo, get your kit. You, you, you and, er, you, get in the vehicles. Let's go.'

One soldier who should have queued to mount a Land-Rover instead cut away towards the Ops Room. 'Oi! Where the fuck are you going?'

'Just getting my Gimpy [General Purpose Machine Gun], Sergeant Kelly.'

'Get the fuck over here, you muppet. Got a rifle, haven't you? Let's just go.' The privates had grown accustomed to such verbal reprimands. A more severe telling off was known as a 'gripping', or worse a 'throat rashing'.

The two Land-Rovers swung out of Camp Condor. Kelly drove the first, Corporal 'Loz' Loseby the second. They slowed when they passed the ICDC training area and accommodation blocks. 'Hello, anyone? Hello, anyone?' Kelly spoke into the mini-microphone which rested above his jaw. 'Hello, hello, somebody listen to me. Why haven't those mongs got their headsets on?' As the concrete walls of Sabeer's office blocked Personal Role Radio (PRR) broadcasts, Lieutenant James Passmore and Corporal Alan 'Neneh' Cherry had removed their headsets. 'Hello? I don't believe this is happening. Is nobody listening?' His passengers kept their counsel as he leant out the window. 'Oi, you fuckin' muppets. Turn a PRR on.' Kelly shouted again, this time pointing to his ear. 'Bollocks!' He shook his head. 'Let's just fucking get out of here.'

The ICDC were at last being paid by Sabeer. There was enough local currency in his mail sack for any of the volunteers to start a new life. Had he been a less dominant character, they would have stolen the money. Neneh suggested that if the recruits had been paid in dollars he would have been 'in and aboot it, because nothing was accounted for'.

Sabeer resurfaced from beneath his desk with fistfuls of Iraqi dinars. His attitude and appearance shouted 'Go on, try your luck. You and your whole tribe against me.' This was dog psychology: intimidate or be intimidated; kill or be killed. The Iraqis were not scared of him because of his rank, which meant little or nothing to them; they feared him because if they crossed him, or tried to, he would shoot them. The other ICDC officers hated Sabeer because he did not play by their rules. In a bid to have him removed from the hierarchy, they made accusations of theft against him to the British.

Neneh trusted him in a way that ran contrary to his attitude towards Sabeer's colleagues and the ICDC mission. To share military tactics with those who might use them against him offended his every notion of personal security. Neneh's reluctance to embrace the concept of operations was compounded by the fact that there were only 30 lightly armed British soldiers at Condor surrounded by hundreds of Iraqi recruits whose allegiances were unknown.

As his nickname suggested, he was old enough to remember the female singer Neneh Cherry, although his musical tastes leant towards Depeche Mode. As most of the Jocks – the Argyll private soldiers – were born after her period of fame, it was tiresome to explain the origin of his moniker. Neneh had become a father at 16, and his youngest soldiers were only slightly older than his daughter. He was naturally parental towards them, as well as informal. The naked weapons-handling test was one of his initiation ceremonies. Rifles would be laid on the floor in front of the wee Jocks, their faces as white as slices of bread, as they sat hunched in a semi-circle. Their instructor would then appear before them naked but for his boots and a webbing belt. 'Right, lads. First thing is, all youse strip off!'

Arriving at Condor as a new private soldier was akin to arriving at the infantry training depot on their first day in the army. Neneh would try to welcome them to the party but was just so big and at ease with himself he could be overwhelming. He would stand there, letting his comment sink in.

Barely adult, they were beginning a life-defining tour of duty in a country where it was better not to live in the fullest sense of the word, not consciously at least, but just to survive. They lived secretly with their fears, unsure what they should say and how they should conduct themselves. Raised on a diet of Mars bars and chips, the youngest Jocks looked around 14 years old.

The carrot the army dangled before them was two weeks of 'R 'n' R' at the Shaibah Logistics Base at the conclusion of their tours. The base was little more than a supermarket, a pizza restaurant and a flushing toilet, but from 150 km up Route 6 it assumed mirage-like proportions. Stories fuelled expectations. No media organisation could induce the Ministry of Defence to quantify how many female service personnel had been withdrawn from southern Iraq having fallen pregnant, but a fair proportion of these conceptions had occurred at Shaibah. There were also DVDs in circulation of non-commissioned officers having sex with female soldiers in four-tonne trucks, the only place they could get any privacy. Although no Condorite provided first-hand testimony, it was claimed a few female personnel at Shaibah traded oral sex for phone cards in order to call their boyfriends in the UK.

Not all the Condorites would make it to 'Shaibah-Napa' or 'Shaih-Ibiza'. Many would have their tours shortened by wounds sustained in battle. There were also soldiers who failed to return after their fortnight's leave in the UK. It was popular among those who absconded to suggest that they had contracted post-traumatic stress disorder. To those still in Iraq, this was a 'get out of jail free card', cynically used by 'shirkers' to the detriment of soldiers genuinely affected by combat stress. Battalion headquarters attempted to lure them back, but this was not an issue on which anyone wanted to shine a light. The location of battalion headquarters in Canterbury, 500 miles to the south-east, was unhelpful to a Scottish regiment, particularly where welfare issues were concerned.

After visiting Condor only a few weeks before the tour's end, a psychologist concluded, 'You're probably the craziest guys I've met. But you are also the sanest people in this country.' Those who had missed the biggest enemy engagements and had never fired their weapons in anger were among the worst affected. All their frustration had remained pent up, and no amount of illicit boozing or Viagra could release it. They would return to Britain as combat virgins. They knew the first question their friends would ask.

Neneh's family home north of the Solway Firth offered no clue as to his profession. He did not think it unusual, but it was rare for soldiers not to display medals, regimental paraphernalia or pictures of themselves in uniform. 'I was an electrician for four years before I signed up,' Neneh explained. 'I don't remember chrome-plating my pliers and putting them up on the wall. I know I'm in the army, and I don't need reminding.' He chuckled at Kelly's preoccupation with soldiering and thought 'Angry Dad', as his Condor 'children' had christened him, displayed obsessive-compulsive disorder tendencies. They complemented each other by virtue of their differences and offered a balance of command within the platoon. With the geometry of the camp so confined, personality clashes could be cancerous: differences had to be settled swiftly and, if necessary, painfully.

Condor was more vulnerable than the battlegroup headquarters at Camp Abu Naji, and an enemy attack would overwhelm the camp before any rescue party could arrive. In such a nightmare scenario, it was predicted that the ICDC would flee. Some of their number had expressed the wish to remain neutral. They would defend Iraq but wanted to sit out the contest between Coalition Forces and the insurgents.

Desperate ideas had been discussed for the defence of the camp, such as placing every weapon on top of the perimeter wall to give the impression of a stronger defensive force. Neneh's commanding officer, the erudite Lieutenant Colonel Jonathan Gray, was more sanguine. He had first flown over the camp in a helicopter a few months before the rest of his troops deployed, leading an advance party of Argyll and Sutherland Highlanders on a reconnaissance mission of the area. He regarded the security situation then as 'stable and benign'. While lawlessness and violence were endemic, little of it was directed at British forces. Gray saw Condor as an ideal base for the six-month process of recruiting, training, mentoring and monitoring the ICDC. He envisaged that his Jocks would not just train the Iraqis but live alongside them, play football with them, laugh and joke with them, and become their trusted mentors. He considered this essential to the new national guards gaining the necessary confidence to see the job through. As he put it, such a strategy was the sine qua non of his concept of operations, especially given the fierce tribal loyalties in southern Iraq. Gray's buzzword for the ICDC was 'adequacy'; their shortcomings were to be excused.

'When I thought about everything that went into creating an army, it was unbelievably challenging,' he said. 'This army needed weapons, radios, uniforms, barracks, food, vehicles, fuel, policy, rules of engagement and a rank structure.

'Status in local villages was undoubtedly a factor in who was given what rank. It was also the case that a second lieutenant needed more authority than his rank in the British Army bestowed to command an Iraqi company. So they were promoted. The Iraqis seemed to respond to the rank of captain. So every British lieutenant was given this local rank. Of course, had the Iraqi Army not been disbanded there would not have been the need to form the ICDC. My confidence that it could work was based on the fact that Iraqis wanted security and jobs. The ICDC offered both.'

Gray and his non-commissioned officers would have to agree to differ on that, as they did about a great deal.

Dark humour prevailed at Camp Condor, and the narrower the shave with death, the funnier the yarn. One lazy afternoon, Kelly, Passmore and Private Bains had a shooting contest with AK47s on the adjacent airfield. Bains selected as a target a rusting metal object, shaped like a tuna can but twice the size, and placed it on top of the bund line – a raised muddy bank. Last of the trio to shoot, Bains's first round brought him victory. He held his trophy aloft and noticed the wires which protruded from it. Back at Condor he told everyone how he had out-shot his sergeant and platoon commander. His can was kicked around the television room for weeks until it was Private Kev Challis's day to clean the camp. He knew a few people had their suspicions about this can and had been throwing it against the walls, thinking it might have been a mine and they could make it explode. All the rubbish was disposed of in a burns pit, so Kev threw the can onto the pile, anticipating a blast. Nothing happened, and he walked off. A few minutes later, the camp was shaken by a detonation. He ran back to the pit to see litter falling from the sky and a crater in the ground. Everybody ran towards him.

'What happened?'

'What the fuck was that?'

'Oh, I just threw a mine onto the burns pit,' Kev said, as though it was nothing.

'You what?'

'I thought it was dead, like . . . well, maybe. It was smashed up a bit, and people had been sticking screwdrivers into it and nothing had happened . . .'

He and some other Princess of Wales's Royal Regiment (PWRR) bods were standing in a half circle near the fire when Neneh arrived, naked as usual. 'OK, first things first, just tell me naebody has been killed.'

'No, corporal. Challis just threw the can onto the fire.'

'Fucking typical of you, that is, Challis, ya bell end.'

Seconds later, Lance Corporal Mark 'Keegs' Keegan arrived. 'What the fuck's going on? I thought we was bein' mortared.'

'Right, Challis, ya prick,' said Neneh angrily. 'You can spend the next hour picking up all the fucking rubbish that's blown everywhere!'

It was just as well the camp was not being attacked, Kev thought, since nobody had run towards him carrying their rifles. Kev, who was English and in spite of his tender age of 20 was more operationally experienced than any of the Jocks, did everything for fun. He loved the army: the adventures, mishaps, mischief and being away with your mates in a strange country, like one long school trip. He was more laid-back than most and refreshingly reticent towards displays of personal machismo. An early picture of the English lads on tour showed them standing by a Land-Rover. Everyone but Kev puffed their chests out as if they had been weightlifting beforehand. Kev sat thoughtfully on the front bumper, his hands cradling his chin as he looked up with big eyes – more bohemian child than typical squaddie. On his first day as a trained soldier he had been presented with the General Purpose Machine Gun, the 14 kg support weapon, as his to use and carry. What he liked most about having the Gimpy on field exercises was that he was excused from running around. While his mates ran breathlessly from bunker to bunker in front of him, simulating assaults on enemy positions, he got to lie on the ground and fire off rounds.

Fortunately for Kev, what went on at Condor stayed at Condor, while the absence of senior officers contributed to the high degree of horseplay. Lieutenant Passmore held the highest rank and answered to a company commander stationed some distance away. Major Adam Griffiths could not be everywhere at once and had two other platoons living and working with the ICDC in isolated locations at camps Sparrowhawk and Jennings. So Griffiths and Passmore kept in touch by satellite phone.

The Condorites had complained about communications on the first day of the tour and would do so on the last. In spite of black spots across the province, a signal attenuated by dry air and flat ground, and the fact that callers were often transferred to a recorded-message service, the satellite phone remained the optimum channel. To their chagrin, they had been refused permission to purchase Iraqi civilian mobile phones. Instead, the signals officer had visited from Abu Naji. He twiddled dials and got the HF and VHF radios to function. None of the Condorites possessed his level of expertise, and the sets soon played up again.

Major Griffiths commanded B Company, 1st Battalion, the Argyll and Sutherland Highlanders. He was the only one of Gray's company commanders to have attended staff college, and Gray rated Griffiths' men as his battalion's foremost infanteers: hence B Company were deployed to Maysan Province, while A and D Companies were based closer to Basra and battalion headquarters. Although Gray did not initially believe that his men were in great danger – in late 2003, he had driven through the provincial capital of Al Amarah armed with just a pistol – Maysan was the most hostile of the British-controlled provinces. Back then, Gray was 'very optimistic' about what could be achieved, as there was still a high degree of support for the presence of British forces and a gratefulness for the deposing of Saddam Hussein. Raising a new army would be a 'very tangible demonstration of progress', as well as being central to the exit strategy for Coalition Forces. 'I was seized by the enormity of the task but invigorated by the challenge,' he said. 'I knew that the Argylls would be up for it.'

Gray's battalion could trace its lineage back to 1794, when the Duke of Argyll formed the Argyllshire Highlanders (91st Regiment of Foot). In 1881 the regiment merged with the Sutherland Highlanders (93rd Regiment of Foot) and took the new title of the Princess Louise's Argyll and Sutherland Highlanders. Probably its most famous engagement was during the Crimean War. At Balaklava the regiment, led by Sir Colin Campbell, won immortal fame when the men, dressed in red tunics and carrying swords, formed two ranks and repelled the charge of the Russian cavalry. Campbell told his men, 'There is no retreat from here. You must die where you stand.' The London *Times* correspondent William H. Russell wrote that all he could see was a 'thin red streak, tipped with a line of steel'. This was interpreted as 'the thin red line', and from that day the description has been synonymous with the Argylls. The 1st and 2nd Battalions fought in the Indian Mutiny, in Zululand and in the South African war of 1899–1902. During the First World War, the regiment was expanded and served on the western front, and in Macedonia and Palestine. During the Second World War, the Argylls engaged in France, Malaya, Abyssinia, Crete, North Africa, Sicily and Italy. And in 1950 the Argylls were victims of a US napalm attack in Korea, with heavy losses – an episode in the battalion's history known simply as 'Hill 282'.

It was to Gray's chagrin that the regiment, now reduced to a single battalion, had not deployed overseas since Aden in 1967. To huge public acclaim, the Argylls, led by Lieutenant Colonel Colin 'Mad Mitch' Mitchell, had out-fought Arab terrorists to gain control of Crater. Mitchell's methods were uncompromising, and he had been ordered to 'throttle back' by the general officer in command of Aden, Major General Phillip Tower. Mad Mitch relished the fact that his methods had brought complaints. He always wanted to dominate any situation – something of which Paul Kelly would have approved.

There was not a subaltern in the British Army who would have found Kelly easy to command. The self-confessed officer-hater liked things done his way or not at all. The best Passmore could hope for was that Kelly would pretend to do as he asked. Although Passmore's command was compromised by Kelly, Griffiths thought no less of him, knowing how obstructive Kelly could be. Passmore, who stood out in his 'mega-Gucci' German body armour, had been handpicked for the job, and his promotion to captain was imminent.

A headache for the lieutenant was his section commander's reluctance to impose his prescribed level of discipline. When the private soldiers drove Land-Rovers up the steeply sloped walls of the accommodation bunkers, Neneh watched them, his forearms crossed. 'You haven't stopped them?' Passmore asked, his eyes raised towards the giant Scot.

'Why would I?' Neneh replied, laughing.

A corporal of long standing, Neneh subscribed to the maxim that subalterns should be seen and not heard. Neither did he make a natural spoilsport.

As Kelly continued his journey to Qalat Salih, three British vehicles approached from the opposite direction. The road narrowed, but he kept his speed high and stared fixedly ahead. The vehicles swerved violently and bounced off the rocky ground to avoid a collision. 'Fuck you,' he thought, as he saw a cloud of dust and shingle rise in his rear-view mirror. Such contempt was typical of Kelly. He drove on, faster, towards the main highway.

Kelly's black hair was buzzed to the scalp, and his skin was monkey brown. A pair of wings sewn onto his right sleeve signified his completion of the Parachute Regiment's 'P Company' selection course and the jumps cadre at RAF Brize Norton. He was married, a Londoner, it was thought, and from his appearance he was aged in his mid-30s. He spoke little of his past. If you had offered anyone besides him a seat on the next flight home, they would have taken it. But the conflict nourished Kelly and he fed it. He was also dedicated to the protection of his soldiers, whom he allowed to vent their frustrations through horseplay so long as they stripped, polished and reassembled their A2 rifles daily.

Weapons maintenance, a chore in European conditions, was even more frustrating in the desert. To clean the inside of a barrel, a square of flannelette was fed through the eye of a short, metal rod attached to a length of rope. The 'pull through' was dropped down the barrel then retrieved by pulling on the rope. The flannelette cleared the carbon as it worked its way back up the chamber. Sometimes they had to do this five times until he was satisfied. Kelly would point the barrel skywards and peer through it. The most tedious job was to clean the bolt carrier assembly, which separated into six pieces: firing pin, retaining pin, cam stud, cam-stud recess, ejector and locking splines. Traces of oil, brushed over the weapon's working parts, were removed from the exterior with a dry rag and magazines emptied of rounds to clean out the grit.

The A2 was bemoaned as a 'range weapon': the harsher the environment, the worse it performed. Nonetheless, it was highly accurate. Whereas the AK47 suggested its inventor had poured his soul into it, in whose image had the A2 been created? It was not a weapon for which the men developed affection.

Kelly's CV said everything about a regular infanteer's life before Iraq: six tours of Northern Ireland, one of Bosnia and not a single firefight. That was until one evening four weeks before. Kelly and Neneh had spent the afternoon of 11 February teaching fire-and-manoeuvre drills. The ICDC did their Keystone Kops impressions, running and firing in all directions until their British mentors could watch no more. The two non-commissioned officers' evening task was to shake up the corrupt police officers and carjackers who terrorised drivers on the highway. Iraqi policemen would stop and search cars in good condition then communicate via radio with bandits hidden a few hundred metres away. The bandits would then climb out of roadside ditches and push boulders onto the carriageways. And the police would flash their lights to warn of any British military vehicles while the armed robbery took place.

That evening Kelly and Neneh were ready to leave camp; the ICDC were not. 'Here we fucking go again,' Kelly said. 'Neneh, I'm getting really bored of this shit. Every time we turn up, they are late. Then we have to spend our nights driving up and down that same road.'

Neneh gripped a few of them: 'Get a move on, ya wee tit. What are ye doin', ya piece a shite?'

They took two Land-Rovers to top and tail the ICDC convoy; the Iraqis drove everywhere in pick-up trucks. Around 20 Iraqi police officers loitered at the highway checkpoint, their faces grey and shifty in the darkness. The traffic was backed up for a quarter of a mile as the menfolk stood in clusters around pick-up trucks and cars. Rumour had fed upon rumour; the Ali Babas (thieves) were on the highway.

Kelly gave the car drivers his hard-fixed stare. They seemed in fear of their lives and rebutted his offer of an escort to where the British-controlled sector ended and the Danish zone began. Kelly's appetite for action had been whetted and for Neneh to have demurred would have been futile. The night air was heavy and still as they pulled away. The slow rumble of their motor engines provided the only sound.

After a few minutes of driving, a rudimentary barricade appeared. 'Strange the stones are still here, eh? Get your lads out, Neneh, and we'll have a look.'

Kelly stood in the yellow funnel of light from the headlamps. Hearing gunfire, he dived for cover behind his Land-Rover. He cursed his idiocy: he should not have stood there. The remainder of his section jumped into a ditch. In the confusion, the ICDC fired at the British soldiers instead of the car thieves.

'Rapid fire!' Kelly screamed. 'Enemy position, 30 metres to our front right, behind a mound.' He let off a full magazine towards a shell hole, and those with night-sights saw one robber flee. They shot at him, which constituted a breach of their rules of engagement. Flares illuminated the ground, and Private Harris fired a General Purpose Machine Gun.

Kelly chuckled. 'Nice one, Harris. You're not useless after all.' He remembered Harris's cock-ups: he had once got flannelette stuck in his machine gun barrel and another time had poured petrol into the camp's diesel generator. Harris wore his spectacles with pride and wiped them with an expression of inward concentration before replacing them on his nose. Even then he stumbled into trouble.

'What is it, Harris?' Neneh had once asked him, awoken as the private shuffled around him.

'Oh, no, nothing, corporal. You're all right.'

'No, Harris,' he pressed through his drowsiness, 'ye've just woken me up. What was it ye wanted?'

'I just wanted to say that any time you want to sit in my chair, that's fine.'

'Harris, ye prick! Ye woke me up just to tell me that? Oh God, what are ye like?'

Harris was on a different frequency to most of his fellow Jocks. 'Hey, Glaister [another Jock], which bank are ye with?' he had once asked.

'Err, Royal Bank of Scotland, I think,' Glaister had replied, confused. 'Why?'

'Aye, because they've got some really good mortgage deals on the noo.'

'I'm 20 years old, Harris. I don't think I'll be buying a house.'

Neneh, Kev Challis and Private Jay Lawrence were cracking jokes from the safety of a bunker. Their laughter unnerved Kelly when he arrived at their position. Fear did strange things to people, he thought. 'Neneh, your guys provide some fire support. I'm going for that first bunker. You two,' Kelly stared at the soldiers nearest to him, 'come with me.'

It was a 30-metre crawl towards the bunker, under intermittent fire. When Kelly turned to give his support duo their last orders, he blinked at the empty space behind him. The pair were sitting in Neneh's trench; they had not heard his command.

Kelly decided it was safer to continue his advance alone than retreat across open ground. His stealthy approach surprised the gunmen, whom he arrested without further shots being fired. He pulled his plasti-cuffs from his webbing and tied them up. In preparation for the return journey, the prisoners were laid face down on the floor and blindfolded. The ICDC took turns to smash them on the head with rifle butts.

'You wanted to sack that off earlier, mate!' Kelly told Neneh excitedly. 'I want the prisoners loaded onto the back of my vehicle, OK?'

'Aye, nae dramas.' Neneh gave the Iraqis a curious look. They appeared to be skinny, weak and terrified.

'We'll take the prisoners back to Condor,' Kelly said. 'Major Sabeer'll know what to do with them [he would issue a beating]. There's no way I'm handing them over to the Iraqi police – they'll get let off immediately. We're going to drive northwards, back towards the police checkpoint with our headlights off. Get some guys on top cover, and we'll use our night-sights.'

Kelly signalled his return to camp by flashing his headlights and honking his horn. 'Find me Major Sabeer,' he ordered one of the ICDC. The dazed prisoners were dragged from the vehicle and made to lie on the floor. Kelly saw one private pose for a picture.

'Get your fucking foot off his head, you dick! The last thing I fucking need is pictures of you in a newspaper.'

While Sabeer interrogated the robbers, 6 Platoon gathered in the television room to check kit, tally expended rounds and agree an official version of the night's events. On his arrival, Major Griffiths asked questions, suspiciously thought

Kelly, about the level of force used. As his young soldiers were high after their first enemy contact, Kelly feared they might say something that would incriminate them. 'The boys did well, sergeant,' gestured Griffiths. Kelly sneered in the face of compliments. His instinct was that a pat on the back was just a 'recce' for the knife. 'Just one question,' Griffiths continued. 'Why was a 40 mm grenade fired?'

'What do you mean, sir?'

'Why did Private Thomas fire a 40 mm grenade during the contact? Was the enemy using RPGs [rocket-propelled grenades]?'

Anger throbbed in Kelly's chest at the suggestion his response had been disproportionate. 'Sir,' he began, 'Private Thomas fired a 40 mm grenade to the rear of the second enemy position to stop their escape. If I had had any 94 mm anti-tank weapons [a round with a much bigger calibre], I would have fired those as well.'

Kelly's soldiers knew he had been desperate for an enemy contact. Nobody in the platoon had fired a 40 mm grenade before, and it had seemed like a good opportunity. Tommo's fellow privates envied his luck. Griffiths thought that Kelly had been looking for a scrap, too. The major's view was that it was not for the Argylls in their ICDC training role to engage insurgents – or, as in this case, petty thieves. It was the resident infantry battalion that was responsible for local security. The Argylls were not part of the security infrastructure. Their role was to mentor the ICDC to the point where the Iraqis could impose their own security. However, Kelly maintained that because the car thieves had fired first, all bets were then off. Griffiths countered that it was the Argylls' responsibility through their actions to persuade the ICDC to throttle back on their own aggressive instincts; firing grenades at low-grade criminals did not constitute such a demonstration.

Neneh was more frightened the following day than he had been during the skirmish. As part of their routine post-contact investigation, the Royal Military Police wanted to visit the scene. He feared the fleeing car robber would return to haunt him. How would Neneh explain his corpse pierced with gunshot wounds? Ever the pragmatist, Sabeer calmed him with cigarettes and a chilling suggestion. 'If there is a body, I will get rid of it. Nobody will know. If you need me to place weapons there, I can do this also.'

Welcome to Maysan Province. This was how things worked. Thankfully, there was no body at the scene and no investigation. Neneh chuckled. Sabeer's solution to dump a corpse and plant a weapon had been presented as if it was an everyday occurrence, neither to be questioned nor met with comment.

2

Rinsing

The plan was to have a couple of hundred Iraqis [the size of an ICDC company] in each base, possibly with a battalion HQ or logistics element 'collocated', in army parlance. A platoon of Jocks would live in a fortified, defendable inner bastion into which the Iraqis were not allowed. Thus the Argyll platoon commander would mentor the Iraqi company commander, the section commanders the platoon commanders, the senior Jock the section commanders and so on. Everybody in the Argylls was mentoring somebody. I was mentoring the former naval officer Brigadier Dhia, who I appointed as the 70th Brigade commander; the youngest Jock was mentoring a handful of *jundies*. It was a big ask but one I knew the Argylls would relish.

Lieutenant Colonel J.D. Gray

En route to Qalat Salih, Kelly said this ought to be that and that ought to be this, as if he had memorised a plan for everything. But he did not have a plan to compensate for the failings of the ICDC and neither, in truth, did his commanding officer. Every day Kelly cursed their laziness, dishonesty and routine absence, especially when they skipped duties but sent a brother or cousin in their place so they could claim pay. He mulled over the incident involving Elliott, too. Had the recruits paraded at 0800 as instructed, business would have been concluded before the temperature had climbed to its peak and nobody would have lost his temper.

Kelly and the other instructors had until the end of June – when the United States returned limited sovereignty to the

Coalition Provisional Authority – to produce soldiers capable of imposing security across a province that straddled the world's most notorious heroin-trafficking route. The drug was grown in the south-western provinces of Afghanistan and moved through Iraq en route to Jordan and Europe. Narcotics was a primary source of income in Maysan. Unsurprisingly, drugs and violence shared a common territory.

The explorer Wilfred Thesiger had said of the marshland Arabs, 'You can usually get on terms with people here by helping them kill something.' No Condorite bought into Thesiger's creed, not even Lieutenant James Dormer, the nearest of the Argylls' officers to the intellectual 'soldier–poet'. The reality was that these people kidnapped children and held their families to ransom, flooded their own villages in order to receive additional aid money (which they fraudulently used for their own purposes) and stole life-support machines from hospitals. So why would anyone want to get 'on terms' with them? There was only love and hate here, and the distinctions were often blurred. The conundrum that was inter-family warfare had been explained to James Dormer as 'Me against my brother, yes, but both of us against our cousin.'

The sun exposed the cracked, barren earth no longer suitable for agriculture. When he drained 80 per cent of the marshlands, Saddam destroyed an existence undisturbed since biblical times. Amid 6,000 square miles of water, the locals had caught fish with spears, farmed water buffalo and slept amid clumps of bulrushes. A refugee's testimony spoke of what was lost: 'The birds died, the animals died, the people died. There is no water, there is no life. We are naked in our misery.' A time-lapse film shot over the course of his dictatorship would have captured beauty and natural wealth ebbing away. Only the brick foundries and the chimneys shaped like naval cannons remained. They fired puffs of grey smoke into an empty sky as tiny female figures, the 'work whores', hurried about the circular bases. Their male co-workers watched from the tea tents.

Eventually, the town made its presence felt when squat houses built on either side of a dual carriageway appeared. Newly imported cars competed for shade beneath spiralling palm trees. Kelly and his men drove a circuit of the town and passed a football pitch, where an important match had drawn a large crowd. They continued on over a pontoon bridge and swept past the hospital until they reached the police station, where Kelly expected to meet Major James Faux. There were protesters outside, shouting about the weapons seizures and house searches. The marsh Arabs were a proud people. To enter an Arab's home without invitation, no matter how apologetically, brought him dishonour. Honour was more important than facts, a belief which led to the denial of self-evident truths. They were particularly irate at such an incursion that day, as it was a Friday, the Islamic holy day.

The soldiers formed a protective cordon around the Land-Rovers as Kelly and Loz marched towards the entrance. 'What you lookin' so happy about?' Kelly asked Loz.

'Paul, you're in trouble over that roadblock.'

'Why? What?' Kelly pretended to scan the horizon, as if too distracted to hear him.

'You know, those Land-Rovers you almost smashed into on the way here?'

'Yeah? What about them?' Kelly hated it when Loz pricked his ego. As a pair they were like identically charged magnets, repelling each other at close quarters.

'Well, that was Major Griffiths driving the first one. He went mental and flagged down my wagon. Colour Sergeant Roberts, who was with him, asked who was driving yours. I told him it was you and how we'd been crashed out on a quick-reaction force. He started effing and blinding regardless. Anyway, he told me to tell you Griffiths wants to see you when we get back.'

Kelly and Loz were pitted against each other for the respect of the younger Condorites. After the privates lapped up Loz's stories of his service in the Airborne brigade's 'Pathfinder' unit, Kelly would suggest that he had not spent sufficient time in Sierra Leone to win his campaign medal and had bought his gong – a scurrilous assertion.

Four Iraqi prisoners were knelt with their heads against the outside wall of the police station and their hands bound behind their backs with plasti-cuffs. 'Who are they?' Kelly asked abruptly. He was unacquainted with the soldiers guarding the prisoners.

'The one in the police uniform was shooting at us,' one of them responded. 'As we followed up, he ran through this building. When we caught up, we found him, the three others and this large weapons stash.'

'Bonus,' said Kelly. 'Where's Major Faux?'

When he walked inside, Kelly saw rocket-propelled grenade launchers, warheads, pistols, silencers, magazines, 800 rounds of 7.62 mm link and 12 AK47s. Some officers would have tasked a corporal or sergeant to tally up the weapons bounty; Major Faux did it himself. He was a rare officer.

'Sergeant Kelly, cheers for joining the party. How's it going?'

'Well, sir, I should be asking you that, I think. What have you got here, then?'

'Oh, a bit of everything: RPGs, AKs, mags, link. We're waiting for the explosives experts to arrive to lift this lot and then get the hell out of here as soon as possible.'

Kelly doubted it was worth the wait. The explosives team was always busy when he needed them. The standard operating procedure in their absence was to throw rocket-propelled grenade warheads in the river rather than risk an explosion en route to camp. Faux logged another rifle serial number as his soldiers shuffled the weapons and ancillaries into neat piles. Loz arrived with a camera and asked Kelly to take his picture beside the stash. He obliged, reluctantly, as Faux continued. 'The locals want those four fucking idiots back, and they're not having them.'

'No, sir.'

'Come outside, Sergeant Kelly, and I'll tell you what I've got in mind.'

The protest had intensified, and the tang of cordite from the earlier skirmish hung ominously in the air. All males of rifle-bearing age in Qalat Salih were routinely armed, and militia factions of political parties such as the Daiwa, the Supreme Council for the Islamic Revolution in Iraq and the Office of the Martyr Sadr were the law. Criminalising residents for weapons possession was akin to issuing speeding tickets at a motor race. Opposition to such a futile policy manifested itself in attacks on British patrols. The military wing of the Office of the Martyr Sadr, known as the Mahdi Army, was better recruited by the week and sought control of Route 6. Corporal Alcock of the Argylls had received a nasty surprise while on patrol a few weeks earlier. He had not heard of the Mahdi Army or Moqtada al-Sadr when he reached a roadblock manned by heavily armed gunmen dressed in black. 'Who the fuck are they?' he wondered as he dismounted from his Land-Rover; they were not dressed like Iraqi policemen. There was a Mexican stand-off while he radioed battlegroup headquarters. But nobody there had seen gunmen dressed and equipped in this manner. The rules of engagement precluded an attack unless the Mahdi Army demonstrated lethal intent. The dark figures stood defiantly without moving to shoot him. Eventually, he withdrew. With no network of paid informants or spies, intelligence gathering was ad hoc. Incidents such as this told soldiers more than any briefing. Their next best option was the Internet, while even at Lieutenant Colonel Gray's level of battalion command the understanding of what was going on in southern Iraq was, as he conceded, 'superficial'.

'OK, Sergeant Kelly,' Faux lifted his voice over the mob, 'I want you to put your vehicles either side of the road to give us cover until our quick-reaction force arrives. When they do, they will then take up your positions. At that point, I want you to take a patrol across the bridge and up past the mosque to the end of town to get a general feel of the mood. The sooner the boys from Abu Naji turn up, the better. The last intelligence report suggested the insurgents are going to launch a major attack from here. We could have another Majar al-Kabir on our hands.'

'Roger, happy with that.'

Kelly knew Faux was referring to the bloody engagement in Majar al-Kabir the previous summer, when six Royal Military Policemen were murdered at the town's police station. Seven paratroopers were wounded when their Chinook helicopter was attacked, and a sergeant won his regiment's first Conspicuous Gallantry Cross. At the time, he had thought that he would die. The Red Caps' deaths constituted the largest loss of British life in combat since the Falklands War. At one point the Paras had been just 100 metres from the Red Caps' location, yet did not know they were there. Neither did the British battlegroup's commanders, who orchestrated the ill-fated rescue mission. The number of Iraqi fatalities and wounded on 24 June 2003 was estimated at 75 to 100.

'As you might have heard on your way in, Sergeant Kelly, they've been saying over the Tannoy speakers how we've attacked the police station and that everyone should fetch their weapons. It could get a bit tasty here later if we don't fuck off soon.'

As promised by Faux, the reinforcements arrived not long afterwards. This freed Kelly and Loz to drive another circuit of the town. The threat was more palpable, as chants reverberated off buildings and gunmen waved AK47s from windows. 'All this over one weapons search,' thought Kelly. He recalled his disagreement with Faux over 'rinsing'. The Light Infantry's policy was to rinse residential areas of weapons and then throw objectors into the nearest canal. They were stoned until they admitted where their guns were hidden. A week earlier, Kelly had led a patrol through a local village when the crowd had reacted aggressively. Unbeknown to Kelly, Faux's men had been rinsing there a few hours earlier. Kelly had been furious that the actions of one British call sign had compromised the security of another – a disturbingly frequent occurrence. Kelly prodded Faux about it the next day. It was the first time they had met. 'You could have got us killed yesterday in that place!'

'I am sorry about that,' Faux replied, somewhat taken aback by the sergeant's tone.

'This is our area of operations as well, you know. We patrol here most days.'

'OK, OK, sergeant. If we are going to do something like that again, we'll make sure you're on board. I'm sorry if we caused you a problem.'

Kelly accepted Faux's invitation, and the following day they seized rocket-propelled grenades and heavy machine guns.

Kelly still hoped to leave Qalat Salih that day without a shot being fired. The sight of an off-duty ICDC recruit he recognised gave him an idea. Kelly persuaded him to collect Major Sabeer from Condor. A resident of the town, he might be able to help the British talk their way out.

Kelly addressed his men: 'Confirm everyone's made ready, keep an eye out and let's talk to each other, OK?'

His soldiers pulled back the cocking handles of their rifles and ensured their magazines were correctly fitted. Both procedures had to be undertaken to prevent a stoppage.

Marching to the rear of his Land-Rover, Kelly found one private with his head leant against the inside of the cargo hold. His weapon was on the bench below, beyond arm's reach. 'What the hell do you think you're fucking doing?' The soldier righted himself. It was hot inside the vehicle. 'Get the fuck out, get your fucking arse down here and get the fuck over there,' Kelly said, clenching his fist. 'And cover our backs.'

When the explosive-ordnance team had made safe the weapons and artillery, Kelly was ordered to return to the police station. His Land-Rovers formed a defensive shield in front of the building as the prisoners were escorted outside. The crowd had grown in size and volume, angry at Major Faux's rejection of a plea from religious leaders that the captives be released.

'Sir?'

'Yup?' Major Faux faced the junior soldier who had addressed him.

'The locals have built a barricade with concrete blocks up at the top of the main street by the police station, blocking any vehicles getting through.' This meant they were trapped.

'Right,' Faux's words quickened, 'we'd better get that moved. Where's Sergeant Kelly?' No answer. 'Get him in here, will you?' A private ushered Kelly back inside the room, where the piles of AK47s had assumed a tottering height. 'Sergeant Kelly, I need you to move forward with your call sign to the corner of the police station. Remove the barrier the locals have built there.'

'No problem, boss.'

'The explosives ordnance guys are pretty much ready to go. All the weapon systems are safe to be moved. I don't want that barrier slowing us down. We'll be moving out as one, extracting the weapons and the prisoners together.'

'Sir, I'll take my two Land-Rovers up there with me, so we can just jump in and leave when ready.'

Every soldier besides the two drivers marched in a protective cordon around the Land-Rovers and pushed back the crowd. The lead wagon was driven by John 'Smudger' Smith, a teenage private soldier. He was a scrappy wee laddie more likely to be seen on a street corner swigging Buckfast Tonic Wine or racing to a chip shop on a BMX. Smudger's mates at Condor were the likes of Private Richie 'Fieldmong' Fieldman and Private Alan 'Aldo' McDonald, kids who did not think about the politics of Iraq or whether the Argylls were to be amalgamated into some Scottish super-regiment. All that was 'shite faer officers tae think about'.

As they neared the barrier, each of Kelly's soldiers was given an arc in front of, adjacent to or behind him to observe. On his instruction, they kept their rifles at waist rather than shoulder height so as not to incite the crowd. Direct confrontation had to be avoided or, at the very least, delayed. Kelly was anxious not to communicate his fears as his men lifted the concrete blocks and debris. 'We don't want to instigate this,' he said. 'Work fast and stay calm. Don't go pointing your weapons at people willy-nilly. They're more likely to shoot at you if you do.'

They saw men on a nearby rooftop draw fingers across their throats. It was a signal. The first stone was light and only the size of a child's fist, yet within a minute the air was full of rocks, which struck heads and shoulders. Kelly's men retreated hurriedly to the Land-Rovers to recover their helmets. As they had no time to fasten them properly, the insides cut into their scalps. The stoning continued as they returned to the roadblock. Sensing something terrible was about to happen, they tore at it desperately. 'Keep your weapons down!' Kelly repeated.

A fat bearded man shouted loudest from the rooftop and gestured dramatically. He lifted a rocket-propelled grenade launcher from beneath his right arm and propped it on his shoulder. The warhead that extended from the chamber flashed white then orange as it began its journey on a downward trajectory towards Smudger's Land-Rover. When it slammed into the engine block, the force of compressed air shot him through the open passenger door and onto the tarmac, his webbing and combat jacket ablaze. Standing only one metre from the explosion, Kelly was blown off his feet. When another rocket found the same Land-Rover, the seismic process of the vehicle being lifted and dropped was repeated. Flames rose and smoke billowed skywards.

'Tommo, de-bus! Get the fuck out of there!'

Tommo frantically squeezed his body out from behind the steering wheel of the second Land-Rover. Secondary fragmentation had dented the doors of his vehicle and cracked the windscreen.

As Kelly struggled to regain his balance, the fat man reloaded. It was a race between them as to who could fire first. Kelly raised his rifle and let off a burst. Fat man peered downwards as poppy-shaped clots blossomed on his chest. Kelly willed him to fall, but the British rounds – 5.56 mm as opposed to the 7.62 mm calibre rounds used by the Iraqis – seemed too light to put him down. Finally, he slumped backwards out of sight. But Kelly's men were now engulfed, and rounds snapped in the air. On the same rooftop, a dark figure appeared. He was armed with an AK47 and carried additional magazines in his chest webbing. His all-black attire suggested that he belonged to the Supreme Council for the Islamic Revolution in Iraq or Mahdi Army.

Kelly felt rounds brush his ears, followed by a burning sensation as molten lead tunnelled through his hand. A fraction of a second later, the round burst through his wrist and splattered his face with tiny clumps of flesh and blood. Immediate comprehension was impossible, but Kelly would later swear that he saw further rounds miss him by centimetres. He gazed down at what resembled a raw piece of meat. 'Oh, well,' he thought. 'That's my left hand gone.'

3

Boys Don't Cry

Lance Corporal Steve Wells was convinced that the day was the hottest of the tour so far. Having lunched, his rest was interrupted by Steve 'Ronaldo' Rennie, one of the Scottish lance corporals. 'Mr Passmore wants everyone besides those on guard duty to deploy to Qalat Salih. Kelly's having a bit of trouble.' This sounded like just another public-order situation to Wellsy as he searched for his helmet and baton. He wished he had a shield and that his helmet had a plastic visor.

Ronaldo was a close friend of the recently deceased Andrew Craw, who had accidentally shot himself, and there had been some doubt over his deployment for that reason. He would later draw the shortest straw, being put on radio duty and establishing an Incident Control Point outside Qalat Salih. Ronaldo would be joined by Griffiths and later Lieutenant Colonel Bill Ponting, Faux's commanding officer. Having initially decided to let Faux handle the situation in his own inimitable way, Griffiths was requested by Lieutenant Colonel Ponting to assess developments at close quarters then report back. Alarmed by what he was told, Ponting deployed himself.

While on his pre-deployment recce of Maysan two months before, Griffiths had spent an unnerving sixteen hours in Faux's company, during which time the pair had been engaged by local gunmen on four separate occasions.

Griffiths had returned to Britain shell-shocked and told his wife that the province was 'like the Wild West'. He formed the impression that Faux was a courageous officer but also a maverick. Rinsing reflected his style of soldiering.

Neneh was in Sabeer's office when one of the Iraqi interpreters casually mentioned a local disturbance he might want to investigate. Neneh did not expect it to amount to much so deployed on a whim. 'No need faer night-vision goggles,' he thought. 'I'll be back in an hour. More use faer a pad and a pen, right enough.'

This excursion at least constituted something to alleviate the boredom. There were days when they just sat around Condor and slagged each other off. On one afternoon they had dragged two rusted anti-aircraft guns into camp from the old airfield. They did not work, but at least the labour killed an hour.

Neneh's area of professional specialisation, as his size suggested, was heavy machine guns. That afternoon he was equipped only with his rifle and 120 rounds. He was to act as Passmore's second-in-command.

Wellsy, who likened Qalat Salih to one of Northern Ireland's hardcore Republican enclaves, its inscrutable inhabitants forming a 'tight-knit community', mounted his Land-Rover at Condor. The smoke tower from Smudger's Land-Rover had taken up residence on the horizon. 'They'll be setting fire to tyres again,' he muttered in his north Hampshire burr. Basingstoke was not an hour from London, yet Wellsy's vowels were ploughed from the earth. He was nobody's fool, earning his first stripe while still a teenager. It had been to his chagrin that his mate Keegs had been promoted to lance corporal weeks before him – surely an administration error at battalion headquarters. Wellsy's sense of responsibility impressed his seniors. His face appeared older than 21, as if wizened by wisdom. Although he would have blushed at the suggestion, he personified the British Army's double-quick knack of developing school-leavers into effective junior commanders. He might have been the least articulate of those who spoke at Orders Groups, but his thoughts, if not his words, were clear.

Infantry platoons were broken down into three sections, each with a section commander, a corporal and a section second-in-command. In addition to relaying Neneh's instructions, Wellsy's responsibilities included a thorough check of the Land-Rovers before departure to ensure they were 'polled up' with sufficient petrol, oil, lubricant and water, and that they remembered to bring the breakdown kit. He also confirmed that the vehicles' radio systems, bolted onto the dashboards, functioned properly. Passmore carried the satellite phone.

The minimum number of vehicles to travel in any party was two, and standard operating procedures dictated that two soldiers should stand in 'top cover' positions. One was armed with a machine gun, the other a rifle. It was also customary that the machine gunner strapped his rifle to his back as a fallback in case, as sometimes happened, he ran dry of ammunition. As those at Condor had been deployed in Iraq to train the defence force, they had received fewer rounds than other infanteers stationed in the same province. Their vulnerability had been further exposed when their Minimi light machine guns were withdrawn after Craw's fatal accident.

Neneh and Wellsy's Land-Rovers closed in on Qalat Salih. Tyre tracks criss-crossed the crusty landscape but led nowhere. Warehouse roofs denoted signs of light industrialisation. Posters of Shia clerics and anti-Coalition Forces graffiti adorned the walls. At the police checkpoint,

Parachute Regiment soldiers reported that they had heard sporadic gunfire inside the town. Though he had never been in a 'contact' before, this persuaded Wellsy to 'make ready'. He tilted his weapon towards him in his right hand and leant across with his left to pull the cocking handle. Only Kelly got away with having his safety catch permanently off; Wellsy kept his on. Two of the Paras, a major and a non-commissioned officer called Glen Cooper, agreed to join the patrol, while Passmore, who had travelled to Qalat Salih with Neneh and Wellsy, attempted by radio to ascertain Kelly's position. He wanted to avoid the scenario of two groups of British soldiers being unable to locate each other and fighting running battles through the streets.

'If he pops up again, shoot him,' said Wellsy in response to the top-cover soldier's report of an armed man who bobbed up and down behind a stone wall. Wellsy leant across the bonnet and peered through his magnifying sight towards where the private had suggested the gunman had appeared. 'Boss,' he said to Passmore informally, 'the top-cover lad said he saw someone. I had a look but couldn't see a weapon on him. I've told him to keep eyes on.'

Aware that the Land-Rovers made easy targets, Passmore ordered his men to dismount. Their boots thudded on the tarmac as they did so. Such a dangerous situation was new to everyone, and now was their last chance to tighten belt webbing, tug on helmet straps and ensure the range drums on their rifle sights were aligned. Wellsy glanced across at 'Wee' Ritchie Payton. One of the youngest Argylls and only weeks out of training, he would have been questioned about his age if he had tried to buy cigarettes.

Payton was also on Neneh's mind. 'Don't fucking shoot at anyone, and stay close to me,' he suggested sternly. The boy–soldier carried the light support weapon, an arm so loathed it was forced upon private soldiers as a 'dicking' to underline their lack of status. It was renamed the 'Crow's Cannon' or 'L S Trouble-U'. Although highly accurate, it was bemoaned for having heavy bi-pod legs that weighed down the front end of the weapon. It was also a bit 'tap, tap' – it did not make the reassuring thud of a belt-fed weapon such as the Gimpy.

'We're going to go in on foot,' Passmore announced. 'We'll leave the wagons here, then fire and manoeuvre down the main street until we find Paul Kelly. Apparently, he's at the police station.' Like most police stations in Maysan, the building was shabby, with a protruding stucco frontage, flaky paintwork and a narrative written into its walls by small-arms fire.

Neneh used a 'comms' gadget known as a Press-to-Talk: a bracelet with a button that wrapped around his rifle stock. This way he could keep two hands on his weapon as he spoke: 'Paul, where are ye? Can ye hear me? We're just at the top of the toon and heading your way.'

The handset of Wellsy's PRR was stuffed into his left breast pocket. He flicked through the channels but reception was so poor he could not distinguish voices. He and Neneh were approximately one kilometre from the barricade.

The butt was a snug fit in the crease of Loz's shoulder. He closed his left eye as he focused on the gunman who had just shot Kelly. The dark figure on the rooftop was magnified to the power of four by his rifle sight. Breathing cycles and sight pictures, alien to the Iraqis, were second nature to him. He concentrated, exhaled and fired a short burst. The rounds sucked the breath from his enemy's body. After a few seconds, the blood ceased to flow and the dark figure collapsed. He had saved Kelly's life, not that such an act would calm the waters between them. Loz lowered his weapon while his eyes readjusted. There would be other targets – many other targets. He had to maintain all-around awareness.

Smudger's body armour and webbing were extinguished and pulled off his body. He was groggy, his expression vacant. His rifle was in the furnace of his Land-Rover, its plastic parts melted.

Blood streamed from Kelly's left wrist. An exit wound was always bigger than an entry wound; the round had wiped its feet and deposited debris of flesh and bone upon its departure. Kelly had to think like a commander, not a victim. So, before dabbing at the sticky bodily matter that coated his face, he did a headcount and issued a set of quick battle orders. He told his men to 'Fire and manoeuvre back to the baseline position'.

Every window, doorway and roof was a potential enemy firing position, and there were too many to observe as they retreated. Ambushes had occurred across the town, and clusters of soldiers converged on the Badr house from all directions. Outnumbered and outgunned by enemy fighters, they were grateful for its walled courtyard. The sonic boom from heavy shelling echoed off its high walls, while RPGs were fired towards the compound from the police station.

The likeness of British Forces in Maysan and flies on an alligator's back, identified by Lieutenant James Dormer, seemed apt. Earlier that day, the Cambridge-educated subaltern had recced the move of his Argylls platoon. En route from Abu Naji to Condor, he and his platoon sergeant Stuart 'Hendy' Henderson had overheard a radio message broadcast by Kelly before the contact had begun. He had said he was 'putting in a cordon'. James and Hendy had offered assistance, but Kelly had said it was not required.

There was a staggered withdrawal from the area of the barricade along the main street towards the Badr house.

Loz extracted before Kelly, who, as platoon sergeant, played 'Tail End Charlie'.

'Loz, Loz, where are you?' Kelly now asked over the radio.

'I'm inside the compound to the north. Don't shoot to the north! Repeat, don't shoot to the north. We're coming in.'

'Confirm you have my team with you!'

'Roger that. ETA one minute.'

Kelly sprinted towards the Badr house, leaving a trail of blood in his wake. 'Tell your guys not to shoot to the north,' he implored one of Faux's signallers upon his arrival. 'I've got a team 20 metres in that direction, heading this way.'

He nodded and added Kelly to his casualty list. 'What's your zap number?'

'Kilo, Echo, figures 5, 9, 4, 6.' Kelly repeated the composition of letters from his surname and the numerical sequence from his army identification code.

'Yup . . . Zero?' said the signaller, speaking to the Ops Room in Abu Naji.

'Roger, receiving. Over.'

'Contact in Qalat Salih. A vehicle has been blown up.' He paused while the receiver scribbled the information down at the other end. 'And we have two, repeat two, confirmed gunshot-wound casualties. Over.'

Kelly realised how much blood he had lost and cursed himself for not having held his left hand higher. When he told Loz to go inside, Faux suggested he did likewise to receive medical attention. Despite his assault vest and desert-issue shirt being leathery with blood, Kelly stayed put.

Faux's leadership impressed Kelly and Loz when he deployed soldiers armed with the Minimi light machine guns in the key defensive positions. 'Get on that wall. Lamppost with the flag on it. Bottom left. Two enemy. Engage.' The Minimis made a terrific rattling noise. Everyone wanted to fire one, but although it was their best offensive weapon, only one in eight soldiers was equipped with it.

Kelly eyed the under-slung grenade launcher bolted onto Tommo's rifle; he had not fired one before. Reluctantly, the private conceded it and accepted Kelly's rifle. He had traded down; Kelly had traded up. More targets were shouted out. Hunched beside a wall, Kelly feared he had left insufficient clearance space for the grenade when he fired the weapon. The warhead shot over the masonry, but only just, and there was a loud bang. He did not know what he had hit, but it sounded fantastic. Satisfied, he went inside and shouldered his way along a drab concrete hallway.

The Badr house was used for interrogations, and there were blood stains underfoot. The air was so dense he could have written his name in the millions of dust particles. Two casualties had been carried inside: Smudger and a private from the Light Infantry called Harrison. He had been shot in the thigh, the round narrowly missing one of his main arteries. Everybody wanted to swap their rifle for his Minimi.

Loz took Goacher and Kuryawa upstairs, while Kelly barked from the ground floor, 'There is a clear field of fire into here from the alleyway outside. One RPG through the window and it will kill everyone!' Four Iraqi prisoners were positioned as a human buffer. Their heads would deflect incoming small arms or be taken clean off by a rocket-propelled grenade. The course fabric of sandbags covered their faces. They would be blind to any incoming missiles. Typically for Iraqis, they were well dressed in slacks and shirts, but their clothes stank. Smudger was placed near them for want of space but out of the line of fire; his internal blast injuries would be diagnosed later.

As Smudger eyed the prisoners venomously, Elliott was tasked to stay with him and ensure he did not lash out at them. There was something different about Elliott now. It seemed the dangerous nature of his predicament had persuaded him to behave more responsibly than when he had been guarding the ICDC.

Elliott, Smudger and Kelly were regaled in colourful Geordie by the Light Infantry company sergeant major. 'When the shooting began, like, I chased this bloke with a handgun into the police station, right? He had, like, this loudhailer an' all, and he'd been indicating our positions, so we took all this incoming fire. Anyway, I ran after him, and we were both in this corridor. He got a round off at me and missed. I thought, "Right, you're getting it, son," so I fired a burst on automatic, like, and cut the fucker in half!' The company sergeant major wanted to inspire his soldiers. 'Well, lads, this is what you joined the army for, isn't it? I'm loving it!' Not everybody was as enthusiastic.

With his hand dressed and resembling a giant cotton bud, Kelly ran upstairs to see Loz, Goacher and Kuryawa. 'How's it going? Got all your team?' he asked.

'We've dropped a few already,' Loz replied, his eyes drawn to Kelly's bandages.

'You all right, Goacher?' Kelly asked. Goacher was a young private who was always excitable.

'Yeah, fine. How's the hand, sergeant?' he replied.

'Not a drama. I'm off downstairs, lads. Stay back from the windows, yeah? Only two people in each room in case an RPG comes through. Keep me informed over the radio, if you can get through.'

This was Goacher and Kuryawa's last conversation for a while: constant machine gun fire would render them temporarily deaf. Their morale reassured Kelly, but two Light Infantry soldiers were in shock. The first was bent double, his knees hinged, his energy seemingly spent. He retched violently and seemed oblivious to Kelly's approach. 'Hey,' said Kelly. The private soldier's face was flushed. Sweat fused razor-shorn strands of hair to his forehead. He seemed semi-conscious of his whereabouts and actions. The second soldier held his head in his hands as his body folded in on itself. The private's rifle was propped beside him. 'Hey, what do you think you're doing?' Kelly asked. The soldier began to cry. 'You've got a weapon. Cover that fucking wall!' The infanteer emitted a faint, indistinct half-sentence as tears painted stripes down his cheeks. 'You've got to fight,' Kelly cajoled, his tone more sympathetic. But the last vestiges of fight had left the kid. That their non-participation placed others' lives in greater jeopardy tempered Kelly's consideration. He also feared the battle would intensify before it lightened.

Kelly eyed the second lad's webbing pouches, the rough-hewn canvas pockets attached to a belt around his waist. They were easily accessible, and the contents of each was invariably standardised – the private was not long enough out of basic training to have customised his kit. Kelly knew where to find what he was looking for. 'If you don't get on that position, I'm going to take your magazines.' The soldier wiped his face but did not reply. 'Did you hear me?' The private's inert silence continued. 'I'll leave you with one magazine for your own protection, but if you're not going to fight, then I'm taking the rest.' The soldier could not compose himself sufficiently to prevent what now seemed inevitable. It was as though he just wanted to be somewhere else. 'It's your last chance, mate . . . I mean it. Right, give 'em 'ere.' Kelly leant down to open the pouches. 'If you won't use them, I will.' He flipped open the first pocket and withdrew two full magazines of thirty rounds. Each 5.56 mm round of 'ball' ammunition consisted of a copper bullet wrapped in a brass casing. Inscribed into the base was the manufacture date and the symbol of a cross inside a circle

– the NATO designation. The tracer rounds, which also acted as target illuminators, were at the bottom and signalled the soldier was about to run dry.

The sight of the distressed soldiers stayed with Kelly as he stuffed his buckshee (free) magazines away. He had never seen combatants on his side look so frightened, giving the appearance of having submitted to a false inevitability of death. Displays of cowardice – he did not like to use the word, but that was what they were – were seldom spoken of or exposed. At least the men were not Condorites. Had they been junior soldiers whom he had raised as his own, he would have been deeply disappointed.

Kelly met Faux and the company sergeant major by the front gate as the officer spoke into his satellite phone: 'We need support. This thing is getting out of hand.' Faux listened and repeated what had been said to him: 'Four Warriors en route? Yup . . . Good . . . OK. Out.'

Having suggested Kelly remain inside for his own safety, Faux appeared to be surprised to see him. 'Our commanding officer Lieutenant Colonel Ponting has "stood to" the whole battlegroup if we need them,' Faux said. 'You've heard about the Warriors. There will be an airborne reaction force as well with a Chinook.' Knowing how low ammunition supplies were, this update on the quick-reaction force reassured all those present.

Neneh and Wellsy's first indication of incoming fire had been the little dust clouds that puffed up by the roadside. Now they came under more consistent attack. When Wellsy sprinted across the highway, he crashed into Lance Corporal Rush on the other side. They laughed. To laugh was usually the best response. Next, they heard a familiar polyphonic trill.

'Where's that coming from?'

'Fuck knows.'

The Para major fumbled agitatedly inside his assault vest for his mobile.

'Ah, it's him!' Wellsy said.

The officer acknowledged his embarrassment with raised eyebrows, as if his mobile phone had rung during a wedding ceremony. 'Sorry, guys!' He held the offending handset at half an arm's length and ascertained the caller's identity before he answered. 'Hello, love . . . Yup . . . Can't really talk now.' Her words came as a tide, his were driftwood. 'Yes, I've got to go . . . I'm in a bit of a situation . . .' He smiled at the soldiers around him, and his facial expression appealed for sympathy. 'Talk to you later . . . Bye.'

They were on the move again, in pairs, each covering their partner's advance. Wellsy was on one knee, his rifle butt wedged into his upper body as he moved the weapon from left to right. Local youths made 'fast moves' on the periphery of his vision. 'This is the real deal,' he thought. He was nervous and excited. To respond effectively in such situations was why he had been eager to deploy to Iraq, not to train the ICDC.

He listened as Passmore explained the whereabouts of the police station and the directions to it. Spying its rear entrance through a gap in the brickwork on the street, Wellsy saw how exposed to enemy fire his approach would be. He heard the shout to advance and sprinted ahead. He was one of the first to enter. Once inside, his throat was gripped by a sickly aroma. He looked down and thought he was going to vomit. A stream of fresh blood ran the length of the narrow corridor. The soles of his boots were sticky with blood. He attempted to rub them dry on the loose-fitting cloth of his combat trousers.

'What can you see?' shouted a voice from behind.

'I've, I've . . .'

'Give me the layout.'

'I've got rooms on my left and a stairway.'

As Neneh and others brushed past him, Wellsy turned into one of the rooms. His eyes were confronted by two men, the first knelt in prayer, the second slumped against a wall. Gunfire had ripped open his stomach. He appeared to be on the cusp of death. 'There's two men here! Unarmed, I think.'

When he looked closer, the first man's body was rigid with fear, and his head rocked backwards and forwards. His comrade slid lower down the wall as his body drained itself of its guts. Wellsy averted his gaze. He had not seen death before and could not afford to be traumatised by the sight. 'Where's Sergeant Kelly?' he asked.

'Yeah, he was supposed to be in 'ere, wasn't he?' another soldier replied. But Kelly had moved to a position a few hundred metres from the police station.

Whether he rested the butt of his weapon on the ground or he gripped it between his legs, it was fiendishly difficult for Kelly to change magazines. For him to use the under-slung grenade launcher required another soldier, Tommo invariably, to 'drop a bomb in' first. There was little feeling in Kelly's left hand, which no longer seemed to belong to his body.

Faux was sitting upright against a wall, the River Tigris behind him, his rifle across his lap. Kelly could not get over how calm he was. But, then, the officer, unlike him, had not been wounded.

Dave, a Light Infantryman, and Tommo set their Minimis atop a wall, pulling the bi-pod legs apart until they snapped straight on the uneven masonry. They could fire with superb accuracy and power at targets across the river. Satisfied with their positions, the pair dived back down behind the wall.

'You know where you're gonna fire, yeah?' asked Dave.

'Yup,' replied Tommo.

'OK. On the count of three. One . . . two . . . three!'

Dave and Tommo jumped up and squeezed the triggers, releasing a torrent of rounds. The percussive power of the Minimis in tandem was awesome.

When the noise died down, Kelly attempted a radio conversation with Passmore. Foiled by poor reception, he ended the transmission with, 'Just fucking get over here . . . I hate fucking officers!'

Wellsy had heard Kelly more clearly. 'Sergeant Kelly, can you hear me? It's Wellsy, are you there?' There was no response. Wellsy was outside the police station, the closest he had been to Kelly's location since the search had begun. At camp, Kelly's presence made the other Condorites feel claustrophobic. The irony of him pursuing someone he dreamt of escaping was not lost on Wellsy as he took cover.

Passmore scanned the skyline. 'You see that flat rooftop over there? It's a block of flats or something.'

'Yes, boss.'

'We're going to get up there and get some eyes on. It's a nightmare getting comms. I don't think Sergeant Kelly's far from here, but we need to establish his precise location.'

They came under heavy fire as soon as they moved. 'Payton, get in there!' Wellsy stared at the Jock until he squeezed himself against a wall. Wellsy and Rush identified the positions of three gunmen. They were identically dressed, apart from one whose black outfit was embellished with a green headdress. He lowered himself behind the rooftop wall. This concealed position, combined with the steep angle of fire, made him a difficult target. Wellsy watched as Rush's strikes peppered the masonry just a couple of feet below him.

'Rushy, up a bit, mate,' Wellsy suggested as he himself took aim. The Iraqi was seemingly unaware or untroubled by their fire. But when he raised himself fractionally, he moved into Wellsy's crosshairs. A brush of his left forefinger confirmed his safety catch was off, and Wellsy compressed the trigger. He guessed that two or three seconds elapsed before the Iraqi dropped his rocket-propelled grenade launcher and fell backwards.

Wellsy was in disbelief that in his first contact he had struck a human target. Keegs was going to be sick with jealousy. To have been left behind at Condor was bad enough, but to learn Wellsy had a notch on his barrel would compound his frustration. It might have been unspoken, but from their point of view the purpose of being in Iraq was to put down live rounds. As young, enthusiastic infantry soldiers, it was what they lived for.

Rush suffered a stoppage. He crouched low to pull the cocking handle back and forth until the stillborn round was ejected.

Ahead of the section of British soldiers chasing Kelly, Neneh and Glen agreed to cover each other as they crossed the highway, with the Para to proceed first. At least that was the arrangement as Neneh understood it. Glen just ran off. Seconds later, a round missed the Scot's head by inches. There had to be a good reason why Glen had not stopped; whatever it was, Neneh felt let down and alone. 'Fuck it!' he shouted. It was hard not to feel vulnerable when he was such a big target.

Neneh was coming under fire from the police station, which had been reoccupied by insurgents. He feared the longer he spent in the town's rabbit warren of narrow streets, the harder it would be to escape. Who got shot, where and when, was just a lottery. He vented his frustration when he caught up with Glen, who was standing in the open a little further down the street.

'Payton, get into cover,' Wellsy snapped again. Having quit smoking, his desperation for a cigarette now shortened his temper.

Everyone heard a loud crack a few seconds later, and they all turned towards where their ears had located the sound. Glen's facial expression was now one of deepest resignation. 'Are you all right, mate?' Wellsy asked.

Glen twisted his body around and pointed over his shoulder. His body armour looked dog-chewed. Wellsy and Rush ran towards him and dragged him into cover. Both pulled field dressings from their webbing, but two dressings were no use without a bandage. They stuffed one of the square-shaped cotton pads back into an empty packet and withdrew a length of fabric to hold a single dressing in place. Glen was mute as his body armour and shirt were pulled off. There was a long, thin insertion across his lower back, as if he had been cut with a knife.

'It's just a graze, mate,' Wellsy said, breathlessly.

Glen was convinced that this was false encouragement. He told himself that the worse the wound was, the more other soldiers would seek to reassure the victim. 'Look, mate,' he sighed – they were not really mates and had only been acquainted a few hours – 'just tell me how bad it is, yeah?' Glen patted his lower back.

'Seriously, mate, it's just a graze!' Wellsy's face was flushed with relief, but Glen still thought he was being tricked. 'If it was a proper entry wound then you'd have an exit wound, wouldn't you? You ain't got one, 'ave you?'

Foolishness and relief now replaced Glen's fear of death. His body armour had repelled the round, which he later discovered lodged inside the fabric. The armour was so torn up nobody would want to wear it again. 'Well, I had thought that myself,' Glen retorted. Normality resumed when the

Para major mocked him: 'You'll do anything to get off PT, won't you, Glen?'

Not usually talkative, Payton suddenly had plenty to say: 'Thank God you moved me!' It took a few seconds before Wellsy realised what he meant. Payton had been sitting in the same position as Glen until just before the shots rang out.

Privately, Wellsy accepted the likelihood of being shot so long as it was while he was doing his job properly. He would continue to take the calculated risks this entailed. It would sicken him to be hit by a cheap, lucky shot.

Wellsy moved off from the others to continue his search for Kelly and his team. His technique for moving swiftly under threat of fire was a hybrid shuffle-cum-sprint with his legs bent and the top half of his body sloped forwards. His next obstacle was a wall. He took a long run-up and kept his speed high. He hoped forward momentum would translate into vertical lift when he jumped. But a jagged edge of rock caught on his kit. He was halfway up the wall and halfway down. As his fingers grasped for purchase, he felt 'proper scared'. He heard the rat-a-tat of small-arms fire nearby. His arms were heavy; his mouth burned dry. All his natural energy seemed spent. The obscenity quotient in his thoughts and speech rose accordingly. Fuck the webbing, or whatever was going to get ripped. The tension released, and he crested the wall.

In the sanctuary on the other side, he took comfort beneath the flight path of enemy ordnance, knowing it was destined for elsewhere. But the sound of footsteps disturbed his repose. He jerked his head sideways and aligned his eyes with the junction between alleyways. He righted himself into a firing position and felt his fingertip against the warm trigger; the slightest increase in pressure would dispatch a round. The footsteps grew louder. It was a moment of all moments: utterly life changing or ending. Yet he hesitated, and this momentary paralysis saved Neneh's life. The Scot stood in front of him and smiled broadly. 'What's the fuss?'

'Fuck me, Neneh. I almost shot you dead!' Wellsy gasped.

'Aye, is that right, marsh man? Well, just as well ye didnae, eh?'

Relief washed over Wellsy but could not refresh him. He felt utterly done in.

'Have a ciggie, man, ye know ye want one,' Neneh said.

'Nah, Neneh, I don't smoke.'

'Ye might as well. It could be yer last, eh?'

'Yeah . . . Thaaanks for thaaaat . . .' Tiredness extended the natural drawl in Wellsy's voice. 'Where's everyone else?'

'Coming after me, I s'pose.'

Right on cue, Payton crashed over the wall and landed on top of Wellsy. 'Come on, youse two,' said Neneh. 'Get on with it. We've gottae find Paul Kelly.'

Wellsy, Payton and Rush, who had made up ground from behind, scuttled after Neneh. They had tired of this never-ending urban assault course.

'Get doon there, marsh man,' said Neneh.

'Sorry?' Wellsy had no idea what 'marsh man' meant – it was a derogatory term for the English.

Neneh needed to clear the ground on the wall's other side. 'Oan tha floor, where ye belong.'

Few at Condor picked an argument with Neneh, such was his size. Reluctantly, Wellsy got down on all fours and his spine compressed beneath fifteen stone of infanteer. Neneh could not resist the temptation to give Wellsy's head a wee kick on his way up. Payton did likewise, but only accidently. With no enemy in sight, they all climbed over and continued their journey until they reached a padlocked gate.

'Fuck it!' Rush said, shaking the lock in his hand. 'I'll shoot it off.'

'Yeah, right,' said Neneh, as he watched him take aim. 'This isnae Hollywood, Rushy. I'll just get oot of yer line of sight before ye try, eh? If ye fire now, ye'll hit me.' Neneh trotted to one side. Rounds pinged off the padlock. 'Told ye. We'll just have tae climb over the wall.' Neneh lit another cigarette and smiled at Wellsy, whose resistance was on the wane. 'If ye get shot, remember: ye couldae had yer last ciggie off me.'

A grenade exploded nearby, close enough to suggest that the enemy had located their new position. As they moved on, they heard snatches of Kelly's voice in their headphones. He said repeatedly that he was 'near the police station'. But that could not be right, could it? They had just come from there. But the radio traffic only flowed one way; Kelly could not hear them.

They began to ascend the external stairs of a small residential block. The group now consisted of eight men, and every step they took increased their vulnerability to sniper fire. As he climbed, Wellsy saw blood on the shirt of the soldier in front of him. He slapped him on the shoulder.

'Oh, sorry, it's you Glen. I didn't know who you were, and I thought you'd been shot, but that must be from before.'

'Yeah, it's me,' he replied. 'Sod being left there.'

The Para took a drag on a cigarette. ''Ere, 'ave a fag.'

'Not you as well. I've got Neneh, our corporal, telling me to 'ave one because it might be my last.'

'He ain't wrong.'

'It's been seven months since my last one. If I can get through today, I don't think I'll ever smoke again.' Wellsy was worried he might relax if he smoked a cigarette.

The same stairs led inside to a landing where two soldiers were tasked to secure the floor area. Another pair did likewise on the next level. The stairway narrowed before Neneh and Rush reached the rooftop. The descent of the sun beneath Qalat Salih's tallest buildings was ominous. Without night-sights and navigational aids, and with such erratic communications, they feared their chances of survival would fade with the light. 'Only a fucking hour,' Neneh thought to himself, remembering that was how long he had reckoned they would be gone from Condor. 'A fucking big miscalculation on my part.'

For all the energy expended to reach and climb this building, there was no sign below of Paul Kelly. A massive palm tree blocked Neneh's view of where he thought his platoon sergeant might be. En route to the next rooftop, Neneh heard Rush describe how an old man had burst out onto one of the landings and attacked him with a candle stick. Rush might have embellished the story, but it amused nevertheless.

Wellsy heard a young baby cry. 'Weird to hear something normal, isn't it?' he muttered.

Incoming fire pinned Rush down. When the gunmen broke cover, Neneh slotted them. Wounded Iraqis were carried along the main road towards the hospital. Wellsy now expected to be shot. There had been so many near misses; surely his luck was spent?

4

Lights Go Down

Outside Camp Abu Naji James Dormer cupped his eyes and counted the Warrior armoured vehicles emerging from the dust cloud. The half-eaten dirt track bowed beneath the weight of thousands of kilogrammes of mechanised firepower. Just a few metres separated each vehicle, and as elephants linked trunks and tails, so each Warrior's gun extended towards the rear of the next. Drivers adjusted their helmets and completed radio checks; crew members ensured the Warriors' main weapons – the 30 mm cannon and the 7.62 mm chain gun – were ready for battle. The chain gun was originally designed for a helicopter, its ammunition fed from above in long strips of rounds known as link. The weapon was prone to jamming, but experienced gunners learned to anticipate stoppages. The rumble of V12 engines ensured each Warrior would be heard before it was seen. With a maximum road speed of 75 kph, the journey to Qalat Salih would be short.

James's visit to Condor had preceded Kelly and Passmore's departure, and neither had expressed anxiety about their excursion, so he was taken aback now. On his fact-finding mission James found Passmore's men had taken up residence in the best accommodation. He and his Jocks would have to clear the rubble from their quarters. The relocation was driven by the intention to centralise ICDC training and to improve security at Condor. James's jundies (aka 'ragheads', 'flip-flops', 'sand-pakis' or, for officers' usage in front of top brass, 'people of indigenous origin') were based at Sparrowhawk, the airfield adjacent to Abu Naji. They were to move into the ICDC camp next door to Condor. By his own admission, James was as green as young officers could be, and the Argylls' notice to move to Iraq had arrived at battalion headquarters only days after him. Kelly ate the likes of Dormer for breakfast. 'Your plan is shit, you're shit. How the fuck do you think that'll work?' Kelly would say whenever James's suggestions deviated from his. Dormer did not envy James Passmore for having Kelly as his platoon sergeant; Hendy let him know more subtly when he strayed.

James's mode of transport denied him his wish to tag along with the quick-reaction force. He and Hendy drove a soft-skinned Land-Rover – this mission was for 'armour only'.

Empty bullet casings were scattered around Kelly. He rolled onto his right side and tucked his left elbow up beneath his armpit. This area would soon go numb beneath his body weight. His oppos had adopted more conventional 'prone' positions on their stomachs: their left hands cradled their rifles while their right hands were held in trigger position. The exception was the lantern-jawed Faux, still crouching on his heels, his legs drawn up tightly beneath him and his back resting against the steeply sloped concrete wall. Kelly cocked his head and stared into the near distance. The afternoon light would soon dissipate, but the abandoned Land-Rovers and a juggernaut loaded with oil barrels remained visible. He and Tommo had established a routine to operate the under-slung grenade launcher: Tommo would drop a dildo-sized missile down the tube, and Kelly would squeeze the trigger. Kelly's third attempt scored a direct hit, killing an Iraqi policeman.

His grenades spent, Kelly returned to his rifle. Again he relied upon Tommo's assistance, this time to load fresh magazines. The locals fired AK47s and Dushka heavy machine guns, and threw bundles of explosives sealed inside canvas bags into the courtyard of the Badr house. The building was close enough to Kelly's position for him to hear Loz shout target indications to Goacher: 'GPMG [General Purpose Machine Gun] gunner, 100 metres, reference house to the right of the alleyway, door open, lone gunman. Rapid fire!'

Kelly had an idea. 'Major Faux, I need to get back to my vehicles. There are weapons still in mine and radio equipment in the other.' The enemy took Kelly's request as their cue to launch another attack. As the ground around him shuddered, Kelly assumed Faux would advise him to wait. Not a bit.

'Yup, good idea. Get your troops up there, Kelly, make your way to the vehicles and get them back here.'

'Yes, sir.'

'Try to tow yours back with the good one.'

'Yes, sir. Will do.'

'Me and my big fucking mouth,' thought Kelly. He knew there was no room for manoeuvre with Faux, and as it had been his suggestion, he felt obliged to proceed. But he was running low on ammunition: his standard issue of four magazines were long gone, and he was tearing through rounds confiscated from the non-combatants.

Kelly pressed 'send' on his PRR. 'Loz? Loz? It's Paul.'

'Yeah, Paul, hearing you.'

'Get your team out here with me. We're going up the road to recover our vehicles and bring them back here.'

Fearful his wounded hand might touch the floor, Kelly shuffled his body around awkwardly, and repeated the plan for the benefit of those crouched behind him: 'My blokes, listen in. We're going to bring the Land-Rovers back. Line up on me. Loz's team will join on the end, and we'll fire and manoeuvre towards the vehicles.' And to Tommo he said, 'Mate, once we reach the vehicles, tie a rope from yours so we can attach the burnt-out wagon and drag it back behind us.'

'Yeah, no probs, sergeant.'

Kelly was surprised not to have seen or heard from Loz already. He spoke into his radio microphone: 'Loz, let's go. Get the blokes out here now.'

'Yeah, roger that, Paul. I've just been briefed by the company sergeant major. I'll wait here. I'm sending my team out now.'

Kelly spat out his response: 'Get your fucking arse out here now. Get your team lined up with mine and let's get these fucking vehicles.' Kelly was convinced that Loz wanted to put his men in the line of fire before himself. It would forever be etched into Kelly's consciousness that Loz was untrustworthy. Loz's friends disputed Kelly's interpretation of this episode.

The atmosphere was charged by their disagreement as they progressed up the street. The acrid aroma told them Smudger's Land-Rover was close. Its metal chassis was twisted and the rifle rack melted. The magazine was still attached to Smudger's weapon, but there was a large hole in the casing where rounds had exploded. Costly kit in his day-sack had also been destroyed, including a Combat Weapon Sight and medical supplies. Kelly cautiously stretched out his good arm and grasped the weapon. He was pleased to deny the Mahdi Army a trophy of war.

Finally, one of Passmore's section, standing on a rooftop, saw Kelly, and they began to make their way down to their wounded sergeant. Kelly was no more than 100 metres from where their search for him had begun. At the same time as his position was identified, the first of the Warriors arrived. The vehicle commander flipped the hatch open; this heightened his personal vulnerability. His crew jettisoned crates of 5.56 mm ammunition and water bottles, which skidded across the main street.

'Fucking hell, he's risking it,' Kelly muttered. Out of the vehicle commander's line of sight, a rocket-propelled grenade launcher was primed and aimed directly at him. The warhead slammed into the hull. His crew responded with cannon fire.

Kelly's and Passmore's steps quickened noticeably as they approached each other.

'Hello, sir, how's it going?' Kelly asked Passmore. 'Come to join the party?'

'Not bad, Sergeant Kelly,' Passmore replied. Inevitably, the conversation steered towards Kelly's wounds. 'What happened to you?'

Kelly felt obliged to hold up his left hand. 'Tried to catch a round,' he said dryly. Passmore smiled, not unkindly. 'Are you coming back to the Badr building with us or staying here?' Kelly asked.

'Lead the way, Sergeant Kelly. We'll head down there.'

On their march to the same location, Neneh and Wellsy shared a joke about how they had initially mistaken the Warriors for Iraqi tanks. They had heard a rumbling noise and had assumed the worst.

Kelly was particularly pleased to be reunited with Neneh; the Scot was his senior section commander. 'Hello, mate. Glad you could join me,' Kelly said.

'What the fuck have ye been doing, ye fucking idiot?'

Kelly laughed and replied, 'Making friends, mate. You know me.'

'Ye havenae seen any Paras around, have you, Paul? One's been wounded, but we've lost the others.'

'No, mate. Didn't know any of them were in town.'

Just then, the paratroopers emerged from a crowd. Wellsy

watched agog as they guided a group of local elders towards Major Faux; after all the rounds he had put down, he thought the talking was over. He reminded himself that he was not one for petty protests: 'Leave the officers to sort this out – the ceasefire or whatever's happening to the prisoners. If they fuck it up, they fuck it up. Just get on with your own shit.' Wellsy stood tall as the sky bruised above him.

The meeting was terminated and Faux briefed Passmore: 'The enemy are moving more heavy weapons into the area and almost have us surrounded.'

'Right.'

'I think we're going to have to release these prisoners after all. It might be the only way to appease this crowd. They're getting very angry. The loudspeakers have been giving it everything all afternoon, inciting them to do this and that . . .' Passmore nodded. 'It's our CO's call, though, what happens. He won't want to lose face. We can't afford to give them a victory. That would be fatal.' The thinking was that even a small victory would strengthen the insurgents' hand. However, it might also have been beneficial to show clemency to the townspeople of Qalat Salih who were caught in the crossfire between a minority of insurgents and the British Forces. 'That probably means we'll be staying here for a while,' Faux continued, 'until the situation has been resolved. Like I said, we don't want them thinking they've won.'

'No, absolutely not.'

'We're very low on ammo, but a lot of enemy weapons we've captured are loaded. Just have to crack on with them.'

It was clear to Neneh and Wellsy that the British had outstayed their welcome. As darkness fell, and it fell quickly, the Iraqis established new positions on the rooftops. They had also used the passage of time while negotiations took place to replenish their ammunition stores.

'If we don't get out of here by the time it's fully dark, we won't be getting out of here at all,' said Neneh, matter-of-factly. 'We havnae got any night-vision goggles. I left mine at Condor.'

'Yeah, fuck it,' replied Wellsy. 'Mine are in the Land-Rover.'

As sweat chilled through his shirt, Wellsy had the feeling icy fingers were gripping his shoulders; his body temperature dropped. 'The LI [Light Infantry] commander says we're staying here until we've sorted this out, apparently,' Wellsy said with a jittery voice.

'Aye,' Neneh replied, 'that's easy tae say when yer outside the town, right enough. It's no so easy here, eh? We're outtae ammunition.'

Wellsy took a photograph of Kelly which captured his platoon sergeant slumped against a wall with his eyes closed, as if he had seen enough. Kelly had begun a mental journey towards abstraction, his mind a dark, distorting mirror. He convinced himself he was destined to die there. He pictured his wife and children – those his death would punish most. So, this was not an appropriate moment for Wellsy to dig up the past: the time in Northern Ireland when Kelly told him, only half jokingly, that were Wellsy ever to be wounded, Kelly would take his photograph first before he administered first aid.

When Major Sabeer arrived at the Badr house, he seemed unperturbed by the gunfire, while his friend and interpreter Safar, who had accompanied him on the journey from Condor, translated the announcements broadcast from the rooftop speakers: 'You will encounter greater forces that will come down upon you. People are coming from other villages with bigger weapons. Release the prisoners, otherwise you will die like the men in Majar al-Kabir.' A suggestion was then broadcast in English: 'Leave the town. Get out of Iraq. Go home.'

Kelly smiled wryly. 'If only we could get out,' he thought. As for the size of the battle, he did not think it could get any bigger. He had run dry, having fired in excess of three hundred rounds, around three times his personal allocation, as well as grenades. Other soldiers were on their last magazine. Those in the Badr house mocked the gravity of their situation. Every incoming rocket-propelled grenade or Chinese rocket was met with an 'Ooh' or 'Ahh'. Their laughter carried towards Kelly's position on the evening breeze. 'What do they think they are, missiles or fucking fireworks?' he wondered. Other soldiers vomited, their stomachs rejecting the piping hot water that had been stored in the Warriors.

Wellsy and Neneh approached the house from the street outside. 'Where is he?' Neneh asked.

'Who?' the soldier replied.

'Smudger, faer fuck's sake!'

'He's with the POWs.'

His friends' arrival sparked a reaction inside Smudger, who kicked out at the POWs. Responsibly, Elliott held him back.

At a briefing for junior commanders, Passmore told Wellsy that it was likely they would remain in Qalat Salih overnight. He was then tasked to secure the rear of the building. Wellsy took Elliott, Kuryawa and Payton. He had followed Neneh's instructions throughout the contact, but Wellsy wished he had got a few more rounds down and had got himself into some offensive positions. At least Payton was still alive. Keeping his rounds down had also reduced the likelihood of him wounding an innocent bystander.

Wellsy's men were stretched along the wall, but, such was

the darkness, he could only identify them as individuals when he was crouched beside them. He stared into their eyes, seeking confirmation of their awareness of the task at hand. 'You know what you have to do, yeah?'

'Yeah, Wellsy, watch for anyone coming over that wall.'

'You've bombed up, yeah?'

'Yeah, got a fresh mag on, mate.'

'Good.'

'Do I tell them about the grenade threat?' he wondered. 'Is it worth giving them something else to worry about?'

''Ere, lads, this is serious shit, right, and we want to get out of 'ere alive. You need to know this, right? I can hear footsteps behind that wall, and if they throw a grenade over, we ain't gonna see it till it goes off.'

Wellsy heard something or someone move in the bushes. Instinctively, he heard a gunman changing his stance, a sound he had made himself on hundreds of field exercises. He charged into the long grass. A goat sprinted away. 'Fucking hell,' he groaned. 'I could do without that.'

The Light Infantry company sergeant major slapped Kelly on the shoulder. 'Ammo is critical, right? I want your team to centralise all the AKs and 7.62 millie and the RPGs – anything we found earlier. We've run out, so we'll have to use theirs, OK?'

'Yup, no problem.' Kelly helped himself to an AK47, four magazines of 7.62 mm and a 9 mm pistol. He felt better for getting back into the swing of the firefight.

Shortly afterwards, though it was difficult to judge the passage of time, the senior officers gathered at the Incident Control Point ordered the casualties to be extracted from inside Qalat Salih. It was their judgement that the threat had diminished sufficiently to allow this to happen. 'Sergeant Kelly,' said Faux, his voice carrying above the exchange of gunfire. 'I thought I told you to leave this town three hours ago?'

Kelly returned his gaze with gratitude. With Neneh *in situ*, he could justify his retirement from the battlefield. 'Yes, sir,' Kelly sighed. 'I'll be on my way.'

'Get yourself to the Incident Control Point on Route 6. The whole battlegroup is waiting outside to flatten this place if the gunfire doesn't stop soon. There is a Chinook waiting to take you to hospital at the Shaibah Logistics Base, OK?'

'Yes, sir.'

Kelly said his farewells and turned to Neneh. 'You're on, mate. I'll see you later.'

Kelly and Smudger were driven out of Qalat Salih in a Snatch Land-Rover. They saw Major Adam Griffiths, Colour Sergeant Brian Meldrum, armoured fighting vehicles and infantry reinforcements. Kelly's eyes lowered as he glimpsed Meldrum's approach; he loathed Meldrum and slandered him at every given opportunity.

'Where's your rifle?' Meldrum asked abruptly. Kelly wondered if Meldrum might have asked him about his condition.

'How should I know?' He could not be bothered to explain he had given it to Smudger.

'I need to know where your rifle is.'

'Fuck off, Brian.'

Their exchange was interrupted by unarmed Iraqi police officers, who asked if there were Coalition Force fatalities. 'No,' Kelly snapped.

'Iraqis dead?'

'Yeah, loads.'

'Chopper inbound,' someone shouted. Lieutenant Colonel Ponting wanted to congratulate Kelly. When Ponting enquired about Kelly's condition, he responded with a rather gruesome comment about the Iraqi death toll. He wished immediately he could retract it, but the conversation ended and he was guided towards the rear ramp. Twenty pairs of eyes stared at him as he emplaned. He was confused at first why the other passengers looked at him as if he was a threat. He had forgotten that there was blood all over him, he was armed with Iraqi weapons and was as dark-skinned as an Arab. At best they might take him for a member of Special Forces. He would prefer that.

'Straight to the front, guys,' the medical crash-team doctor said, beckoning to the casualties. 'Just sit down there.'

Soldiers attempted spasmodic bursts of conversation, but the twin-turbine engines drowned out their voices. The rotors blasted warm air in all directions. The Chinook shook and seemed more likely to bore a hole in the ground than achieve flight. The buffeting forced passengers to cling to their seatbacks and each other. Finally, the bird rose and tilted forwards. The ascent raised the pitch of the rotors to a higher, more strained note. Transition lift had begun. Onlookers cowered against its backwash and coughed because of the 'av-gas' fumes. The Chinook would be a slow and easy target for any insurgent armed with a rocket-propelled grenade launcher as it travelled south.

Soon after Kelly was evacuated, an agreement was struck. Despite all prior refusals to release the prisoners, they were to be granted freedom, but the first Land-Rover to extract under the auspices of the peace deal came under fire and one of its front tyres burst. Incoming fire continued as it reversed back to the Badr house. Wellsy and Passmore mounted an unarmoured wagon. 'There's no way I'm driving out of 'ere blind,' Wellsy said, so he cut a hole in its tarpaulin roof. He and a private soldier from the Light Infantry stuck out their heads.

Staring at each other, their faces were grey and anxious

in the darkness. Something cold rippled up their spines. Wellsy was 'bricking it' now, and he did something he had not done before: establish the blood-group details of his partner. Although a transfusion would be impossible on the vehicle, the fact that they were both O positive somehow reassured him.

Passmore, who was sitting in the back of the Land-Rover, grabbed Wellsy's leg when he opened fire. 'I just wanted to keep a few heads down, sir,' Wellsy explained. 'There was a few blokes acting suspiciously, like, on one of the rooftops.'

They reached the Incident Control Point, where the Warriors were parked in an all-around-defensive position. They were safe at last. Major Faux addressed them with elegiac understatement: 'What happened today, boys, was out of your control. You were great. But you might not be able to sleep tonight.'

Neneh smiled dryly. All that philosophical stuff about taking life was 'officer shite'. He knew he would sleep soundly; Wellsy likewise.

The padre added, 'Gather in. Don't feel bad about what you've done. You did what you had to do, and you've looked after your mates. If you do have any doubts, call your families when you get back to camp. They will let you know that you made the right decision when you pulled the trigger.'

In truth, this was something they had to work out for themselves. They began to as they sat in a circle smoking. Wellsy finally lit a cigarette. 'We've been in a contact, then,' one of them said, 'and a pretty big one at that. We got out of it, too.'

'It's not how you expect it to be, though, is it?' another countered. 'I didn't know what the fuck was going on half the time. So much confusion, you know? It's just mad.'

'There were so many near misses,' added Wellsy. 'I almost

shot Neneh by this wall. And he had a round miss him by, what, a couple of inches, or something?'

'Aye, man. I reckoned after that and you trying yer best tae slot me that it wisnae gonnae be ma day, ye know? But, right enough, here I am.'

'What about Paul?' Wellsy said. 'I didn't know he was hurt so bad. But I guess we couldn't see beneath his bandages. I thought he was all right, as it goes. He was just sitting there by the wall a bit quiet, like. He was a bit shocked, but it must be a bit worse than that.'

Wellsy was desperate to see his best mate when he returned to Condor. A wicked smile spread across his face. 'Keegs, Keegs, he's gonna be sick with envy. Wait till I tell 'im,' he thought.

It was not rocket science to understand why the locals had reacted with such aggression to the presence of British Forces: it was Friday, their holy day of the week. They were better let be after prayers at the mosque. The Light Infantry had poked a hornet's nest and subsequently scores of Iraqis had been either wounded or killed.

On the eve of the war, Lieutenant Colonel Tim Collins had famously exhorted his soldiers that they should be sensitive to the culture and customs of the inhabitants of Iraq. British Forces had failed in that respect in Qalat Salih that day.

It was noisy aboard the helicopter. 'What happened?' asked the doctor.

'Sorry?'

'I said, what happened?'

'Oh, gunshot wound through the hand.'

'Have you had morphine?'

'No.' Kelly paused. He wondered if the doctor might be impressed. If he was, it did not register facially.

'I'm just going to place a drip in your arm.' The doctor found a vein, removed the cap off the phial and squirted the liquid. 'Let me have your weapon. Is it loaded?'

'Yes.'

'Give it to me. I will get someone to unload it for you.'

Kelly was emotionally attached to his weapon. 'I want to keep it. I want it back after . . .'

The doctor handed Kelly's AK to another soldier, who executed the normal safety procedures: NSPs in infanteer speak. Satisfied that it was safe, the soldier returned it to the doctor, who promised Kelly he would be reunited with it later. Kelly wished he could have put a name tag on it.

'Have you got anything else?' the doctor asked.

'Just ammo.'

'I'd better have that as well. Do you want morphine? I can put it in through the drip if you want.'

His wound was numb; he had never had morphine and had hoped not to do so. But he accepted. 'Yup, I'm happy with that. Yes, please.' He was hooked up. 'Cheers, mate.'

Kelly saw the soldier tasked to hold his drip bag was slumped to one side. 'Get that up, will you?' snapped the doctor.

When the soldier righted himself, Kelly recognised him. 'Shit, mate, I'd forgotten about you,' Kelly said with a smile. 'Doc, this is Private Smith. He's survived two RPGs. He got blown up in a Land-Rover.' Smudger lifted the drip above his head as if it was as heavy as a barbell.

Eventually, the helicopter landed, and the doctor walked Smudger and Kelly towards the field hospital. 'Who's receiving, who's receiving?' he called to the medics huddled around the entrance. They ignored him and continued smoking.

'Wankers,' thought Kelly.

Once inside, doctors fretted around him, while Smudger was laid out on the other side of the ward. 'We want to remove your clothing, cut it off . . .'

'What?' Kelly was alarmed. 'I don't think so, mate. I'll take it off myself.'

'No, you don't understand,' a nurse said, trying to reassure him. 'We don't want to damage your arm any more than it has been.'

'Listen to me. You are not cutting anything off me. I bought this assault vest myself, and this is my own desert smock and body armour. It cost me a lot of money. I'll take it off myself.'

Kelly went into full awkward mode; perhaps his dose of morphine had not kicked in yet. 'And what about him?' he asked. 'What's happening with Smudge? You're not touching me until I know he's all right. Nobody's doing anything for him.'

'Sergeant Kelly,' the doctor said sternly, 'you need an operation on that hand. We still don't know how bad it is.'

'No, mate, I'm not going anywhere. Not until you tell me all my blokes are OK. So you'd better go and find out, hadn't you?'

The doctor shuffled away. When the nurse removed his blood-soaked bandages, his hand was twice its normal size. Kelly saw her eyes drill into the entry wound. 'Nice hole,' she said. His wrist was open, with bits of flesh flapping around the edges. The exit wound was moist and glazed. 'Come on, get them off,' the nurse said, the corner of her lips turning up.

'Sorry?'

'Your trousers . . .'

'Don't think so, nurse.' Kelly's objection was weak. He looked back up from undressing to see a camera pointing at him. 'For fuck's sake!'

'We always take pictures of the wounds when the casualties come in.'

'I want copies!' His flabby chest, not his wounds, made Kelly self-conscious. It also disconcerted him to remove his clothes in front of another woman besides his wife. 'Just keep my man boobs out of the shot, will you?'

When the doctor confirmed Kelly's men had extracted without further injury, he agreed to let them wheel him into the operating theatre.

The bosses at Condor wanted to keep up the tempo. 'Guys, guys, I know you're all fucking knackered, but there's some essential drills to go through now. We need you to check yourselves, make sure you have not got any little wounds, that you haven't taken any shrapnel or secondary frag and that. There's water and chocolate waiting for you in the television room. You can all have a seat in there while you go through the re-supply drills. If you lost kit, we'll have to account for all that being missing, all the little gubbins and shit. OK? We'll have to get it back from Abu Naji.'

The television was on, but Wellsy did not register the programme – it was just pictures and noise. He had lost that level of comprehension. When Wellsy spoke to Keegs, the latter's determination to disguise his envy only made it more obvious.

Wellsy held his rifle in one hand and his assault vest in the other as he shuffled from the TV room towards his bed space. Dumping his kit on the floor, he collapsed exhausted. So much for Major Faux's suggestion he might find sleep elusive. He had never craved it more and was convinced that the heaviness of his arms and legs would confine him to bed for days.

5

The Concept

I flew over it [Condor] on the recce and visited it on the advance party to inspect the rudimentary engineering works that had been carried out to make it fit to be used as a base. I always saw it as an ideal base by virtue of its position: isolated yet in proximity to Route 6, which, with the assistance of the ICDC, we had to defend. The conditions in what was no more than a collection of hardened aircraft shelters were basic to say the least, but I knew that the Jocks would soon make it into a home from home. I had learned never to underestimate the ability of the British soldier to 'adapt and overcome' adverse conditions.

Lieutenant Colonel J.D. Gray

When 6 Platoon had first secured tenancy of the larger accommodation bunker, Wellsy moved in with Corporal Steve 'Izzy' Izzard and a mix of junior non-commissioned officers, while Keegs, Kev Challis and Rob Schwar chose digs along the corridor. The other Steve Wells – there were two soldiers of that name at Condor – Lee Gidalla and a private soldier who had collected the unfortunate moniker 'Horsehead' shared another room. The camp's medics and chefs shacked up in the smallest room. This had already become known as the jinxed room, because their record of personality clashes and setting themselves on fire forced a rapid turnover of personnel during the first months of the tour.

Kelly had hated the first chef from the off. 'If I get my guts blown out today, this is what everyone's going to see:

one of your fucking pies!' The chef was a young lad whom Kelly had thought would have benefited from being more proactive. He had wanted him to 'stag on', do a few hours in the Ops Room and on the camp gate. The lad had replied that, as a chef, it was not in his remit. When he had refused Kelly's order to clean his rifle, Kelly had grabbed him by the throat. Kelly had then applied to have the chef charged for insubordination but discovered that a complaint had been lodged against him for assault. Company Sergeant Major George Lees had strived to find a compromise but both men had been immovable. Kelly had received an unofficial wrist slap, and the chef had been transferred to somewhere less enclosed and tribal.

Condorites did not take easily to outsiders, and one of the replacement chefs was ambushed with flour and eggs. The caterers warranted greater sympathy: the cooking facilities at their disposal were minimal. Loz Loseby's answer to their mediocre cuisine was to douse every dish in sweet chilli sauce, a less offensive, more practical form of protest.

Condor was like a squat for the disenfranchised, their existence seemingly forgotten for weeks at a time, at least until the Qalat Salih siege and the arrival of 7 Platoon.

Jonny Gray's visit left Neneh irate. They chatted as both drew heavily on cigarettes. 'So, how are things? What was the contact in Qalat Salih like?' Gray asked, seeming eager to share his experience.

'Aye, nae bad . . .'

As Neneh outlined events, they were interrupted by a female officer who belonged to Gray's administrational entourage. 'Sir, your transport is about to leave.'

With that, Gray dropped his cigarette, ground the butt with his heel and marched off. Knowing Neneh's contempt for officers and those who discarded fag ends, the private soldiers who witnessed this scene were bent double with laughter.

'That fucker has really rattled my cage,' Neneh snarled. 'It's gonnae take me a long time not tae want tae punch his lights out.'

As Neneh was the first Argyll non-commissioned officer for decades to experience a proper battle, he felt entitled to a little more respect. But Gray had given him the impression of abruptly losing interest. It was not for Neneh to be sympathetic towards Gray's other priorities: the 5,000 ICDC recruits who were now in training in camps across southern Iraq. The best non-commissioned officers focused on the nuts and bolts of daily soldiering and the welfare of their men.

Gray would have liked to have spent longer at Condor and to have said farewell to Neneh properly, but Gray had commitments to juggle. He also remained troubled by a recent visit to Baghdad, where he had witnessed the approach of the US 1st Armoured Division to ICDC training. Rather than embedding and living alongside the volunteers, they merely dispensed wisdom and largesse from behind mirrored sunglasses on rare visits to the Iraqis' barracks. Gray did not believe this was going to achieve results and concluded there was a 'doctrinal gulf' between the British and American approaches. He later commented, 'Individually, there were many intelligent and capable US officers who could see what we were doing and wanted to adopt a similar approach, but it seemed that institutionally the US Army and ourselves were poles apart on a tactical level.'

It was all the more disappointing because a group of US generals had visited Basra the previous week and had been impressed with the progress of British-trained ICDC units at Camp Steven. 'Brigadier Nick Carter and I had prepared at length for the visit of General Petraeus, who was to assume responsibility for security-sector reform across Iraq,' Gray said. 'We decided that instead of one of us briefing him, Brigadier Dhia and the ICDC commanders should do so. They gave a Staff College-style briefing about ongoing ICDC operations and capabilities, and General Petraeus continually asked if the Argylls were Special Forces. I said, jokily, "They are to me."'

Neneh was summoned before the Royal Military Police. The Red Caps wanted a blow-by-blow account of the Qalat Salih siege. 'Did you offer a challenge?'

'A challenge?'

'A warning. You're supposed to give whoever you shot at a warning before you open fire.'

'Er, no, I didnae. We wis in a firefight.'

'Hmm, I don't know what we'll do about that. Tell me where or who you fired at.'

'Well, I shot at this window, this car, this doorway . . .'

He was interrupted. 'You mean you didn't shoot at selected enemy targets who fired at you first? You're only supposed to fire aimed shots, not at buildings and vehicles. You've breached the rules of engagement. Do you know what they are?'

'Look, this isnae Northern Ireland, man. Ye cannae be usin' the Yellow Card rules or whatever. We had to put suppressing fire doon in order tae fire and manoeuvre. We had a call sign in there stranded, and we didnae know where they was.'

'How many rounds did you fire?'

'Got through my four magazines, so that's one hundred and twenty. Then we'd all ran out, and the AK47s got distributed. There was a lot of firing going on with those as well, but I couldnae put a figure on it.'

'How many rounds?'

'Well, I dunno.'

'You shouldn't be firing AKs really, either. You're not officially trained on it. So we can't mention that in your statement.'

'Aye, nae bother.'

Although his rank was corporal, Neneh stepped up to become platoon sergeant in Kelly's absence. Such was his popularity, the Condorites hoped his promotion would be approved instead of a fully fledged sergeant being parachuted into the camp.

Drawn from the 1st and 2nd Battalions of the PWRR, the deployment of 6 Platoon as part of B company, 1st Battalion, the Argyll and Sutherland Highlanders, stemmed from a chance meeting between Lieutenant Colonel Gray and his friend Lieutenant Colonel James Cameron of the PWRR at an inter-unit boxing night in Northern Ireland. They privately agreed to the transfer of the PWRR soldiers to the Argylls on a temporary basis. This was mutually beneficial, as Cameron had bucked the trend by having too many recruits, while the Argylls needed a few more. The two-year-loan deal was completed 'under the radar', as Gray recalled: 'The plan was nearly scuppered by Headquarters Infantry, who tried to allocate the manpower elsewhere, but we won through in the end. Brigadier Jamie Balfour, the director of infantry, never lost an opportunity to wind me up about this deal, however, which he never fully supported. It was ended shortly after I handed over command.'

There was no talk of deployment to Iraq when Gray first met the PWRR composite platoon in Canterbury in October 2003. He told them he would treat them as Argylls for the duration of their attachment. The biggest sweetener was that because the Argylls belonged to 16 Air Assault Brigade, they would participate in some marginally more interesting infantry exercises, i.e. with an airborne or heliborne element, and they could also attempt the Parachute Regiment's exhaustive P Company selection. If they passed this course, they could attempt to qualify as military parachutists.

Private James 'Larks' Larkin and Jay Lawrence passed P Company – which included weeks of speed marches, log and stretcher races, assault courses and 'milling' (a form of boxing) – only to miss their jumps course when it clashed with an exercise already written into the Argylls' training calendar. Larks, a tousle-haired 21 year old from Hampshire, could remember when Kelly had held up his joining instructions against a window. He had read them excitedly through the glass until his sergeant mouthed the words, 'No way. You're on exercise with the rest of us.' Slots on jumps courses for non-Para Regiment soldiers were, in Larks's words, 'as rare as rocking-horse shit'. Larks's sense of injustice lingered; he knew how proud Kelly was of his wings so could not understand why he seemed so determined to deny him his.

With their English interlopers in tow, the Argylls had left Kent in early January 2004. James Dormer was among the first to deploy, and upon arrival he and Adam Griffiths drove up Route 6 into Maysan, the canvas roof of their Land-Rover snapping in the strong breeze. Neither he nor his company commander were clear as to the specific nature of their task and how ICDC mentoring would work.

Condor was far removed from Sidney Sussex College, Cambridge, where James had read English. The 23 year old was the only Condorite, perhaps the only British soldier serving in Iraq, to have appeared on the BBC quiz *University Challenge* and was an unlikely apprentice in the profession of arms. He was also too perceptive to last a day longer in uniform than the natural expiration of his short-service commission. While at the Royal Military Academy,

Sandhurst, General Sir Mike Jackson, the chief of the general staff and the Paras' colonel commandant, had asked James, 'What can you do for the [Parachute] Regiment?' James had responded, 'Well, sir, what can the Parachute Regiment do for me?' His answer was not well received.

Second lieutenants were the private soldiers of the officer class. But at least private soldiers only got squeezed from above. From day one, 'subbies' were confronted by corporals, sergeants and warrant officers with decades of experience as well as captains, majors and colonels, who it sometimes seemed were waiting for them to fail. Having joined the army with notions of helping the impoverished, the slow pace of reconstruction in Iraq compounded James's objections to the invasion and occupancy. He was not alone. Gray had been against the invasion and believed the majority of his generation of army Staff College graduates held similar views. He did not believe it constituted a 'just war'. The joke was that if Condor had been a constituency, it would have returned a 'Bring Back Saddam Hussein Party' candidate with an overwhelming majority.

Gray had been sufficiently impressed to welcome James from Sandhurst into the battalion and was untroubled that his newest subaltern had only twice visited Scotland; at least James was a Cambridge man. Gray's battalion railed against contemporary ambivalence towards class, pursuing an agenda of gentrification, including Scottish dancing lessons and the requirement for subalterns to spend £5,000 on seldom-worn uniform. James tolerated rather than embraced the traditions of a regiment in which everyone from the commanding officer to the most junior soldier was branded by their tongue: the former for sounding aristocratic, the latter for constructing a linguistic Hadrian's Wall. James found the dialects of his teenage Jocks beyond even vague comprehension. In spite of his paternal care towards them, they had already christened him 'Doormat'. Hendy ensured they stripped their rifles for cleaning but excused James the chore. As Richie Fieldman put it, 'He didnae want tae treat that sprog officer like the wee boy he was.'

James and Hendy could both remember their first meeting. 'Gottae put a hand on his shoulder,' Hendy had muttered, having steadied many a naive subaltern before. James feared Hendy thought he was a 'twat'. The fact that his sergeant spoke without moving his mouth rendered any advice he might proffer indecipherable.

Gray set the tone operationally and socially, and his air of omnipotence filled the ceilings of Saddam Hussein's palace in Basra – the makeshift battalion headquarters for the duration of the tour. Even his sharpest critics acknowledged his intelligence and political savvy, overcoming the Argylls' manpower losses to carve out their unlikely niche in the ICDC training role. Gray's Jocks had previously sat out British operations to Afghanistan and Iraq in Belfast; indeed, the Argylls' tours of the province had been arranged to let others go to war. Enough was enough. He was personally driven towards becoming the first Argylls commanding officer to deploy operationally overseas since Mad Mitch in Aden.

With the battalion facing amalgamation into the proposed Scottish super-regiment, or even disbandment, this was a vital personal victory. Prior to commanding the Argylls, Gray had worked in the office of the chief of the general staff at the Ministry of Defence in Whitehall, so had known that infantry restructuring was on the cards for a long time. He recalled, 'I always sought to portray the Argylls in the best light, even engaging in a bit of spin from time to time.'

Nobody was more committed to the concept of the ICDC

than Gray – perhaps because he did not have to suffer teaching the recruits on a daily basis. He also thought ICDC training would suit the Argylls' skill set. He used his contacts among the senior staff at land headquarters formally and informally to ensure his battalion got the job.

'I became aware of the emerging SSR [security-sector reform] theme in the autumn of 2003,' he said. 'SSR was then, and arguably still is, a strategic enabler to the exit strategy for Iraq. That summer the Argylls had just finished a two-and-a-half-year tour in Belfast, where we had been thought leaders and expert practitioners in public-order operations developed over seven consecutive marching seasons and also in the Holy Cross school dispute and its aftermath. We had taken on the role of training the trainer across Northern Ireland, both for the police and military, and had earned the praise of many in doing so. It was clear that we were the pre-eminent battalion in the army to train an internal-security force in IS/COIN [Internal Security/Counter Insurgency] operations.'

The ICDC was the brainchild of the head of the Coalition Provisional Authority, Paul Bremer. Heavily criticised for the disbandment of the Iraqi Army, he intended the ICDC as a 'rural gendarmerie' capable of securing each of Iraq's provinces.

In November 2003 the Argylls had been placed on seven days' notice to move, and in December Gray had flown to Iraq for a three-day reconnaissance mission. 'On arrival in Basra, we were briefed by Brigadier David Rutherford-Jones, the Commander of 20 Mechanised Brigade, and his very capable chief of staff, Major Alastair Aitken of the Black Watch. The task was to raise, train and deliver an operational brigade of national guards (called ICDC at that stage) for internal-security duties within six months, while my old friend Lieutenant Colonel Andrew Cuthbert would be taking care of the police and border guards. Secretly, I was pleased to have the blank sheet of paper – raising a new army – as "Cuth" had more constraints and pre-existing issues to overcome. I was seized by the enormity of the task but invigorated by the challenge. I knew that the Argylls would be up for it, and we set about designing the concept of operations over two sleepless days. We were allocated a helicopter and flew over the brigade area, dropping in at, or just flying over, possible locations to base the ICDC. One of these was Camp Condor in the south of Maysan.

'The British brigade in Basra supported the ICDC embed programme from the outset, and further discussions centred on the logistics of the plan. I explained the requirement to requisition dozens of locations across southern Iraq in which to base all the companies, battalions and brigade headquarters of the new ICDC. We left Iraq after a manic three days having agreed a plan and leaving 20 Brigade with an enormous list of enabling activities, most of which were preparatory engineering. During the recce, we discussed the lay down of the new ICDC brigade and its need to have a footprint across the area if it was to dominate the ground. Where we could, we would locate bases alongside or even within Multinational Forces bases, not least because we could all see the possibility, even then, of handing over bases to the Iraqis as they became able to assume responsibilities. It was clear from the outset that we would need to establish some new bases from scratch, in particular to dominate the vital main supply routes. Route 6 was one such route, and we decided to establish five new bases along that route. One of these was Camp Condor.

'Embedding at every level was essential to the process of recruiting, training and mentoring, as my battalion would effectively provide the Iraqi chain of command until such time as the Iraqis could take over responsibilities for themselves. I drew on British military history for inspiration.'

What had seemed entirely possible when Gray had visited Iraq in late 2003 looked less so by March 2004, as the Mahdi uprising took flight. It rankled with British officers that their US counterparts had neglected to inform them of their intention to assassinate or capture Moqtada al-Sadr, which triggered the rise of the Mahdi Army. As the Argylls were not part of the security infrastructure, decisions to enforce the unpopular weapons-disarmament policy and rinsing were not theirs to make either. Gray later said, 'The timing of the uprising could not have been more unfortunate for us. In February 2004 we were in a position in certain areas of Basra Province to plan the handover of security to the ICDC units.'

Rather than encouraging British forces to adopt a more aggressive stance, this unforeseen development should have led to a doubling of efforts on the security-sector-reform front. Law-abiding locals needed convincing that it was worthwhile to support the British, rather than side with the insurgents. Suspending weapons searches on Islamic holy days might have been a good start.

The fate of the poorly manned Scottish infantry units focused everyone's minds. At the time, three of the British Army's six worst-recruited infantry battalions were Scottish, and the Scottish infantry division was heavily reliant upon Fijian and Caribbean soldiers. Major General Andrew Graham, the Argylls' bagpipe-playing colonel-in-chief noted, 'This reinforces the impression that Scotland can no longer produce the infantrymen to man seven battalions, while providing so many soldiers to other arms and services. The storm clouds threatening our regiment have been gathering for some time. We all face losing a part of something that is very personal and very precious.' How the Argylls would fulfil their obligations to 16 Air Assault Brigade remained to be seen.

Gray's subordinates wondered at his mastery of Whitehall presentations but mocked his sense of theatre when he strode onto the parade square at Howe Barracks, Canterbury, and said, 'As you can probably tell from the way I am dressed, we're off to Iraq.'

Seeing his desert fatigues, his men scoffed. 'Aye, I think we couldae worked that oot for ourselves.'

Smudger, Aldo, Private 'Diesel' Reid, Richie and Private Kristopher 'Fishlips' Henderson had grown up on the streets of Scotland's toughest cities; they had already had their chips of commanding officers and 'crow' English officers telling them what 'tae dae'. The Jocks lived amidst their country's drug- and crime-riddled working class – a United Nations report condemned their homeland as the 'most violent place in the developed world'. According to the World Health Organisation, they were three times more likely to meet a violent death up the road than down it. In order for the Jocks to maintain their sanity in Iraq, it was key for them to strip away morality and sensitivity until only their basest selves remained, something they were perhaps accustomed to doing at home.

Gray banned any drinking until the battalion returned to Kent in July. As he put it, 'Jocks are great soldiers – it is in their blood. Their humour is disarming, and as such they are at their best in close-quarter internal-security environments where they have to win the hearts and minds. However, over 20 years I had learned that Jocks, alcohol, guns and terrorists did not mix well. So I made the decision to have a "dry tour", although I delegated to company commanders "opt out" authority for specific events.'

His Jocks had no intention of disentangling themselves from their country's twisted relationship with alcohol.

'Buckie', an inexpensive and intoxicating brew, was an intrinsic part of their lives. Whoever said that civilisation started with distillation had not tasted Buckie or the tinned whisky sold by the ICDC. Gray's edict merely meant that the Jocks' friends and families poured the wine from its glass bottle into plastic Coca-Cola containers, which were cheaper to post and less likely to break in transit.

Buckfast Tonic Wine was first credited to French monks who settled at Buckfast Abbey in the 1880s. Spanish wines known as *mistellas* were imported, to which the Benedictines added tonics according to an ancient recipe. The additional ingredients are now listed on the bottle: sodium glycerophosphate, dipotassium phosphate, disodium phosphate, vanillin and 37.5 milligrams per 100 millilitres of caffeine. The resulting concoction, with a 15 per cent alcohol content, is sold with the disclaimer, as if it was required, that 'The name Tonic Wine does not imply health giving or medicinal properties'. A cocktail of Buckie and Irn Bru together was somehow renamed 'Bamgria'.

Buckfast – or 'Fuckfast', as it is also known – is a social poison: some of Glasgow's poorest neighbourhoods are known colloquially as the 'Buckfast Triangle', and Helen Liddell, the former Scottish Secretary of State, once blamed the tipple for the anti-social behaviour of delinquent youths across the west of the country, where 70 per cent of the drink's sales originate.

As a youth, Neneh had made a pilgrimage to the monastery in Devon. Richie was also savvy to this subculture. All this street-tough private looked for was a good time – the rest was just propaganda. 'I couldnae give a fuck aboot the morality of the war. What a load of shite. Those marsh Arabs aren't even human, choppin' each other's hands off, an' that. They're just sick animals. I cannae believe how people can treat each other like that. Saddam knew the only way tae treat 'em was tae treat 'em brutally – that's tha only way ye can keep 'em in check. That Saddam wis canny, man – had tae be tae have stayed in power so long. Did a better job than us of keepin' control aroond here.'

Twenty years on from his time as a football hooligan, Hendy's chest and arms carried the scars of 'fighting withdrawals' from pubs in Dundee and Edinburgh, when the beer glasses had rained down. The Aberdeen supporter and former Scots Guardsman was as tall, sinewy and deceptively strong as he had been in his late teens. His Jocks were his primary concern, and whereas violence had once been for pleasure, there was a strict purpose to it now. Hendy was responsible for their discipline, and his method of punishing bad soldiering or disobedience was to 'square away' offenders, usually by way of a blow to the stomach or jaw – a practice that, however barbaric, reflected the extremity of their existence. Violence was so interwoven into the fabric of the Jocks' lives, there were no complaints when being squared away replaced press-ups and shuttle runs. Some were even apologetic for making Hendy go to the trouble, knowing that there was never any personal malice behind his chinnings.

Hendy supported Gray's ruling on a dry tour, acknowledging his Jocks were 'bad for the bar'. He also knew they would circumnavigate the prohibition order. James concurred: 'You simply cannot trust a Jock with alcohol. If you give them a sniff of it, they'll be on it all the time. They can't help themselves. They don't know any different.'

More surprising was their appetite for Viagra, readily supplied by the ICDC. What was the point of taking a tablet and getting the biggest erection of your life when, as Hendy put it, 'ye were only going to bang one oot in tha bogs, like'? Richie said he intended to get rich after the war selling the tablets in Clydebank at inflated prices. 'You've got yer Free Trade coffee in Starbucks that's benefitin' the farmers in the Third World. I'm just daein the same with the jundie an' their tablets. Nae harm in that.' He reckoned Indian Viagra tablets were the strongest, accelerating then decelerating his heart rate until he felt like passing out. 'I tell ye, ye've got tae beware of the low-flying spunk around here,' he said. 'Everyone's just lying there in their wank chariots [beds], bangin' them oot. What else is there to do around here?'

The biggest threat to his profit margin was the temptation to spike his mates' water bottles; there was nothing funnier than a Jock cutting about with an unexpected and uncontrollable hard-on.

Richie and the rest were inclined to get their kicks today, for tomorrow a rocket-propelled grenade could blow their heads off. After two days without sleep, Andrew Craw, a 21 year old from Alloa, had accidentally killed himself with a Minimi. There was no medical equipment on the range, and his colleagues had to drive for an hour and twenty minutes to summon a rescue helicopter. He was pronounced dead on arrival at the field hospital. An official review attributed the accident to sleep deprivation, pitiful medical back-up, the shortage of oil to clean and maintain weapons, and the fact that the Minimi instruction manuals were missing. It was the first time he had fired the weapon. The final ignominy for his parents was to discover that had he died after 6 April 2004 they would have received £73,992 in compensation, four times what they were to receive as he had died in January. They won permission to challenge the Ministry of Defence in the High Court; the case is ongoing.

After the accident, Gray felt that he had no choice but to suspend Minimi usage across the battalion. 'Shortly after we arrived, Lance Corporal Craw killed himself handling a Minimi. There followed several negligent discharges. I took the view that our rudimentary training had not been sufficiently comprehensive and that we risked further accident or injury through poor weapon handling. I issued the order to withdraw the weapon but delegated authority to reissue it to company commanders in the event that the threat changed.'

Whether or not 6 and 7 Platoons would rub along more amicably at Condor than in Canterbury, where the English accused the Jocks of breaking into their rooms and tearing up a St George's Cross, only time would tell. Major Griffiths' comment that 6 Platoon were the best soldiers in B Company heightened the animosity between the two tribes. The PWRR boys – nicknamed the 'PW Ha Has' by the Jocks – were cocky. As one PWRR private put it, 'They [the Argylls] seemed to be in the Dark Ages about kit, such as the Minimi, and had a Northern Ireland mindset. They were one of those bullshitty traditional regiments, with all these customs you had to remember. Everywhere you went you were expected to swing your arms about and bang out salutes to people. We were used to being a bit more chilled out.' In the Jocks' defence, the PWRR had selected many of their best privates, junior and senior non-commissioned officers, and an experienced lieutenant in James Passmore. 'It wisnae difficult tae get one decent platoon outtae two battalions,' Neneh reminded people.

The English were intent upon preserving their identity, rebutting the invitation to exchange their berets for Tam o' Shanters. They kept their PWRR staple belts but adopted the Argylls' drop-zone flashes and the 'Screaming Eagle' badge of 16 Air Assault Brigade.

The two tribes had not done much drinking together, because the Jocks were banned from many Canterbury pubs. As Hendy put it, 'It didnae take a squaddie to know a squaddie,' especially when they failed to disguise their accents. Both the English and Scottish blamed the Royal Irish Rangers, who had been in barracks in the city before them. When Kev Challis went out drinking with a Jock, he gave him a local name and address to remember when questioned by the nightclub doormen. The plan went awry when the Jock blurted it out in his native twang. 'It's nae Scottish in there tonight' had become a familiar cry.

Rob Schwar seemed allergic to life in the Argylls and always found himself in trouble. By his own admission, he was a 'little shit'. His mates forgave him, but he took it for granted that Passmore and Kelly distrusted him. His passage to the Gulf had been delayed while bones in his right hand healed – injuries sustained during an after-hours fight in Canterbury, not in the boxing ring. In his mind, the battalion hierarchy were convinced he had injured himself deliberately to postpone his deployment. Whatever his opposition to life in a Scottish battalion, or the prospect of six months in Iraq, he insisted he would not have taken his protest that far.

If 6 Platoon could have picked any platoon sergeant for their tour, it would have been Paul Kelly. His departure was a blow, to the junior soldiers in particular. It was said that he was less effective working alongside soldiers who objected to being dictated to. In addition to the standard-issue white cards – which listed the rules of engagement – Kelly had written up various 'actions on' for typical scenarios and sketched out where each member of a section or platoon should sit aboard a helicopter, according to what weapon system they carried. But no private had to stack his socks in straight lines at Condor. As long as the walkways between bed spaces were clear and webbing and weapons were immediately to hand, Kelly was satisfied.

Passmore knew he would encounter less obstruction to what he as platoon commander wanted to achieve without Kelly. He could be so obdurate that it had often been easier to do as he wished. One of Kelly's sayings was, 'I don't do officers, I don't do bullshit.'

The weekly kit and weapons inspections continued in Kelly's absence, but whereas he had insisted upon conducting these himself, Neneh delegated to his section commanders: Loz, Lee Gidalla and Izzy Izzard all knew a dirty rifle from a clean one.

Lots of the men had customised their kit, and privately purchased assault vests were an alternative to belt webbing. The vests looked pretty sharp and made life easier getting in and out of vehicles. Whatever could not fit into an assault vest or webbing pouch was carried in a day sack. Each soldier had two sets of uniforms, known as DPMs (Disruptive Pattern Material), which he handwashed. Ablution facilities were basic, and there was only sufficient water running through the TSUs (Temporary Shower Units) for 'ship showers', i.e. they got wet, soaped, rinsed, then towelled-off. On one occasion Neneh punished a soldier for using too much water. Everyone knew the rule: only two pushes of the button. Neneh had watched and counted seven pushes before making his presence known. 'You're for it,' he said, smiling wickedly.

'What? I only pushed it twice, Neneh.'

'Did ye fuck! Get dried off, go and get yer clothes on, and get yerself back in here. Ye're going tae sit in here in the heat for hours, sweating yer balls off and counting the number of times everybody presses that button. A wee bit of willy watching will teach ye.' The soldier went AWOL on leave in the UK shortly afterwards, as did the erratic Private Elliott.

Kelly had sometimes given his soldiers practical tasks to keep them mentally alert: Wellsy's had been to construct outdoor showers; Colin Beeney's to build a barbecue area. But they could not escape health-and-safety regulations, even in Iraq. Despite the presence of a qualified, if slightly reluctant, chef to prepare the meat, the barbecue was banned. In the Ops Room and satellite TV area, the communal porn stash had already been 'had away' by somebody on night-time stag duty. While BBC News 24 was an excellent information source, it was no compensation. Kelly had enjoyed watching Al-Jazeera. 'You can see all sorts of shit on this channel,' he had said. This was true, but the channel also inflamed local opinion against the presence of Coalition Forces, with fatal consequences later during the tour.

Major General Andrew Graham CBE, the Argylls' colonel, was serving as deputy commanding general of the Multinational Corps. He was based with the Coalition Provisional Authority in central Baghdad, a more salubrious location than Condor. More than three-quarters of a century had passed since the Argylls had last soldiered in Mesopotamia, and General Graham's tour was a personal crusade. His grandfather, Second Lieutenant Reginald Graham VC, had served in Iraq in 1917 when the Jocks suffered heavy losses against the Turks. Severely wounded, Second Lieutenant Graham was evacuated to a casualty clearing station, eventually being withdrawn for convalescence in Bombay. Upon rejoining his company in Basra for New Year's Eve celebrations, he wrote in his diary, 'Great rejoicings. Rather too much for me, I regret. The sergeants tied me up. However, there was nothing for it since, as they said, it simply had to be.'

General Graham was in the thick of it in March 2004 as the number of attacks against Coalition Forces doubled against previous months. With the rate of attacks peaking at 85–90 per day, the general's staff were instructed to assess the feasibility of his visiting the site of his grandfather's battle.

This process was effusively written up by his aide-de-camp for the regimental magazine *The Thin Red Line*:

> What made this date [22 April] and battle special was that General Graham's grandfather had won the Victoria Cross during the Battle of Istabulat, and, understandably, the General wished to visit the site of the battle and the approximate spot where his grandfather had won his VC. As it was only a 45-minute helicopter flight, it was more than feasible. Luckily, I had been warned some months previously of the intention to visit Samarra and the plan to find the spot where the VC was won. With the aid of Major General Graham's grandfather's diary, which contained detailed sketches of the battle site, and with the aid of some aerial photographs provided by the 1st (US) Infantry Division, the unit in charge was able to pinpoint the area where the medal was won. It was now necessary to contact the unit who had Samarra in their area of responsibility. In this instance it was the 1st Battalion of the 26th Infantry, of the 1st Infantry Division from North Carolina. I initially had a tough job explaining to the Ops Officer of the battalion why a two-star British general would wish to go to Samarra on a specific time and day.

Eventually, the Americans closed a public road to the Iraqis and deployed M1 Abrams tanks to facilitate the general's battlefield tour. The author, Lieutenant Stuart Young, signed off by saying, 'It was a very memorable day.'

Weapons seizures were so bountiful nobody could climb aboard a Land-Rover at Condor without first clearing a path through stacks of AK47s. Soldiers with sequestered weapons were like children with toys, fiddling with all the working parts and discovering operational differentials. The airfield adjacent to the camp became an unofficial venue for shooting parties. Targets were made out of whisky cans and posters of topless models ripped from *FHM* magazine and stuck to wooden pallets. Using an L96 sniper rifle, Passmore shot a crow perched above a derelict aircraft hangar. James Dormer and Hendy watched it fall in slow motion, landing with a silent thud. No 'sniper ninja', Passmore surprised himself with his accuracy, not least as he was using 7.62 mm rounds intended for use in a General Purpose Machine Gun rather than custom-made sniper ammunition.

Condor measured only 60 metres square and was fenced off from the much larger ICDC camp next door. Both lay amid an enormous horizontal expanse of flat, dusty ground that included an airfield once occupied by the Royal Air Force. The Anglo–Iraqi treaty of 1930 had paved the way for Iraqi independence two years later, whilst preserving British tenancy of such locations. During the Second World War, Winston Churchill had ordered the overthrow of the Rashid Ali government when it sought to abrogate the treaty entitlements.

In the spring of 2004 the camp was home to two companies each of six hundred ICDC, but with the shift rotation system, only four hundred were present at any one time. Most of the Iraqi recruits commuted to and from their homes on bicycles or on foot. James Dormer penned an early assessment of their capabilities: there was little discipline as British soldiers would understand it, and the ICDC were 'unruly' and 'dirty'. Left unsupervised, those who held rank failed to ensure their soldiers completed set tasks, while those ICDC holding the rank of corporal were 'totally ineffective'. As much as he sought to convince them that they belonged to the 'ICDC tribe', those of more influential tribal lineage threatened any senior ICDC figure who sought to discipline them. James also found that the ICDC were fearful of arresting locals with status and that they let too many vehicles pass unchecked through Vehicle Checkpoints; the recruits claimed to know all the drivers and passengers and vouched for their good characters.

Keegs loved rifling through vehicles for AK47s and pistols, knowing he could keep some of the bounty. What frustrated him was the rule that he could only search men. He knew the Ali Babas abused the courtesy of Coalition Forces by hiding arms and ammunition beneath their wives' dresses. This was a consideration he could only observe for so long. Keegs was a 'squaddie's squaddie', always rolling up a fag and looking for mischief, despite his promotion. In the view of their fellow Condorites, he and Wellsy shared the same appalling musical tastes: their combined age was little over 40 yet they listened incessantly to 'power ballads'. Horsehead and the more trendy bods were into rap. Neither Keegs nor Wellsy could say 'rap music' without screwing up their faces. It was said that they were so 'army barmy', they may well have come straight from the womb 'cammed-up' and dressed in DPM.

James's suggestion that the ICDC might be incapable of fulfilling their security brief met with a brisk rejoinder from Gray's staff: 'This comment is unhelpful!' So his reports became counter-factual. But no amount of spin could disguise certain failings. Towards the end of a military-tactics lecture, one Iraqi recruit communicated that he needed a toilet break. He was asked to wait but instead defecated on his hands and threw it out the window. He then sat down as if he had only disposed of chewing gum.

Extra effort was put into ICDC training on days when Griffiths visited, but not everyone believed the establishment of an effective branch of the civil powers, let alone the ICDC, would bring stability after the withdrawal of British Forces. One of James's pay-off lines to battalion headquarters read, 'What will never be achieved is the imposition of British Army standards and practices, which are incompatible with Iraqi culture.'

As he came from a weaker, less populous tribe, Major

Sabeer cared little for the pecking order and preferred to rule by personal intimidation. The private soldiers likened him to Clint Eastwood, while Kelly thought him a 'brilliant bloke' who should have been commanding officer of the ICDC, not a mere company commander.

Few other officers were trustworthy, certainly not Captain Hussein.

'Who is this man?' James asked.

'Ah, Mr James, he is a very bad man,' replied Captain Hussein.

'Then what is he doing in my camp? And why is this man still a sergeant? I sacked him two days ago.'

'Ah, Mr James, he is a very good man.'

'No, he's not. He's lazy and useless.'

'But he comes from good family, Mr James. He has status in Qalat Salih.'

The two Jameses divided the 'hundreds of square kilometres of fuck all' around Condor into separate but adjoining areas of operation. Qalat Salih, aka 'Dodge City', was included in 6 Platoon's sector, while the village of Al Kahla straddled the border and was patrolled by both 6 and 7 Platoons.

On one of their first patrols, Larks, Lawrence and Gidalla narrowly avoided committing war crimes. They responded to the sound of gunfire seemingly engulfing their Land-Rover by de-bussing and performing a fire and manoeuvre. Peeling around one building, instead of an insurgent force they saw a funeral procession. The Iraqis had only been firing into the air, a popular pursuit.

'Oh, shit,' one of them said, watching the Iraqis flee. 'What the fuck do we do now?'

Gidalla stared at Lawrence and Larks. 'Just get your kit and yourselves back on the wagon, and we'll forget all about this, eh?'

'Yeah, fair one. Must have been "happy fire".'

Larks blamed his 'bullying' of the ICDC on having just passed P Company and being all 'Airborne this' and 'Airborne that'. But it was unrealistic to expect Parachute Regiment standards here. Gradually, he learned that humour was a more effective motivational tool. Having fired the rifle since they were kids, the Iraqis handled the AK47 with ease. He bluffed his way through lessons, having been introduced to the weapon only minutes earlier. He taught the ICDC 'pairs fire and manoeuvre' but refused to teach four-man contact drills – when a quartet of soldiers position themselves so each has their own arc of fire while advancing in formation towards a target. 'Give it a few years and we'll be back here fighting this lot and they'll be using these against us,' he said. 'There's no fucking way I am teaching it.' Later, the ICDC would be told always to 'go left-flanking' when under fire. The hope was that their movements could be anticipated in combat.

Confiscated weapons were also handy for shooting disease-ridden dogs. Soldiers fell ill at such a rate that James ordered all wild animals seen on the camp perimeter to be shot. He thought the Jocks might have done this of their own accord, but they were too frightened of their quartermasters to use ammunition with such licence. 'If one of those wire-haired mongrels comes anywhere near you, wherever you are, just fucking shoot it, OK?' he told them. 'They've got rabies. They're all infected. Don't get bitten. I'd rather deal with a dead dog and a grumpy QM [quartermaster] than have another one of you lot fall ill.'

'But Captain James,' said Hussein, shaking his head, 'here the dog is part of the tribe, just like a man. If you kill their dog, they will kill you. It is enough to start a blood feud.'

'Well, I would like to see them try,' James retorted flatly.

The dysentery epidemic meant one of the Portaloos was

always reserved for sufferers, and soldiers were banned from using their own battlefield utensils in the canteen. James wished the ICDC officers would do something about the flies. Every work surface in their offices and accommodation was covered in an inch-deep layer of insects. He could not discuss anything with them without their insistence that the tea-boys prepare refreshments. Young, male servants were a throwback to their Iraqi Army days, and James grimaced as they dished out the sugar, the flies only buzzing away as the spoon submerged into the hot liquid.

For all Captain Hussein's apparent obsequiousness, James was aware of his Machiavellian methods. 'Captain James,' Hussein once said, wringing his hands, 'there are very bad people here. They are part of the insurgency – they are not your friends! But I will find them out. I have also been out on my own mission and captured weapons.' He bowed as he pointed to piles of rusting mortars and rocket-propelled grenades. 'These belonged to insurgents. But I took them away from them.' James invariably discovered that Hussein's claims were bogus. The weapons were his – he just no longer wanted them.

Whenever James wanted something done, he used Sergeant Hassan. He was instantly recognisable, for he shunned ICDC uniform in favour of US combat trousers, a black-and-white-striped Juventus football shirt and wraparound sunglasses. It was not until July that James discovered Hassan belonged to the Mahdi Army. 'Oh, fuck, I've relied on him for months. What am I going to do now?' James said, quivering. 'I'll just have to pretend I have not heard about this. The Iraqi Police Service is full of insurgents as well, so there's no point getting him arrested. I can't believe my best man was a terrorist all along!'

It was not unusual for locally employed civilians (known as LECs) to live double lives, and, apocryphal or otherwise, the dying words of the Abu Naji camp barber had passed into Condor folklore: 'By day I am with you; by night I am with my brothers.' He had been identified as one of an armed gang ambushing British Forces near Route 6. Other LECs were sacked after pacing out the distance between the refectory and camp perimeter at Abu Naji.

Captain Hussein's habit of holding James's hand as they strode around Condor disturbed him, but one LEC known as Bob took fraternising a stage further. His shop sold Coca-Cola, cigarettes and alarm clocks shaped like mosques which played the *adhan*, the Muslim call to prayer; Viagra, porn and whisky were also sold under the counter at 'special prices'. Bob was a familiar sight, riding his bicycle around Abu Naji, where he lived for his own safety. He was a typically plump Iraqi gentleman, winding down in life – until the day he exposed himself to a private soldier and requested oral sex. The private fetched his rifle and chased Bob around the camp. Custom at his shop dropped off thereafter.

6

Exile

There were those who enjoyed having their meals brought to them, watching nurses complete laps of the ward and lying around idly – and there was the irascible, brooding Paul Kelly. Having dozed fitfully, he was now fully awake and could keep neither still nor quiet. He obsessed with what might be happening at Condor. Neneh and Loz would be taking charge of his platoon, making light of his absence. 'The bastards! Do they not know they need me?' he thought.

The hospital was divided into many parts, and he was unsure where his ward fitted into the general plan or how close it was to the operating theatre where he had spent the previous evening. Craning his neck, he could see a long corridor and imagined other wards connected to it. He vaguely remembered stirring in the night and a nurse straightening his bedcovers. His own ward had filled, and a woman was sitting up in the bed opposite him. She worked in the army supermarket at Shaibah Logistics Base and had broken her arm falling out of a Land-Rover. Beside her were a husband and wife from the Royal Air Force who had been involved in a car crash in Kuwait – apparently, an Al Qaeda sympathiser had purposely driven into them. He could not tell what their injuries were.

Kelly was wound tighter than a magnet's coil. He suspected his ward was occupied by malingerers, although everyone else was probably as eager as him to be discharged. His sense that too much coddling might be going on at Condor, although unfounded, overwhelmed him. He was suffering from anti-REMF (Rear Echelon Mother Fucker) syndrome, a condition affecting frontline soldiers trapped with those deployed, in military parlance, 'so far back in theatre they sent their washing forwards'. His symptoms were a shortening of temper whenever REMFs sought to engage him in chit-chat. His fear was that they might accidentally find they had a mutual friend serving in the Gulf, thus providing genuine cause for conversation from which it would be difficult for him to extract himself.

Beneath layers of fresh bandages, his hand was bulbous and useless. Surgeons had cut his palm open, removed metal fragments deposited by the round and sewn it back together, leaving stitches in a zig-zag pattern. When he returned to Britain, he would not be able to hold a fork, let alone a rifle. His left hand was already his unlucky hand. He had lost his ring finger after falling out of an observation tower in Northern Ireland some years before.

Shaking himself awake from anaesthetic-induced lethargy, he recognised Glen and Harrison, the Light Infantry soldier whose first name he had forgotten. Another infanteer called Dave was in hospital to have a piece of secondary fragmentation from a grenade blast removed from his arse. The quartet discussed the contact endlessly. Kelly was particularly proud of his first-time efforts with the under-slung grenade launcher.

'Hey, we're on the radio,' one of them said, hearing the announcer mention British soldiers wounded in Iraq.

'"The Army has launched an investigation into a firefight which left seven British soldiers wounded. Violence broke out on Friday while the troops were on patrol in the village of Qalat Salih, south of Amarah," the Ministry of Defence said.'

'Have they? Now that's honest of them.' The soldiers were adamant that the Ministry of Defence watered down enemy and local fatality figures and friendly casualties, excluding information pertaining to the intensity of the resistance encountered.

'*The soldiers came under fire after arresting a suspect they believed had shot at them.*'

'Yeah, fucking heavy fire, bastards. They paid for it, though.'

'*The Ministry of Defence said it would hold an inquiry partly because three Iraqi civilians were believed to have been killed.*'

'Three?'

'Thirty-three, more like!'

'Oh, man, that is priceless!'

'The MoD is so fuckin' cheeky about keeping the death-count down.'

'Yeah, it doesn't play well with the natives.'

'*Four British soldiers were taken to a military hospital near Basra.*'

'Shit.' They glanced at each other. 'That's us!'

'*General Ismail Kazem Adhzar . . .*'

'Who's he then?'

'*. . . chief of police in the area, said British troops had clashed with the Badr Organisation, the armed wing of the Supreme Council for the Islamic Revolution in Iraq. He said a person opened fire on a British patrol before taking shelter inside the group's local offices.*'

'So it was them, then – the SCIRI. I can't tell who belongs to which group – Mahdi Army or whoever. One raghead looks pretty much like another when he's firing at you.'

'And what? Just one of them there, was there?'

'Yeah, all those Chally tanks and Warriors, all for one bloke? What are they on about?'

'*Shia Iraqis then attacked the soldiers, destroying a British military vehicle.*'

'Smudger's Land-Rover, mate. Got to be . . .'

'*The Ministry of Defence spokeswoman confirmed the patrol returned fire when fired upon.*'

'Got through enough mags on my own.'

'*They were extracted by a quick-reaction force, and whilst the incident was happening, four of the patrol members received non-life-threatening injuries. The patrol, from the 1st Battalion, the Light Infantry, is based at Paderborn, Germany.*'

'Get in!'

'Hey, what about the Paras?'

'And the PWRR? No mention of us. Cheers for that.'

An Argylls' quartermaster was Kelly's first outside visitor, bringing a phone card which Kelly used to call home. 'It's me,' he said.

'I thought you'd been shot.' Donna had been warned by the families' officer.

'Yes, it is only my hand. I'm OK.'

'Not the left one?'

'Yeah, my lucky hand.'

'Muppet.'

'Heartless cow.' He cried when they watched sad films together, not her. 'I was operated on last night. I've just been told by the doctors that I'm going to be stuck in this hospital for a week. Then they're sending me home.'

'OK.'

'I don't know much else about what is going on, but I'll call you before I leave Iraq.'

'Good. Bye.'

His next visitors entered warily, as if unsure what the reaction to their presence would be. Kelly straightened himself in time to see Gray and the regimental sergeant major standing over him. To Kelly, regimental sergeant majors embodied everything he was not: always playing by the army's rules, making sure everyone's boots were polished and not fighting the system hard enough to get a better deal for those below. Like an Anglepoise lamp, Gray lowered himself to Kelly's eye-level. 'I've heard good things about you.'

'There's a first time for everything,' Kelly thought. For the commanding officer to massage Kelly's ego, even when he was wrapped in bandages and on a drip, was a fatal error. It only exposed how seldom they conversed.

'So, tell me about the contact.'

With the regimental sergeant major looking on uncomfortably, Kelly described the rocket-propelled grenades slamming into Smudger's Land-Rover and how he had been shot. Gray nodded. Kelly rarely lifted his head to establish eye contact. As this awkward, courteous exchange continued, he considered how it could benefit his platoon. 'I want the Minimis back . . .' Gray's reaction suggested he was unaccustomed to such a forthright demand. He readjusted his narrow frame and waited, perhaps for Kelly to soften his request. But Kelly was determined to be the master of this argument. 'We were issued two of the light machine guns at the start of the tour, which were withdrawn after Craw's accident. Now, he might not have had experience on the weapon system before leaving Canterbury, but that lack of experience doesn't apply to all of us. Those of us in the PWRR are no strangers to belt-fed weapons.' Kelly's comment could only be interpreted as an attack on the pre-deployment build-up training. No matter his wounds, he was straying into a conversational out-of-bounds box.

'Maybe that was why they were taken back?' His suggestion that the Minimis had been withdrawn because the training the men had received to use the weapon had been insufficient did not draw Gray into further argument. As his battalion had been almost permanently deployed in Northern Ireland, Gray's men had been amongst the last in the infantry to be issued with enhanced offensive capability equipment, such as the Minimi light machine gun. Gray's soldiers were rarely seen patrolling in Belfast with any weapon besides their standard-issue rifles; their Gimpys were more often than not confined to the range for being too 'warry' and reminiscent of more troubled times. The province was all soft hats and smiles now. Gray would face mutiny if he reissued Minimis to 6 Platoon and no other. And should another soldier suffer an accident like Craw's, he would be held wholly responsible.

'The Light Infantry battalion have got Minimis,' Kelly persisted. 'We took a couple off the guys in Qalat Salih who were injured. It's a brilliant weapon. The PWRR blokes are trained up on it and with what we're exposed to up there, we need it.'

'I'm sorry, I can't do that. It would mean giving PWRR guys their Minimis back but not giving them to our own battalion. I can't do that.' Gray was apologetic, but he had to look at the bigger picture. In spite of the apparent unfairness of some infantry units having the Minimi and others not, he considered returning such a potent weapon to his troops too great a risk.

Kelly's physical incapacity emboldened him. He charged on, disregarding his commanding officer's status. 'Right, I want more GPMGs then. I want GPMGs in replacement of the Minimis – two more!'

'Your platoon will have them in a few days,' Gray replied.

Kelly opened his mouth to reply but no words came. He passed his good hand across his face to scratch an imaginary itch, a movement intended to disguise his satisfaction. He could never have imagined what he could get away with as a wounded war hero. He should take a bullet more often.

'Well, I wish you a full and speedy recovery,' said Gray,

sincerely. Kelly believed he had won a victory. Gray thought that the up-scaling of General Purpose Machine Guns was a measured response to the Shia uprising and not solely as a result of Kelly's request.

'Thank you, sir,' Kelly replied, through a half smile, as Gray turned to leave the ward.

Gray had already dispatched the sergeant's medal citation to London. It covered the contact with the car robbers on 11 February, as well as the action in Qalat Salih on 5 March. Penning this vignette of British military and Argyll history, late at night in Basra, had brought a smile to Gray's face. 'Here I was, an Argyll commanding officer writing our first serious gallantry citation – not just of this tour but for a generation – not for an Argyll but for a PWRR soldier embedded within the Argylls. I briefly mulled over this fact. I could imagine this might play badly with some members of my regiment, especially those not in Iraq and the old and bold of the associations. However, I remembered my promise to the PWRR soldiers when they joined that I would treat them no differently to anyone else. In my mind they were Argylls. So I set about writing the citation. I knew it had to sing so that the medals committee back in Whitehall would sit up and take notice. You can get a bit carried away if you're not careful. The first time I read it back to myself it sounded more like a Victoria Cross than a Military Cross!'

Gray wrote that Kelly had demonstrated 'exemplary leadership' and had been 'truly inspirational to those around him'. He also wrote that Kelly had shown 'little regard for his own safety' on both occasions.

Major Griffiths had penned a more sober first draft. He doubted Kelly's actions merited a Military Cross and told Gray so. He also questioned why his commanding officer dispatched the citation with such haste. They rowed, but Gray got his wish.

On his fifth day in hospital, the temptation to remove his bandages defeated Kelly. But in doing so, not for the first or last time, he made an enemy of his future. The bandages were a mash of fluids, and when he tore them off he felt as though somebody had torched his hand. Over the next 24 hours, no painkillers could soothe him. The stitches on his exit wound burst, exposing a gaping hole in his wrist. Through streams of pain, the same feelings of insecurity and nausea he had succumbed to in Qalat Salih surfaced, while his hand was a tobacco shade of brown. He cursed himself for not asking more questions before surgery and felt his trust in the medical staff had been misplaced. The doctors were glad to shunt him onto a transport aircraft the following day.

Part of the atrophy caused by being in Iraq was the effort to disguise gentler feelings such as vulnerability, self-doubt and love. He could unwind at home, knowing Donna would provide stability. He had always liked her unfussy, practical way. Once home, he would also be glad of home-cooked food to replace RAF catering and hospital swill.

His emotions perplexed him; the regret of leaving his young soldiers was irreconcilable with the joy of being reunited with Donna, Abbygail and Jack. He had two families in two countries. He pondered the subsidence in his memory's landscape. Seemingly well-constructed landmarks had fallen by the wayside. He hoped they could be rebuilt as easily.

The C-17's cavernous interior was twice that of a Hercules' and half as comfortable. When sleep proved elusive, Kelly went in search of company. 'What happened to you?' a young crew member asked. His tone suggested that he feared a senseless question would end the conversation before it had begun.

Kelly affected a manner somewhere between bashfulness and nonchalance. 'Got shot last week.'

'Whereabouts?'

'Qalat Salih. Massive contact. About a dozen friendly casualties. A lot of enemy dead.'

The loadie's eyes widened. 'Yeah, we heard about that one. Sounded like you did well to get out.'

'Well, it was looking pretty bad at one point,' said Kelly, glad of his notoriety.

'Please tell me about it.' These were experiences somebody who called the inside of this giant aircraft his office only dreamt about. 'What was it like?'

Kelly described the firefight, being holed up in the Badr house, running out of ammunition and resorting to AK47s. He spoke easily of the carnage and the procession of British armour claiming occupancy of Qalat Salih: it was easy to revisit scenes he had never left. The loadie was enraptured; the interior of the hull became his cinema auditorium. Kelly did not count the number of times he began a sentence with 'I did this' – the figure would have embarrassed even him. Enjoying his new fame, he also took back every disparaging comment he had ever made about guileless REMFs.

They landed at RAF Brize Norton, from where Kelly was transported to the Ministry of Defence's new medical facility in suburban Birmingham. Finding himself among the walking wounded, he soon demanded to be released. His discharge from the Centre for Defence Medicine was granted with great reluctance and on the condition he visited his battalion medical centre daily for his wounds to be cleaned. He secured a lift home from the Argylls' families' officer, who was returning to Canterbury from Scotland.

The Kelly homestead was set back a few paces from one of those long, straight roads that dissect the Kent countryside. More traffic travelled its width than it was designed for. There were fields on the Canterbury-bound side of the carriageway and a collection of detached houses on the other, one of which was his. A palm tree dominated the front garden.

He would later plant a flag pole and lower the Union Jack whenever the British Army suffered a fatality.

He dropped his kit bag and made his way through to the kitchen. From the window he saw his children's bicycles on the lawn. He was glad of the cleansing wash of normality. But these were just a few drops; he knew he could not achieve a complete sense of belonging while his Condor children remained in Iraq.

Abbygail and Jack were excited to see him and pointed to his wound. He likened it to a big black spider, the exit hole being its body, his stitches its legs.

Kelly attended the medical centre the following morning and stood outside the building for thirty minutes before its opening. His impatience had acquired a physical bite by the time the duty lance corporal appeared. He was unshaven and Kelly was sure he could smell alcohol.

'Sergeant Kelly, would you like to come into the treatment room?' There was a carefree tone to the man's voice. He was unacquainted with his patient. Kelly jettisoned *Cosmopolitan* magazine and hauled himself upright. Shaking the tiredness from his legs, he strained at his mental leash. 'One fuck-up and this bloke gets it,' he thought.

'Is there a doctor coming in to assess me?' Kelly asked.

'I'm sorry?'

'A doctor.' Kelly closed the door firmly behind him. They now shared a confined space.

'No, just me. May I see your hand?' Kelly laid it flat on the table. 'I'm just going to clean out the wound.' Without first putting on surgical gloves, he took a cotton-wool pad and ran it under a tap.

'Aren't you supposed to use sterilized gauze and those little packets of water to clean this?' Kelly withdrew his hand but not his remark.

'Er, yes. I'll . . .'

Kelly snapped. 'Get me the stuff, and I'll do it myself.'

'It's OK, I'll . . .'

'I'm not happy at all.'

'I'm sorry.'

Kelly fired him a glare. 'Give me the supplies,' he said as he stood up. 'Give them to me now.'

'OK, OK.'

'There's no way you're doing this. I'll do it at home. I can't believe it. You expect me to let you clean my wounds? You must be joking! I'm out of here! I'll be back when I run out of the stuff.'

'There was no way I was going to let that idiot treat me!' Kelly slammed his front door. He put the bottles and bandages down on the kitchen table. The painkillers issued in Iraq were spent, and the Ibuprofen from the medical centre proved to be ineffective. He spent his nights downstairs on the sofa, sleepless and in great pain. He should have stayed in Birmingham, where the staff knew what they were doing; he conceded that now. Returning to the medical centre, he was told he must see a doctor before stronger painkillers could be prescribed.

'When? Today? Tomorrow?'

'A week on Monday, Sergeant Kelly.'

'Look, there's a major difference between twisting your ankle and being shot. I have to clean my wounds every day. Do you know how much that hurts?'

'No, Sergeant Kelly, I . . .'

'Two weeks I've been back, and he [the doctor] hasn't returned my calls. Considering the state of me, he should have called on my first day home.'

'I'll make a phone call. You'll have to wait.'

Kelly wanted to grab the medic by the throat. But Canterbury was not Condor.

'Shauncliffe. Tomorrow. Nine a.m.'

'How do I get there?'

'You'll have to make your own way.'

'I can't drive, you muppet, and my wife is at work.'

'Taxi.' Kelly heard sarcasm in his tone.

'Listen to me, chopper, get on to the MT [Motor Transport] and get me a ride to Shauncliffe before I lose my temper.'

At seven the following morning, he shared his transportation with a soldier attending his final medical before leaving the army. With his hand and wrist still heavily bandaged, Kelly was eyed suspiciously when he told the driver and fellow passenger of his intention to return to Iraq. The exchange of glances between them suggested they considered his plan far-fetched.

The walls of the doctor's consultation room were adorned with medical charts and illustrations. Book-lined shelves and an array of pharmaceutical bottles added to the short-lived feeling Kelly was in the right place and his recovery could now begin. His optimism was premature. He could not stop his hand from shaking, while the pain when he flexed his wrist was excruciating.

'Do you have any strength in your left hand, Sergeant Kelly?'

As the doctor could call his bluff with a simple test, Kelly opted for honesty. 'No.'

'Can you open or close your left hand?'

Kelly let his reply slide from his mouth. 'No.'

'Well, Sergeant Kelly,' the doctor leant back and put a safer distance between himself and his patient, 'the truth is we are going to have to downgrade you until you are medically fit to work.' The doctor's fingertips brushed pieces of paper on the desk in front of him.

'Sorry, what did you say?'

'Downgrade you, perhaps for one year?' The Royal Army

Medical Corps doctor glanced upwards from his papers but only momentarily.

'No, no, I'm going back to Iraq.'

A smile tempered the doctor's stern façade; the overall impression he gave was of a teacher censuring a well-intentioned but errant pupil. Those of his patients who wanted to be downgraded accepted his prognosis without question, whereas the headstrong struggled with their pride before they accepted the inevitable.

'Sergeant Kelly,' he sighed.

'No, no,' Kelly interrupted. 'You're not downgrading me. I'll be all right in a few weeks. I'm going back.'

'Sergeant Kelly,' the doctor's tone was intended to appease. 'You can't . . .'

'I can. I'm a platoon sergeant in a rifle platoon. My men are there getting shot at.'

'You have significant nerve damage. You can't close your hand or put any weight on it . . .' Having seen Kelly's wounds, he preferred the evidence of his eyes to the assertions of his patient.

'Being downgraded is great for some people, doctor . . .'

'You're not fit for combat operations.' The doctor's agitation had remained unspoken until then.

'I'm going back.'

'Not for a year.'

Their voices rose incrementally in pitch and volume. Each looked increasingly bemused by the other's failure or refusal to comprehend. The physical space between them filled with Kelly's falling aspirations. 'I would like to see the physiotherapist . . . I would like a second opinion . . .'

The doctor stared down at his desk as if it were a chessboard. Kelly's move had put him in check. His frown suggested he had not anticipated his opponent's strategy. He responded that the physiotherapist was unavailable for a fortnight. They shook hands and Kelly departed.

This appointment was cancelled when an officer with a twisted knee was given priority. A sense of injustice swelled inside Kelly. He was told to play catch with his children in the garden. When the physiotherapist eventually saw Kelly, it took him 15 minutes to concur with the doctor's verdict: Kelly was unfit for Iraq and should be downgraded. Kelly told him if he did not change his mind, he would 'drag him over the desk and beat the shit out of him'.

Donna thought he should stay at home. Her husband had done his fighting, and it was time the army looked after him; this was what all the medical personnel involved in his care had attempted to do since he had been ushered aboard the helicopter. Talk of a medal citation did not placate him. The only benefit to receiving a gong would be the clout it would give him when fighting political battles. He would accept a Military Cross and all the accompanying plaudits on that basis. The reasons why he should remain at home were many and obvious. He just chose not to hear.

The weapon Kelly had jettisoned during the firefight – his standard rifle, not his acquired AK47 – was in the possession of a new arrival at Condor. It had been smeared in the blood of its previous owner when Captain Al Roan received it. Roan had been tasked to reinvigorate the ICDC training programme and later to take command of B Company during Adam Griffiths' period of leave.

James Dormer's notes on the state of the ICDC made for reflective reading:

Discipline: There is a genuine fear of reprisals from a minority of persistent offenders, should the hierarchy take action against them. A published list of fines for disciplinary offences (absence, refusal to obey an order, sleeping on duty, etc.) would be useful in establishing conformity across the entire battalion.

Intelligence: At present there is no intelligence being passed up the ICDC chain and this is something the CMT [Coalition Monitoring Team] is attempting to introduce. What information has been communicated to CF [Coalition Forces] is based on the local knowledge of individual soldiers.

Operations: 3 Company is also tasked to provide a twenty-four-hour guard on the prison in the centre of Al Amarah and two ammunition dumps on the outskirts of the town. The two ammunition dumps are very dangerous: as hazards to the local population and potential sources of supply for terrorists. Both sites are extremely large and, at present, are not guarded effectively.

Logistics: The ICDC have been issued some excellent equipment but little joined-up thought seems to have gone into deciding what they require. Very little kit has actually been issued to the troops, as they have no use for it, and there is little hope of ICDC private soldiers being able to retain a significant number of items put on a 1033 [inventory form]. There is no culture of responsibility and equipment husbandry. The only vehicles the ICDC will willingly use are pick-up trucks, preferably the hired ones with drivers. The Gaz trucks have not been used once.

Police/ICDC relations: There is no formal relationship between the ICDC and the police. Opinion of police trustworthiness and competence is not high. A clear remit for the ICDC as opposed to the police would reduce the doubling up of tasks. Systems for prisoner handling, evidence gathering and joint operations would also allow an effective working relationship to be developed.

7

Pets

The upsurge in terrorist activity manifested itself in skirmishes on Route 6 and nightly mortar attacks launched from the vicinity of the police checkpoint. Nobody would have been surprised to discover uniformed officers were responsible, as they had done much of the shooting during the Qalat Salih siege.

Condorites likened the mortar teams to high-handicap golfers: long off the tee but with little control over their shots. Sweepstakes were run on the proximity of the missiles and the time the first shell would land. On several occasions, Neneh had his platoon 'standing to' with rifles, webbing and body armour in case the aerial bombardment was accompanied by a ground force. But the shelling was so erratic, the frequency of such alerts was reduced as he became less wary. He was even worse the wear for drink one evening when an attack began.

While those opposed to the presence of British Forces could muster numbers and firepower, question marks remained over their tactics and team skills. With the likes of James Dormer's trusted non-commissioned officer Sergeant Hassan leading a double life as a professional ICDC soldier by day and insurgent by night, the training provided by Her Majesty's forces would potentially strengthen these areas. At least Neneh thought so. He likened the mentoring programme to 'selling his soul'.

Keegs was one of Neneh's lance corporals, a rank which

bestowed upon its bearer the expectation he curb the worst of his behaviour. Given their rivalry, Keegs had been chuffed to climb the first rung of the ladder before Wellsy. During his three and a half years as a private soldier, he had pulled every stunt and had a wiretap on what junior soldiers got up to when unsupervised. He knew they dozed off on stag duty and woke themselves up just minutes before they were to be officially relieved. As laid-back as Neneh was, he would have 'sparked out' any private soldier he caught asleep in the machine-gun sangar. Keegs was not going to 'nark' on them, and no matter his promotion or demotion chances he would always be a private soldier at heart.

Keegs and Wellsy had frequent punch-ups: over cigarettes and the camel spiders they hid in each other's kit and for trashing each other's bed spaces. Having been acquainted since basic training, and having served together in Northern Ireland and Bosnia, reconciliation was always swift.

As if there was not already a surfeit of weapons, most of which were legitimately confiscated, Keegs decided to build his own. This would not have been tolerated at Abu Naji.

''Ere, what you doin'?' Keegs's eyes tilted upwards from the pile of empty tins to meet Kev Challis. Kev was still a private soldier and after having thrown the mine into the burns pit was unlikely to be 'upped' soon. Kev got away with less than Keegs and was always the last to bomb-burst away from any scene of trouble. Their friendship was fuelled by alcohol and pranks. They had recently returned to Iraq, having spent a fortnight on leave in Canterbury. Cruising the pubs with no success, Kev blamed his failure to 'pull any birds' on Keegs.

'Oh, 'ello, mate. I'm buildin' me my own mortar, aren't I?' said Keegs, staring at the tins again.

'You what?'

'I'm buildin' a mortar.'

'What, out of baked-bean cans?'

'Yeah.' Keegs hacked into the bottom can with a knife as Kev screwed his face up like he had tasted something horrible.

'How do you do that, then?'

'Well, I got the idea for it off me uncle, as it goes, yeah.' An image of 'the old fella' on his allotment flashed before Keegs.

'What the fuck did he want a mortar for down in Kent?'

'Fuck knows. He just built it, didn't he?'

'What you gonna do, then?'

'Well, I got 'em from the kitchens, right? What you do is you cut, like, a half-moon shape out of the bottom of each of 'em, yeah, and, like, stack 'em up on top of each other.'

'Right . . .'

'But you stack alternately. So the can at the bottom of the stack 'as got the half missing on the one side, and the one above it has it missing on the other side, as it goes.'

'Er, right. What's the point of that?'

'It's for the petrol, when it comes down from the top, it takes it longer and all the fumes swill about . . . I don't fuckin' know! It just works better.'

'How do you stick 'em together, then?' Kev frowned, partly because the sunlight was in his eyes. He was also confused.

'I've got some back nasty [masking tape], and you just wrap it around so it's really airtight – keeps the gases in there. You give the tube a shake first so most of the petrol runs out of the bottom. Stick whatever you like in the top of the tube and fuck it – it should go miles into the air.'

'Fuckin' hell, Keegs, that'll be a laugh,' Kev said, nodding approvingly.

''Ere, pass us the tape. See . . . all the cans have got the half missing on one side then the other.'

'Oh, yeah! Nice one.'

Ten minutes later the home-made mortar was ready for test firing. Keegs lit a match at its base and sent a squashed Coca-Cola can 50 metres into the air. 'Fuckin' hell, Keegs!' Kev was transfixed. 'We're gonna 'ave some fun with this, mate!' Fun meant trouble.

Keegs's Coca-Cola addiction would ensure plentiful ammunition. He consumed ten cans a day and had two rotting teeth loosening in his mouth. He bought crates of Coke from Abu Naji and numbered the cans in a vain attempt to dissuade Rob Schwar from pinching them.

Neneh was fond of the story of how he and Lance Corporal Rush had stolen a pair of day-old chicks from Abu Naji. On the day in question, his accomplice had sprinted towards the Land-Rover, shouting at him to accelerate as he clambered aboard. Rush had finally shut the passenger door as Neneh sped through the camp gates. Keeping one eye on the road, Neneh had glanced at the fluffy white balls, and his throaty laugh had filled the cabin. 'I cannae fuckin' believe it!' he had said.

'I know, mate. I swear, right, I walked in the shop and asked if the chicks were for sale, yeah? And they weren't 'avin' any of it, right?'

'No, no. I cannae believe I'm the getaway driver for a couple a wee chicks!'

'So, I just, like, turned, kept it subtle, had a look if anyone was lookin' and just grabbed 'em. Cool, aren't they?'

The chicks had lifted their downy heads to reveal pinhead-sized black eyes, yellow beaks and peculiarly large scaly feet that bicycled through the air when Rushy held them upright. The two soldiers had laughed all the way back to Condor, where the new recruits had made everyone else laugh, too.

There was sadness when one of the chicks died but great resolve to raise its surviving sibling – or assumed sibling. A protective coop was built using squares of black plastic matting.

'Couldn't we just have one conversation when you're dressed?' Al Roan asked Neneh, who stood wearing only flip-flops, clutching a bottle of baby oil. Neneh was determined only the crack of his arse should remain white. He smiled as he scooped up the chick with his spare hand and exited the bunker. His flip-flops slapped against the concrete. He had discovered the chick's practical purpose, and he kept it in hand as he found a comfortable sunbathing position. When the flies descended, he freed the bird to scamper after them. The chick would occasionally lose balance as it climbed Neneh's contours, but it gobbled up every insect.

The chick's growth rate was rapid, its appetite voracious, yet the Condorites engineered a further method of accelerating its physical development using the muscle supplement creatine. A serving of the crystalline white powder provided protein equivalent to a tin of tuna or a turkey breast. The chick shot from babyhood to adolescence almost overnight. 'If you stare at that chick long enough, it'll grow before your eyes,' said Al Roan, who, coming from farming stock, knew his chickens. Its body grew bulbous, wider than its height, and, for its size, immensely powerful. In hindsight it was unwise of them to place a baby goose in the chick's coop. The timid, endearingly clumsy creature was found dead the following morning. With a finger, a soldier flipped the goose's lolling head over. Its beak was ajar, and there were holes where its eyes had been. The chick had not asked to be morphed into a freak. Unwittingly, it had sacrificed its innocence.

When Keegs and Kev tired of using the mortar to fire tin

cans and tennis balls, they decided the chick should take higher flight. They mentioned the idea half in jest to James Passmore. He dismissed it as lightly as it had been suggested. 'But if he was dead set against the plan, he would have said, wouldn't he?' Kev would pay for his misinterpretation of Passmore's position on the chicken-being-fired-from-the-mortar debate.

The weapon system was prepped, and Wellsy pushed the bottom of a paper cup through to create a cylindrical prop for the chick. They also made the chick a little hard hat to protect it on landing.

'Come on,' said Kev. 'Let's see how far we can get him to fly!' Keegs crouched with a match, while Kev positioned the bird as he would a warhead into the top of the tube. 'Shit! Mr Passmore's coming!'

Wellsy bailed out first, followed by Keegs, leaving Kev holding a mortar tube and a startled young chicken. A livid Passmore cursed Kev's immaturity and insensitivity. 'What the fuck are you doing?' he demanded.

'We were just going to put the chicken in the mortar. We made him some protection, though.'

'Get on guard, now.'

Keegs was still laughing about it as he prepared to visit the marshlands. While Kev was on guard, he was going on a hearts-and-minds patrol with Jay Lawrence, among others. The discovery that Rob Schwar was going to be one of the two drivers on the excursion tempered his mirth. Rob, who had been through basic infantry training with Kev, was a bona fide lead magnet, and the men regarded his presence behind the wheel as a curse.

'We'll get contacted today, then, Rob,' Keegs declared. 'How many times is it you've been ambushed now?'

'Fuck knows, mate. Too many, though.' Rob smiled boyishly.

He had sun-streaked hair, and his skin was honey brown.

'At least you're not driving my Land-Rover. I've got Steve Baker.'

Rob drove Corporal Lee Gidalla's wagon. The battalion boxing coach called Rob 'Billy' after the world light-welterweight champion Billy Schwer. He asked if he was related, but Rob had not even heard of him, despite fighting in the same weight division. Corporal Gidalla had insufficient drivers to enforce army regulations that UK driving bans should be observed on operations. Rob claimed he'd lost his for excess points; Keegs and Kev had been prosecuted for drink-driving.

'It's so fuckin' hot in 'ere,' said Rob, strafing the inside of his thumb across the helmet strap's coarse fabric. 'Fuck it, I won't bother.' He threw it behind him. 'Where we goin' today?' he asked.

'Off the beaten track. South of here, near Al Uzayr.'

'We all polled up, yeah?'

'Yup.'

'Well, we've got some petrol, not sure about the oil and lubricant.'

The sky was as clear as glass, and bright-green grassy hummocks bulged from the otherwise crusty brown landscape. As they drove deeper into the marshlands, sunlight glinted off shallow pools. They reached a settlement at the end of a long, bumpy track. It could not have consisted of more than ten mud huts. Smiling barefooted children ran towards them as they dismounted. On such afternoons, pleasantly warm rather than painfully hot, the troubles of Iraq and their tour seemed distant, if only temporarily.

''Ere, look at these, fellas!' One of the soldiers had found two terrapins.

'They're great, the little slimy buggers.'

'Shall we take 'em back?' They had had terrapins at Condor before, but, to Keegs's dismay, they kept running away. He could never work out why.

'Nah, it never works, does it?'

Keegs laughed. 'Hey, Jay? Did Wellsy tell you that story? Or maybe you was with 'im. He was on patrol one day, as it goes, and his Land-Rover screeched to a halt because they reckoned there was this IED [Improvised Explosive Device] in the middle of the road. Only it was a massive terrapin. Fucking huge, it was!' These were babies, or young terrapins at least.

The soldiers sometimes played a game with terrapins – not a particularly clever one. They would place them on a Land-Rover bonnet and see how fast they could drive without them falling off.

Keegs was bored. He was often bored at Condor, too, when not hoarding AK47s or firing his mortar. ''Ello,' he said, his gaze drawn away from the terrapins. 'Look at that donkey over there!'

It was a male, not fully grown but seemingly well fed. Its head jolted from side to side to dislodge the bothersome flies. Its ears leant forwards out of curiosity. The children followed as Keegs crossed the road; he already had it in mind that he was not leaving without the donkey.

'We'll 'ave the donkey, you have ten dollars,' he said, the note clasped between his forefinger and thumb.

When the farmer raised his head, the wrinkles sewn into his leathery face were pulled tight. Through English eyes, he looked about a quarter of a century older than his likely age. 'Twenty dollar.'

'But we've only got ten.'

'Twenty dollar. Fair price.'

'Well, we can't 'ave it, then.'

Keegs turned away and went back to playing with the

terrapins. Gidalla signalled it was time to leave. The terrapins were placed back in the pool, and everyone mounted the Land-Rovers. The wheels were turning when the old man shouted, 'Mister, mister.'

Its bedraggled state immediately distinguished the second donkey from the first. Then there was its head, which hung low, and the ropes which bound its legs. It appeared not to know the meaning of happiness and was perhaps twice as old as the other animal. The farmer's price reflected its life expectancy. 'Ten dollar,' he said.

Keegs bent down to inspect the donkey more closely. It backed off; human contact signalled danger and pain. It dug its hooves in when the old man pulled its rope. Keegs smiled. The donkey was a creature of its own will. 'OK. Ten dollars it is.'

Keegs pledged to give the donkey a better life. It was otherwise destined to end its days wasted and muscleless. Its thickly matted coat was flea-bitten and its eyes infected. A mane of dark-brown fur ran from the top of its forehead, between its ears and along its spine. Its ears were very long, and opened and closed amusingly as the donkey investigated new sounds.

'Hey, Keegs,' shouted Jay from on top of the Land-Rover. 'I'll give you five dollars towards it when we get back. I'll look after it with you.'

'Yeah, yeah, I don't reckon I'll see your dollars. You can give us a hand, though. I don't think he wants to move.' With Jay and the children helping him, Keegs manhandled the donkey towards the Land-Rover.

'Fuckin' hurry up, Keegs,' shouted Gidalla, knowing his patrol were due back at Condor.

'Yeah, hold on. Sorry, Lee. Jay, you lift its front legs onto the cargo hold, right? I'll get behind it. You'll 'ave to stand over it and keep it still once we're movin'.'

''Ere, Keegs, I can't stop laughing. 'Ave you seen the size of its cock? It's fuckin' massive.'

'OK, lift.'

The donkey emitted a high-pitched screech. It did not want to ride in the Land-Rover.

'Stick 'im on top cover, Jay,' shouted Baker.

Finally, the donkey consented to sitting in the cargo hold, and Jay stood astride it as Baker drove off. It shunted into his thighs in a bid for freedom. With the donkey visible to passing traffic, every kilometre of the return journey seemed longer than the last, while Keegs convinced himself that the donkey had been sighted and its presence on his Land-Rover would be broadcast on the radio net.

'How's he doing back there, Jay?' Keegs asked, leaning over his seat. 'Maybe he's thirsty? Give him some water.'

'Yeah, in a sec. I'm still laughing about his cock.'

A British convoy passed in the opposite direction. 'Fucking hell, Bakes, put your foot down, will you?' said Keegs. 'I'm fucking shitting myself. One of those Land-Rovers was a command wagon. I could tell from those pennants flapping on the bonnet.'

'I'm going fast enough. What the fuck is Passmore going to say?'

Keegs had not thought of that. 'I think he likes animals, though. He likes the chick, doesn't he? Here, Bakes, when we get into Condor, swing the wagon around the back of our accommodation. We're running a bit late, so hopefully most people will be in 'avin' a scoff. I'll sort the donkey out.'

On his visit to the Ops Room, Lee Gidalla did not mention the new arrival. Keegs, meanwhile, led the donkey behind one of the bunkers. His new pet was a sorry but loveable sight, with its fur receding above its nose. There were bare patches on its hind quarters where fleas had fed.

Gidalla's section, Keegs included, sat on the benches in

the kitchen, their mouths bursting with laughter. Passmore's expression revealed his suspicion. 'OK, what is it this time?'

'Nothing, Mr Passmore, honestly.'

When the donkey emitted another anguished snort, they cracked. Passmore marched outside to investigate. He soon returned. 'What the fuck are you playing at?'

'It's just a bit of fun, Mr Passmore.'

'It's a donkey. You can't keep a donkey here.'

'I'm gonna look after it, honestly,' said Keegs. 'We can feed it on food that's left over. I'll even build a pen, so when the OC [Griffiths] comes, we can keep it out of the way.'

'For fuck's sake.'

The terrapins, chick, geese and now the donkey were a welcome distraction. The camp resembled a menagerie; the men doubted Kelly would have tolerated it. As if a VIP, the donkey toured Condor on its first full day in camp and was photographed with the chick sitting contentedly on its back. The donkey ate Keegs's favourite dish, chicken Kiev, and rotting fruit from a cracked red bucket. Having never kept a donkey before, as no Condorite had, Keegs had to learn about its likes and dislikes. His natural inclination to pat the donkey sent it scuttling away. It preferred to be scratched, and scratched hard. Scratching excited its skin beneath its thick, unkempt coat. The donkey rubbed itself against the sides of buildings and rolled on the dusty ground with its head back and its legs tucked up close to its undercarriage. It was less content when confined; there was nowhere to explore within an eight feet by eight feet enclosure, and it upset Keegs to see the donkey stare longingly through the fencing; he had not rescued it from one cell to see it trapped in another. He had Kev's support. They both loved the donkey and reckoned they could tell when it was happy.

Keegs's pet lost human friends when it urinated in the

gymnasium, this being where the Condorites spent most of their downtime. Seeing the soiled, sodden gym mats, Rush cursed the donkey and Keegs. As Keegs considered Rush to be a 'nobody' in the camp hierarchy, he ignored his threats about the donkey's fate if it pissed there again.

Keegs let it out of the pen at every opportunity. ''Ere,' he called out to the chef, 'chuck us, like, any old fruit and that.'

The chef half-filled the donkey's bucket. 'How's he getting on?' he asked.

'Not bad, so long as I feed it once a day. It likes them scraps after dinner.'

'His fur's in a bit of a state.'

Keegs defended his donkey. 'Well, he's as healthy as donkeys can be out 'ere. It's got flea bites and things like that. But he ain't got any injuries or nothing like that.'

'How does he behave around everyone?'

'He's fine. He's never funny when the blokes go up to him and that. He likes a good old scratch! He's entertainment – popular with me and Kev, like.'

'What about the boss? What does he think?'

'I don't think Passmore is that bothered either way.'

'I heard it pissed in the gym.'

'Yeah, Rushy wants to come and lock him up at nights now. I think it's a bit cruel. I'll let him loose. I ain't fussed about anything Rushy says. I don't listen to him.

'He [the donkey] likes walking into the accommodation. I wouldn't want him to piss in there as well.'

Meanwhile, the Condorites had created a 'predator–chick', with excess muscle, increased adrenalin and a bad attitude. They pitched it into zero-sum combat against creatures larger than it would usually have eaten. The creatine-fuelled chick defeated lizards and a weird flying creature that nobody knew the name of. Its appetite grew with every feed and its lust for combat with every contest. Its latest bout was against a camel spider, a creature that when fully grown would be able to run at 10 mph and jump several times its height. This camel spider was an adolescent but much bigger than the chick.

Camel spiders – which actually belong to the non-spider group of arachnids known as *Solifugae* – rely on speed and stealth to kill. They have a regular set of spider's legs plus two pincers called pedipalps: sensory organs similar to insects' antennae. The camel spider uses pincers to locate and kill food, which it cuts into pieces, liquefies and ingests through its pharynx.

The soldiers held the creatures in close proximity, the chick desperate for release, the camel spider stretching its pincers. The camel spider lunged forward first, but the chick outmanoeuvred the pincers and hammered its beak against the camel spider's body. The arachnid lost a pincer when the chick wrenched it out of its socket. The chick was ruthless and skilled. With its victim's innards dripping from its beak and its armoured shell crumpled, the contest was declared over within a minute. The camel spider's famed defences had been wrecked. The chick shook its gullet contemptuously as the latest meal dropped into its stomach.

The chick had looked set to lose the next contest before Richie intervened, slamming his clenched fist down on top of a snake. From then on the chick was considered surplus to requirements. Its mortality had been exposed, and the novelty of its existence as an unlikely predator had worn off. The Condorites wished they had never tampered with a harmless, fluffy baby chicken in the first place. Now it was more likely to be pushed out of the TV room for chirping too loudly than invited to remain and gobble the irritating insects. Unlike the donkey, which had Keegs to oversee its welfare, the chicken did not have a keeper. One day its absence was noticed, but nobody was perturbed. A Jock with missing teeth had bagged it and tossed the package over the perimeter fence.

On what turned out to be the donkey's last night, Rushy locked it up, but Keegs freed it again. Keegs was out on patrol the next morning when the donkey's calling card was discovered in the gymnasium. Neneh's instruction was simple: 'Get rid of it. Give it tae a farmer – leave it somewhere. Whatever you do, just get rid of it. I don't care – I just don't want tae see it again.'

The morning heat was fierce as Larks dragged the donkey reluctantly to the rear of the Pinzgauer all-terrain vehicle. The motor spluttered into life as the animal was hauled on board. Wellsy and Izzy were in the cabin. They had decided to take it to the airfield. Once there, the donkey stood amidst the horizontal expanse, not knowing which direction its life was going to take. Its front hooves were planted close together, and its head was bowed. The soldiers drove back to Condor.

What option did the donkey have but to follow? There was no food, water or habitation where it had been left. Condor was its home, and it had gradually become accustomed to living there, even though it was not yet house-trained. The donkey was also a pack animal. It trotted back to camp.

Again, it was lifted onto the Pinzgauer and driven to the airfield. The soldiers dismounted and offloaded their living cargo. They hoped it would wander off towards one of the villages. But the donkey was sufficiently intelligent – probably more intelligent than the soldiers gave it credit for – to know its way back, even though they had altered the location from where it had first been deposited. It had also been well cared for and had no reason to think it was being permanently expelled. It might have interpreted this sequence of events as a challenge.

The soldiers were amazed when only shortly after they returned, the donkey did likewise. Neneh issued them a handful of spare ammunition. 'Go on, Larks. It will do you good . . .'

Wellsy's superficial encouragement nibbled at Larks, who had not experienced a contact; engaging a party of innocent wedding guests did not count. He accepted the task and for a third and decisive time they drove to the airfield. As he loaded his weapon, he could hear laughter from the vehicle. 'Come on, mate, get it over with.'

'Yeah, Larks, you're supposed to be Airborne and all that. Just shoot the fucking thing.'

'What would you be like in a contact?'

'About time you got some rounds down.'

This debacle had not yet reached its pinnacle, but already he wished it forgotten. Larks was now driven by necessity, because to withdraw would be interpreted as cowardice. The donkey determinedly walked in a circle, so no matter where Larks crouched the creature stood between himself and the Pinzgauer. 'I can't risk a shot now. It'll be deflected,' he said.

'Yeah, yeah, Larks, whatever.'

He sweated in the heat of the moment; nothing in his infantry training had prepared him to execute a pet at close range. He worried that if he missed the donkey's small brain, it would suffer unnecessary pain. His first shot missed altogether.

'For fuck's sake, Larks!'

'You muppet!'

He sighed as he closed in. There were guffaws of laughter from the Pinz. This was very embarrassing. When Larks's next shot clipped the donkey's neck, it let out an anguished groan. From a range of no more than one metre, he fired the fatal shot, and with its final breath the donkey spat blood onto Larks's trousers.

Larks's justification for his actions was that Condor was a small space and soldiers were suffering from dysentery. You could not have a donkey peeing and crapping everywhere, especially in the gym, where some guys spent three hours a day. But Larks was not without sensitivity and would later concede that the situation could have been handled humanely.

Larks and Izzy were doing circuit training when Passmore sensed that something was missing; either that or he had been tipped off. 'Larks. Get over here. Now!'

'Oh, for fuck's sake,' Larks said to Izzy. They both feared what was coming. Larks sprinted towards Passmore, jolting to a halt a couple of yards in front of him.

'And fucking stand to attention in front of me.'

'Yes, sir.' This sudden injection of formality alarmed Larks, as Condor was welcomingly free of parade-ground discipline. The platoon commander's stare shocked him into obedience. Larks drove his right boot into the ground, straightened his back and stiffened his arms.

'Where's the donkey?' Passmore asked.

'It's at the end of the runway, sir,' he replied, stifling a smirk.

'What do you mean, it's at the end of the runway?'

'It's dead.'

'How did he die?'

'We shot it.'

'Why did you shoot it?'

'Because it was peeing everywhere. We tried to let it go, but it just kept coming back.'

'You're a wanker, and you're out of order. Go and get a shovel.' Larks returned, anticipating the worst of punishments.

'Right, you're going to dig a hole. The Portaloos are full so your task is to dig shit-pits. And I want them fucking deep, you hear?'

'Yes, sir.'

Passmore found Izzy and Wellsy, and they were ordered to dig with Larks. As Passmore intended, it was the kind of work that turned boys into men. He stood over the offenders as they dug for hours.

'It's up to our knees,' Wellsy pointed out.

The trench was not deep enough to placate him. 'Keep digging. I want it up to your waists.'

When he saw Keegs, Wellsy cocked his head to one side and gave a short laugh. This was the way that so many of their exchanges began. His best mate had taken a weird shine to the donkey and just stared back. If Keegs knew that he had told Larks shooting the donkey would 'do him good', he would be in even deeper trouble.

Later, Keegs broke the news to Kev: 'It's the donkey.'

'What about it? Where is it?'

'They shot it.'

'What?'

'They shot it.'

'Who? When?'

'Larks, an' that.' Keegs pointed to where Larks, Izzy and Wellsy were shovelling earth. 'They reckoned it 'ad pissed in the gym. I'm not so sure, meself.'

'I don't believe it.'

Kev ran to the trench. 'What 'ave you done, Larks?' Kev looked distraught.

'Oh, don't give it all that, Kev. It was pissin' everywhere.'

'I fuckin' 'ate you, Larks, for doin' that. That donkey was well 'appy. It wasn't a slave any more.'

'Yeah, all right, mate. It was a health hazard.'

'Fuck you, Larks. I hate you.'

For a well-meaning soldier with a conscience, Larks knew he had committed an exploitative act. He did not need telling. 'Cheers, lads, it's fucking *Band of Brothers* here,' he told Izzy and Wellsy. 'It's fucking hot an' all. I'll square you guys away when you fuck up, yeah?'

'Shut up, Larks, and fucking get digging.'

Passmore was as angry with Neneh. 'It was an animal,' he implored. 'It was supposed to piss and shite everywhere.'

Neneh, who as a youth had wanted to train as a veterinary surgeon, could not take it so seriously. 'Well, it won't be doing any more pissing and shitting now, will it?'

'You can't just kill an animal like that. What were you thinking of, giving them the ammunition?'

'It was their donkey – they could do what they liked with it. I don't know what yer getting a hard-on aboot. We're killing human beings out here. It was a donkey.'

Later, Neneh told Larks how Passmore had 'wanted to go through him like a dose'. They chuckled as Larks described how the donkey had prolonged the ceremony. There was enough grief going on outside Condor to keep this incident in perspective.

8

Red Eyes and Tears

Playground bully and all-round general troublemaker Jim 'Danger' Faux has been grounded by Mum and Dad after residents of the well-to-do 'Kalat Sally' estate petitioned local police. Local residents decided enough was enough and went to see Danger's dad. He was promptly grounded for a week after being made to promise not to do it again.

This was the Light Infantry's in-house newsletter's interpretation of what followed the Qalat Salih siege. Indeed, Major Faux left battlegroup headquarters less often after the battle than before, as the elders held him personally responsible. Bill Ponting took their vendetta against Faux seriously. That day had seen the longest confrontation between British and local forces of the 'post-war' period. Around 4,000 rounds and scores of grenades had been fired. Estimates of the Iraqi death toll were exactly that. All that could be said was that it was significantly higher than the single-figure estimate offered by Coalition Forces. On the Light Infantry's official website it read:

A firefight left seven 1 LI soldiers injured and three Iraqis dead. The soldiers came under small-arms fire while on routine patrol. The MoD was unable to say why the fighting broke out or confirm if any of the Iraqis killed were civilians. It is not known if any more Iraqis were injured.

The Whitehall committee approved Paul Kelly's Military Cross citation, while James Passmore and the company sergeant major from the Light Infantry were mentioned in dispatches.

Faux later hinted in a newspaper interview that his presence might have inflamed the situation:

> The Iraqis knew that I was in there and who was there with me – they did not like us much because we had taken their weapons off them.
>
> There were eight of us on the patrol in two Land-Rovers. A shot was fired, so we chased and picked up the shooter who turned out to be a local policeman. We traced his steps back and found the house he had come from. We also discovered rocket launchers, ammunition, grenades and 14 assault rifles. At the same time we got opened up on by heavy machine gun fire. We left the Land-Rovers and retreated to the Badr house. By this point we were being shot at from 360 degrees. Everyone was stunned. The sheer amount of fire coming towards us was unbelievable. One of our soldiers was shot through the hand, another through the leg and one suffered shrapnel wounds. If we hadn't got out, it would have been another Majar al-Kabir, where the six military policemen had been killed the year before. They had no weapons and were slaughtered anyway. There were moments of sheer terror followed by sheer hilarity. We were incredibly lucky, and a lot of us could so easily have been killed. It is weird knowing that we should be dead, that I should be dead.

The aftermath of the Light Infantry's tour was shrouded in acrimony. Faux was one of many soldiers questioned by military police detectives investigating allegations of brutality. Video footage obtained by the *News of the World* showed men from the support company he commanded striking protesters after a riot in Al Amarah.

By mid-April it was time for the infantry and armoured units of the main battlegroup based at Abu Naji to be relieved. By coincidence, the infantry battalion to which many at

Condor already belonged would replace the Light Infantry. Wellsy remembered Lieutenant Colonel Matt Maer, the incoming commanding officer, from when Maer had been his company commander.

The PWRR comprised two battalions (1 PWRR in its armoured infantry role and 2 PWRR in its 'light' role) and had been formed in 1992 by the amalgamation of the Queen's Regiment – the county infantry regiment of Kent – with the Royal Hampshire Regiment. The first battalion (1 PWRR) had approximately 600 soldiers based in Tidworth, Hampshire, and would be moving barracks to Germany upon returning from Iraq. Lieutenant Colonel Maer was a chain-smoking police officer's son who had led his battalion since the previous November – when its deployment to Iraq was announced. Aged 39, his last job had been deskbound at the Joint Terrorism Assessment Centre. Maer was as eager as his men to deploy on operations and put into practice what he had learned.

The process by which the baton passed from the sitting infantry battalion to the arriving battalion was convoluted, but all of 1 PWRR were *in situ* by 18 April 2004 – this was 'flag day' and the date of the formal handover. The fully armoured elements of the battlegroup also changed over, the new units being A Company, 1st Royal Welsh Fusiliers, equipped with Saxon armoured cars, and A Squadron, the Queen's Royal Lancers, equipped with Challenger II tanks. The PWRR battlegroup reported to the headquarters of the 1st Mechanised Brigade, as did B Company at Abu Naji and the Argyll companies based in Iraq's second city. Gray's battalion staff shared with brigade headquarters the use of Saddam's former palace in Basra.

The security situation had been worsening progressively across the province month on month, and in the eyes of many the arrival of the PWRR only accelerated this process. Demonstrators thronged around the Civil Military Cooperation house in Al Amarah. This facility had been the offices of those responsible for the regeneration projects in the province. Several hundred Mahdi Army volunteers were active in Maysan Province, and the Condorites witnessed the spectacle of simulated self-flagellation in which men dressed in black from head to toe whipped themselves with lengths of black rope. To a teenager from Dunoon or Dumbarton, this was a sinister sight.

It was with some trepidation that Griffiths returned to the UK on leave. In spite of the addition of 7 Platoon to Condor, his anxieties remained about the Condorites' safety, and these were shared by Al Roan, who would act as company commander in Griffiths' absence. One of the Light Infantry's last sorties, piggy-backed by members of 1 PWRR, was forced to withdraw under small arms and rocket-propelled grenade fire from Majar al-Kabir. This most perilous of locations was subsequently made a no-go zone for all but secretive Special Forces raids in search of the killers of the six Royal Military Policemen. Certain pockets within the Condorites' area of operations had also been ruled out of bounds. However, as nobody was sure which ones, there was no blanket enforcement of such an edict.

Keegs had been determined to prove that Iraqis were abusing the courtesy shown by British forces of waving through female drivers at checkpoints. Finally, he snapped and chased down a vehicle driven by a woman in full headdress. The driver and her female passenger jettisoned rifles as they sped along the highway; eight more were found when the car was stopped. The women had fully loaded ammunition magazines hidden beneath their dresses. Vindicated, Keegs espoused sexual equality at all times thereafter, even searching a woman whilst she was breastfeeding. He joked she was the 'fittest bird' he had seen in Iraq.

That afternoon's Vehicle Checkpoint was mundane by comparison. Keegs stopped more cars than anyone else before his thirst for Coke found him back at Condor by 1600. Keegs collapsed onto his bed and made a mental note to wipe down his weapon when he could find the strength.

Meanwhile, Kev and Rob were out on patrol with Gidalla. Their attention had been caught by a driver accelerating away from them; an AK47 was wedged beneath the rear bumper of his vehicle. The weapon was confiscated but at the cost of a punctured tyre. Sweating, and with oil seeping into their roughened fingers, Rob and Gidalla cursed Kev's driving. They had told him to slow down, although the kid should not have been driving at all, since he did not have a licence. The superstition and fear surrounding patrols when Rob drove had persuaded the others to give Kev a go behind the wheel. They regretted the decision now as they changed the tyre.

'Let me drive again tonight, Lee, yeah?' said Rob. 'Kev can go back on top cover . . .'

'OK, Rob.'

On returning to Condor, they headed directly to the kitchen. Chicken Kiev was on the menu again, which pleased Keegs. His donkey would have appreciated it, too. It still angered him that Larks and Wellsy had got rid of the donkey while he was out on patrol, which was no coincidence as far as he was concerned.

The dossing-about time passed quickly between scoff and the evening's operation, and it was dark as they gathered for Passmore's briefing. They were to conduct a patrol with the ICDC. 'Why is he briefing us?' wondered Rob. 'We never get a briefing from the boss before patrols!'

Passmore's tone was sonorous. 'There is quite a big threat.

The Mahdi Army has been seen in this area. Something could happen.'

'Sounds dicey to me,' thought Rob. 'Fuck it. I'm just a bod. I just do as I'm told when it comes to ops. They ain't gonna cancel it just because I reckon it's iffy.'

'Keep your eyes peeled,' Passmore added, 'be aware and remember your drills.'

'Yes, boss.'

The soldiers broke out of the huddle like gridiron players after the quarterback has called a play. They mounted their vehicles, and Kev and Col Beeney adopted the top-cover positions on Rob's wagon.

'What's all this about dominating the ground, Col?' Kev asked. 'He sounds serious.'

'Yeah, I've got a bad feeling about tonight. We've been confined to camp for a while. I reckon he wants to show them we won't be intimidated. I'm going to get some more field dressings before we leave. You coming?'

'Yeah, I will.'

An unfortunate idiosyncrasy of Rob's was his preference for soldiering during daylight hours. Darkness exacerbated his fears, so much so that he put on his helmet. He usually considered it to be too hot for headgear.

It was Kev and Col's second operation of the day, and their faces looked bleary. Armed with the heavy machine gun, Kev faced the rear and Col forwards. Kev and every other Gimpy gunner cursed the fact that the Danish soldiers had fully armoured vehicles with fixed weapon systems. Such was the Government's 'Pound-Shop' approach to equipping its soldiers, Kev struggled to hold his weapon in place as it rattled against the roof cage. It slipped and slid through his hands as the Land-Rover gathered speed. The vehicle had no armoured capability.

The night air was muggy as they collected the ICDC and

drove towards Al Kahla. The Iraqi recruits had no personal body armour and stood in the back of their pick-up trucks wearing boiler suits and baseball caps.

Rob decelerated as the convoy approached a village. He used his shirt sleeve to wipe perspiration from his forehead and squinted into the darkness. The rudimentary street lights had been turned off. Out of his line of sight, Keegs jumped off the other Land-Rover and, weapon in hand, bounced onto the ground. He approached a portly farmer squeezed into the seat of his tractor. The Iraqi had one hand on the steering wheel and the other on top of a little boy's head, the child perching in front of him. The farmer did not care for Keegs's close attention and gesticulated. It was then that Keegs saw the outline of an AK47 protruding from the tractor engine. Their eyes met. Keegs tugged at the weapon. It was his now, regardless of the farmer's story that it was for personal protection. Keegs slung it into the cargo hold.

On Passmore's signal, the vehicles moved out. Al Kahla was indistinct in the distance but for the cluster of shadowy single-storey buildings that rose up on either side of the main road. The only locals Rob saw were youths crouched behind a market stall, as if ready to leap from their positions. 'This isn't right. This just isn't right,' Rob thought, shaking his head.

Gidalla tightened his grip on his rifle. He would have been better off with a pistol: it was almost impossible to return fire with a 'long' from the Land-Rover cabin. The kids' feet kicked up tiny dust clouds as they sprinted away. Their work as observers was done.

Somebody quipped that it was 'too empty around here' and that things would get 'dodgy'. The shops and buildings on both sides of the road were closed. Rob was rigid with fear.

They were ambushed on the main street. The staccato

sound of light weapons was followed by an Improvised Explosive Device exploding beneath Rob's Land-Rover. The vehicle lifted up then crashed back down.

There was incoming fire from all directions, and as Rob ducked beneath the dashboard rounds passed across the bonnet of his Land-Rover. He was so shocked, he had not yet felt the tiny pieces of secondary fragmentation embedded in his arms. He heard screams from behind him and appeals for him to accelerate. But the ICDC pick-up had stopped in front of him and the recruits were running in all directions. Rob pulled the gear stick into second and wrenched the steering column hard over to his left. The Land-Rover slammed into the corner of the ICDC wagon. Rob reversed and shot forwards again.

'Go! Fucking go!' he heard again.

Either Rob or Gidalla switched off the headlights, making the Land-Rover harder to hit. The engine snarled as Rob floored the accelerator. He did not bother to change gear. Rob drove with his head beneath the dashboard, both arms braced in front of him. He heard screams again – sounds he described as 'pure pain'.

'What's happened!' he cried.

'Who's been hit?' yelled Gidalla.

'Kev's been hit,' Col mumbled, failing to mention he had been too, in his left forearm. He had returned fire even after being shot.

A round had entered Kev's right shoulder blade, tunnelling across and exiting through his right tricep, ripping out a portion of flesh as it surfaced. Kev had then collapsed, leaving his machine gun hanging limply from the roof. Only the netting draped over the metal cage prevented it from dropping off the Land-Rover.

Blood gushed from Kev's arm, bile welled up in his mouth and he felt nauseous. Time hung unmoving about him as he curled into a foetal position. The Land-Rover crested every bump and came crashing down, contemptuous of his suffering. Seconds before he was hit, a rocket-propelled grenade had flashed past his head, and he had seen grenades exploding. Kev remembered firing a few rounds before being hit. He was now delirious with pain. 'I'm gonna die, I'm gonna die. Shit.' When Rob accelerated, Kev slid towards the tailgate. He was within inches of falling off the wagon when Col hooked him back with his leg.

Chunks of Kev's arm muscle were hanging down by his elbow. He thought his arm was going to fall off. 'Fuck, the burning, the burning! This is me finished.'

'Great driving, Billy boy!' Gidalla yelped as they exited the village. But now they came under mortar fire. The road shook beneath the aerial bombardment.

'Col, you all right, mate?' Rob asked with foreboding. Col was bleeding profusely.

'Of course I am, mate,' he shouted. 'I'm from the Isle of Wight, aren't I?'

Although slight of build, Beeney's reputation was as a mean, gutsy soldier. When he went nightclubbing back home, the bouncers working the doors would nod in silent respect. Rob knew Col would downplay whatever had happened to him.

With Gidalla alone squeezing off rounds through the passenger window and both top-cover soldiers badly wounded, the Land-Rover was virtually defenceless. Rob finally answered the vehicle's call for him to change up from second gear. He reached a fork in the road at which he was to turn right, according to the 'patrol matrix' route plan. But too many British patrols, as well as his own, had been seen passing through Al Kahla in recent weeks. If he had been observed turning right there on a previous visit, this was where the enemy might have situated the 'cut off'

– the second phase of the ambush. He turned left, a decision which perhaps saved their lives.

The problem was finding a route back to Condor or Abu Naji. Gidalla told him to look for a place to stop out of range of the mortars. Rob stared ahead, his hands shaking. He was in a rage. He slung the Land-Rover off the dirt track onto some flat ground. Passmore's wagon pulled up behind him. The uninjured soldiers formed a defensive cordon. An Iraqi car approached from the opposite direction; the lights were off on both Land-Rovers and there was nearly a crash. They kicked in one of the Iraqi's doors to persuade him to park elsewhere.

Passmore established communications with the battlegroup Ops Room. Abu Naji, where there was a Field Surgical Team, was his intended destination. Neneh was manning the radios at Condor. He had not heard from Passmore since the subaltern's departure from camp.

'We have two serious casualties, and we will need an ambulance at the gates of the camp on our arrival,' Passmore said, gripping the satellite phone to his ear.

'Roger that.'

The signaller at Abu Naji called Condor. Neneh was expecting Passmore's patrol to return to camp.

'Hello, can we have the zap numbers of your two casualties, please?'

'Sorry?' Neneh replied. 'We don't have any casualties. I don't understand.'

'Yes, you do. They are incoming at our location.'

'First I've heard. Roger. Out.'

Neneh's first thought was that the ICDC had tipped off the insurgents. He stared at the patrol matrix written up on one of the noticeboards. It provided an outline of all patrols due to occur over the next 48 hours. He tried calling Passmore. 'Send a sit-rep. Over. Repeat, send a sit-rep. Over.'

As it was an insecure radio net, he gave no further information. He was confused. 'There's no way Passmore wouldnae have called if he had casualties,' Neneh thought. 'He wouldae informed me for sure.' Passmore had tried but could not get a signal.

'Help me, help me,' Kev implored of his best mate Keegs, who had run across from Passmore's Land-Rover. With no medic among the patrol, Keegs would, in his own inimitable way, help his friend.

'All right, Kev, all right. I'm tryin'. The pain will be gone once I've helped myself to the morphine!' There was an edge of amusement to Keegs's voice. 'Where does it 'urt, then?' Keegs clutched Kev's arm, sending a bolt of pain through his best mate's body.

'Aaargghhh!'

'Oops. Sorry, Kev!'

'Aaargghhh!'

'Hang in there, mate. Now, where's me fuckin' torch? I can't see what I'm doin' 'ere, can I?' Keegs's personal admin was 'in rag'. Being on top-cover duty, he wore an assault vest rather than belt webbing. 'I know where everything is in there, Kev. But fuck knows what's goin' on 'ere, as it goes.' Keegs kept up this commentary as he patted his pockets. His facial expression, if not his voice, acknowledged his welling anxiety. Stooped in front of Kev with both his knees bent, Keegs at last liberated a field dressing from his left-thigh pocket and removed its sterile cover. Pressing the pad against Kev's upper-right arm, he realised his mate's shirt was rolled down over the wound. It was submerged in blood and body matter.

'You're gonna be all right, mate,' he puffed heartily, not believing a word. This was surreal: his best mate was dying in front of him.

'Fuck,' Kev wailed repeatedly. 'Fuck.' Keegs was 'proper fuckin' scared'.

'OK, Kev. I'm gettin' the morphine out now.' The phial seemed tiny in his hand. He freed Kev's morphine from its plastic housing – it was a standard operating procedure of combat medicine to use the victim's first-aid supplies before your own. Keegs had no specialist combat medical training; he simply looked at the red end of the phial, then the yellow. Keegs bit on the yellow end while he pulled the red cap he figured was protecting the needle. Nothing happened. He pressed the red end against Kev's leg; at least he remembered this from demonstrations. He felt the prick of a needle pierce the skin and veins of his own palm; lifting his arm, he saw the needle hanging from his hand. He had attempted to insert the wrong end of the phial into his patient. 'Oh, fuck, mate, you won't guess what I've done. I'm gonna need another needle. Kev, for fuck's sake, just hang in there. It'll be worth it. Sorry.' Keegs ripped the needle out of his hand and slung it behind him. His eyes darted from one end to another of his own morphine: red, yellow, red, yellow.

'Have you done that yet?' Gidalla glared at the phial.

'Nah, I've just pricked myself.' Keegs half-smiled.

'You what?' the corporal replied, disbelievingly.

'Yeah, I don't know what happened. I stuck it in me! I'm gonna give him mine, but I don't know which end . . .'

'Well, which end did you use last time?'

'That's it, I can't fucking remember!'

'For fuck's sake!'

Each looked to the other for the answer. Gidalla could not be too hard on Keegs, as he was not sure which end was which himself. 'Just try it with the yellow end down, and press the red end first.'

Somehow Keegs's torch reappeared, and holding the yellow end against Kev's leg, he used the torch to hammer down on the phial. He moved in closer to keep the sodden field dressing in place. Keegs expected an immediate change in Kev's condition, but it would be some minutes before the morphine kicked in.

Keegs and Kev were the closest of mates, having served together for four years in Bosnia and Northern Ireland. They were friends in spite of the fact that they had little in common, apart from drinking, but that brought a lot of soldiers together. Keegs was sporty; Kev was not. Kev was into cars; Keegs was not. Drinking, smoking and cracking on to birds in clubs were the interests they shared.

'I'm gonna die, Keegs. I'm gonna die!'

'Shut up, mate. No, you're not. You're gonna be in the pubs soon, and the birds are gonna love you for it.'

Kev remembered the drill. They had both been taught to reassure casualties when treating them. 'You're lying to me, Keegs. I'm dying!'

'Shut up, Kev. You'll be all right.'

Kev was kneeling with his head in Keegs's lap. He had lost a lot of blood and could not afford to lose much more.

They spent most of their leave time in the Millhouse, their favourite Canterbury pub, immediately outside the barracks. They did not look or act alike, which was an advantage when out on the pull. With two birds, once they had got them talking and had bought them bottles of something fruity and intoxicating, they could proceed with their patter hopeful that, without too much cajoling and steering, one would start talking more to Kev than Keegs or vice versa. Hopefully, each bird would fancy both men, but if he was honest, Keegs had to concede it was more likely to be Kev, with his soft, almost feminine face and doe eyes. Keegs was no gargoyle, but he was more of a typical squaddie, with his shaved head, St George's flag tattoo and his preference for roll-ups. He got a lot of grief from Paul Kelly and the bods on platoon piss-ups for his lack of success on 'chick ops'. By contrast, the female front was Kev's natural domain.

'You'll be in the Millhouse before me, mate,' Keegs cajoled, although his voice was hollow. 'Think about it, the birds will be all over you even more now.'

'Yeah, yeah, yeah.' Kev was slipping in and out of consciousness.

For reasons he would never want to explore, Keegs found himself stroking his best mate's earlobe. He continued to do so, comforted by the hope that Kev was too sedated to reciprocate and the thought that he was only doing unto another that which, had he been dying, or apparently dying, he would want done to himself.

The patrol had been stationary for around 15 minutes. Kev and Keegs had been oblivious to the mortars until one landed only 20 metres away. It was time to move on again. Keegs was still holding the field dressing to Kev's arm; his mate seemed quieter now, even when tickled. After receiving morphine, Col Beeney assured the others he felt fine as long as he did not move his arm. Gidalla, meanwhile, had found a route to Abu Naji that avoided Al Kahla and the 'Danny Boy' junction, always a potential ambush point. The route led through the marshland wilderness.

On the dirt tracks, Rob could not 'red line it' back as fast as he might. 'You need to turn left in a minute,' Gidalla instructed him.

Rob did so, but the track soon narrowed. 'Fuck, it's a dead end,' he said. His choice of words was unfortunate. Rob, driving, felt the pressure, as did Gidalla, navigating.

'Oh, fuck, fuck!' Kev's faint plea chilled his mates. 'Get me back, quick!'

Rob accelerated his Land-Rover again, bouncing over potholes and rocks. Kev groaned every time he was displaced inside the cargo hold. 'Slow it down,' Gidalla said.

At last they crossed the familiar bridge, turned off Route 6 and rolled towards Abu Naji. Their approach was observed by the sentries manning the sangars – field fortifications built with sandbags and rocks – on the camp perimeter. Medical teams were waiting at the camp gates. They carried Kev and Col from the vehicles onto stretchers and into ambulances. Every time Kev's body jolted, his helmet slid off his head and cut into his wound. He was drowning in waves of pain.

To Rob, suddenly nothing seemed real any more. This was a nightmare, and he raised his eyes skywards. Like most British personnel, his attitude towards life and death was conditioned by years of service in benign environments. He could have soldiered until eternity in Northern Ireland without feeling his life was in jeopardy. Here, fear was never far from the surface – and now it had been realised. He stared back blankly when people asked him if he was all right. He climbed into the back of his Land-Rover, his boots treading a sticky carpet; the day sacks lay in a puddle into which a red stream flowed.

The men spared the Iraqi rounds stood outside the Ops Room awaiting the debrief. They had left their weapons in the Land-Rovers; one of the camp signallers stood guard. They were ushered inside. Keegs dragged heavily on a fag; for the first time he could remember, he was permitted to carry on smoking inside the cramped, hard-shelled room. Command staff moved around the bird table, the epicentre of battlegroup activities. A map of Maysan Province was spread across it.

'We just want a quick account from you all, written down,' an officer requested. Keegs did not recognise him. Someone else – the padre, he thought – produced a hip flask; it was better than a lecture on Jesus, he readily admitted.

Listening to Passmore, Neneh and Al Roan sensed he blamed himself for the contact. 'Lee [Gidalla] had said there was something not right when we had got in there,' he confided. 'Everywhere was shut up. He was just putting this over the net when it all went down.' Passmore's eyes were tired and sad. He seemed on the verge of tears as he explained how he had decided not to return to assist the ICDC once his patrol had extracted. Although he knew that some of the ICDC might have been wounded, the mortars chasing his Land-Rover had convinced him that such a course of action would have been suicidal.

The ICDC had been overwhelmed by the experience in Al Kahla, forgetting their much-practised contact drills. 'Get them out on the ground, and let's use them to stabilise the situation' had been the message from battalion headquarters. 'Let's start taking ownership of the security situation' was another buzz phrase. The ICDC did not like being in the line of fire. The fear now was that, having been attacked, they would retaliate. Whether or not they would do so depended on where Al Kahla stood in the pecking order of villages and which tribes the four wounded ICDC members belonged to. The incident could trigger a blood feud.

They cut off Kev's uniform in the medical centre and bandaged his arm. There was a crater where a huge chunk of flesh had been blown off. Through a semi-consciousness haze, he heard Col ask for his photograph to be taken. Kev passed out again and woke up on a Chinook helicopter, which flew him to the field hospital near Basra.

Looking at his wounds just made Kev feel worse. He wanted to faint or cry. He heard echoes of Keegs shouting at him and saw images of himself sliding out the back of the Land-Rover before Col's outstretched leg rescued him. He remembered firing his Gimpy at first, but then his arm 'fell down'. To think, before this evening he had thought himself bullet-proof. He was not one of those soldiers who feared for their lives. Being shot was something he imagined only happening to others.

His first visitors in hospital were from the Royal Military Police. One of the Red Caps asked, 'Were you wearing your body armour?' He passed out again after that, so Col provided Kev's witness statement. Yes, they had both been wearing body armour, he confirmed.

As part of his report for battalion headquarters, Al Roan had to discover what had happened to the missing ICDC. This meant waking up the 606th's commanding officer at his home in Qalat Salih. It was 0400 by this time, but Roan was buzzing with adrenalin. He and his men deployed in a convoy of two multiples, first to find the ICDC duty officer then to the ICDC commanding officer's house in Qalat Salih. It took some time to locate the building, as it lay within a private compound.

The commanding officer was relaxed about the intrusion and seemed to have been expecting it. When told about the contact, he gave little away. Perhaps he was playing for time, waiting for his visitors to reveal what they knew. At one point, he claimed not to understand the questions put to him. When finally he spoke, it was in quiet, near-perfect English. He explained that one of the ICDC recruits was severely wounded. Others had minor gunshot wounds. After the Land-Rovers had extracted, the insurgents had ceased firing and had rushed towards the ICDC vehicles, apologising for their actions: 'We only meant to strike the British soldiers, not you. Come, let us look after you.' The casualties had been taken to hospital in Al Amarah. Roan reckoned the meeting raised more questions that it answered.

At Abu Naji, Royal Military Police took statements from Passmore, Gidalla and the others. They took three hours over each witness's account – the Condorites wondered whose side they were on.

The news that Gray and his entourage would be arriving at Condor in the morning hit hard; his tactical command group had not earned the moniker the 'Morale Dyson' for nothing. Accompanying Gray would be the most senior ICDC officer in southern Iraq, Brigadier Dhia. Gray wanted to personally mentor Brigadier Dhia through the aftermath of such an incident so that he would know what to do the next time.

Eventually, Passmore and his men made it to their beds. They lay motionless, as if sleep was a blunt instrument that had knocked them out cold.

9

Out of Bounds

Gray's arrival was signalled by a funnel of dust several kilometres away. There was a last-minute tidying-up of Condor. Enemy weapons that had been lying around were hidden away. Such a hurried preparation for this kind of visit was known as 'Operation James Bond'. The gates swung open, and Gray de-bussed and marched directly towards the ICDC commander's office. He emerged several minutes later, reiterating that he and the ICDC brigadier wanted to visit the wounded recruits. Gray's plan was to leave shortly after lunch, having spoken to Passmore.

Nothing as bad as Al Kahla had happened to Passmore before. He had fought alongside men who had been wounded in Qalat Salih, but after last night he felt the weight of added responsibility for Kev and Col's wounds. It had been his decision to patrol in Al Kahla; he had inadvertently directed the convoy into the ambush.

'Why did you leave the Iraqis behind?' Gray asked the shell-shocked subaltern.

'I was still in contact. We were being mortared . . .'

'You should have gone back.'

'I had two serious casualties, sir. We had taken a lot of incoming fire. It did not seem the wisest option at the time.'

'Well, we have lost a lot of face with the ICDC. We left fellow security forces on the ground to be ambushed by the insurgents. How do you think that looks? We're in this together with the ICDC – that's the mission. They need to have faith in us.'

Gray was deeply worried. He saw himself, the Argylls and the ICDC standing at a strategic crossroads, with two serious gunshot casualties of his own and members of the ICDC in hospital. The importance of Camp Condor and the mission had been spoken of at divisional level. Camp Jennings had been allowed to close, but there was no way the mission could be allowed to fail here. It was too important to the overall security-sector reform programme, which, it was all too easy to forget, was supposed to be the main effort of Operation Telic 3, the current phase of British operations in Iraq. Gray could not stay at Condor and sort things out himself. So the officers at the camp had to provide the leadership and the steel to 'earn their pay', as Gray put it.

There was no time for any further inquiry into what had happened in Al Kahla. The Argylls were obligated to coordinate their movements on the ground with the battlegroup at Abu Naji, hence why Griffiths had attended the operational meetings. With the Condorites shaken and the British battlegroup in a state of flux (the Light Infantry were in the process of handing over to the 1st Battalion, the Princess of Wales's Royal Regiment) it had been an awkward time for Gray's trusted company commander to have returned to Britain on leave.

Al Roan thought Gray should have credited Passmore for putting the safety of his men first. 'Fuck the Iraqis,' Roan thought. 'They don't give a shit about us. How dare Gray come up here and tell us what is what? He hasn't got a clue what the situation is like on the ground in Maysan Province.'

Gray called the Condorites together for a briefing. The

lieutenant colonel was from Edinburgh and was educated at one of its esteemed public schools. He sounded about as Scottish as Tony Blair, who had attended the city's Fettes College. Scotland's capital was more class-conscious than England's, and Gray had friends who had never met the likes of those he commanded, the fiercely working-class private soldiers raised on high-rise estates littered with junkies. The Jocks disliked Gray because of what they perceived him to represent – a privileged ruling elite north of the border – yet it fell upon Gray to lift their spirits. 'Last night was a terrible event, but the guys are in good hands. They are going to pull through. You're doing a fantastic job here. Remember, we want to leave Iraq. To do that we have to train these guys, the ICDC, to be ready to take over from us. That's the bigger picture. We've got to keep building bridges. Keep your heads up and stick with it.'

The Jocks, dressed in their football shirts and flip-flops, stared at the ground, the heat heavy on their shoulders. What did they care about the bigger picture? Just hours earlier, two of their mates had been shot. The non-commissioned officers and officers kept straight faces.

Roan saw Gray peering at him through the crowd. The commanding officer wanted to buttonhole him as well; he thought the acting B Company commander was 'wobbly'. Gray led the way towards the makeshift cookhouse. Pie and mash was on the menu. 'How do you think the ICDC are doing?' he asked.

'Well,' Roan pushed his food around, 'there are a few issues. I don't think they are ready to patrol on their own.'

'Is that because of the training they are receiving?'

'No, it's to do with their attitude. They don't want to patrol. Militarily, a lot of them have experience from the Iraqi Army. This really isn't what they want to do. That's where the problem lies – not in their skill levels. By Iraqi

Lance Corporal Steve Wells
during the siege of Qalat Salih.

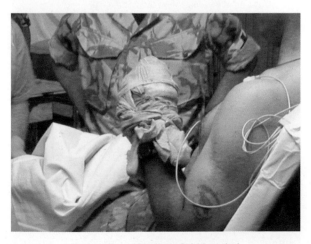

Paul Kelly at Shaibah field hospital.

Snap Vehicle Checkpoints, Iraqi style. Rather Keystone Kops.

Boy soldiers, Aldo and Smudger.

'It's a donkey – it's supposed to piss and shit everywhere.'

James Passmore, right, with 7 Platoon and the donkey.
Hendy is in the sweatshirt.

The chick –
pre-bodybuilding programme.

Lieutenant Colonel Hikmet of the ICDC with Jonny Gray.

Major Sabeer pays the wages.

The cargo hold of Rob Schwar's Land-Rover after
the Al Kahla ambush.

Jonny Gray briefs his shell-shocked troops after
the Al Kahla ambush.

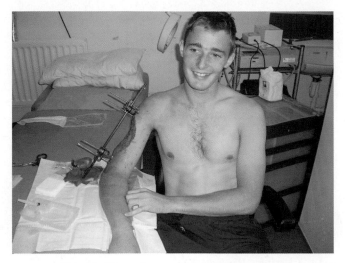

Kev Challis staying positive during treatment.

6 Platoon, otherwise known as the 'PW Ha Has'.

The Jocks go swimming. Paddling pool provided by Richie Fieldman's mum.

James Dormer in Condor uniform.

The aftermath of the attack on the US convoy
outside Al Amarah.

'I had told the sergeant major
to bring "the silver" to Iraq. It
was what proper regiments did.'
Jonny Gray, eyes down, at his
eventful dining-out ceremony. As
he said, 'It was like a scene from
Carry On Up the Khyber'.

Aldo and Richie under fire on Danny Boy day.

By time-honoured tradition . . .

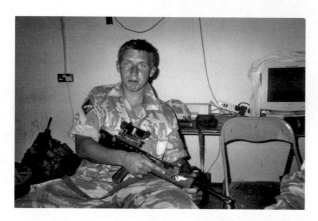

Rob Schwar points to where an AK47 round deflected off the gas block of Jay Lawrence's rifle, saving the latter's life.

6 Platoon on patrol in the marshes.

standards, those are OK. They want to be neutral – not to put themselves in the firing line.'

'Perhaps it is because of B Company,' Gray replied. 'Perhaps it is the way the company is training them? This mission will not fail. The security of Iraq is at stake.' His words hung like an ultimatum. He wanted to hear solutions, not problems. Battalion headquarters had made it clear that the goal was for the ICDC to patrol without supervision. What battalion headquarters might not have known was that the colour-coded reports on 'ICDC effectiveness' bore little resemblance to reality – they were filled in as if everything was going according to plan. A year had passed since the US Ambassador Paul Bremer had come up with the idea of creating a 'capable' Iraqi security force. Roan and Gray were simply the poor buggers charged with making it happen.

'Well, I still think it's about attitude rather than capability,' Roan countered.

'If they are not progressing fast enough, then whose fault is that?' Gray persisted. How would Gray react to being told that the ICDC would simply go home or bask in the sun like lizards if you sent them out of Camp Condor to patrol alone?

'In fact, I am not sure you get it, Al.' Gray had fixed verbal bayonets. 'Do *you* think you are capable of running this organisation?'

'Yes, I do. And I do understand the situation, considering how long I've been here.'

'It's just not good enough. You are in the hot seat here, Al. Like it or not, this is your personal responsibility. You need to convince me you are up to this job. You are the man in the chair.'

'Sir, forgive me for not understanding your intent, but I have never received any direction directly from you. When I arrived, you knew I was to take over 606th, yet you and your staff never gave me any insight to your overall plan. I had to receive this second-hand from Adam.' Griffiths was still on leave.

'My ethos, Roan, is that the security of this nation and the success of British operations in Iraq depend on the Iraqi Civil Defence Corps. There is no one else apart from the ICDC. I say again, this mission will not fail – it cannot fail.'

Gray's only concession was that some of the ICDC were 'useless'. 'But I am still driving this project forward, and so should you.'

'Yup, yup. I fully understand now, sir.'

'Humour him. Go along with it,' Roan told himself. 'Tell him what he wants to hear: that everything is going well, that the ICDC are the solution to stability in Iraq and that he is responsible.'

Gray left Roan feeling bruised and freely admitted later that he did not mind having done so.

Meanwhile, George Lees had conducted the day's pre-deployment brief, including the order of march. The B Company headquarters vehicles, with Lees navigating from the first wagon, would take the lead, with the ICDC in the middle and Gray's Rover Group bringing up the rear.

Roan walked to his Land-Rover in a state of confusion. 'Maybe Saddam was right and we're too soft on the ICDC,' he pondered. 'Or maybe we'll never understand their mentality. We've only been here for a few months – how dare we have the arrogance to think we can change them overnight!'

George Lees was a classic Argyll senior non-commissioned officer and a hater of the bullshit ingrained within the regiment. 'Hey, boss. Boss, wha' the fuck is goin' on?' he asked Roan, who just shook his head. 'Don't you worry, boss. I understand. We'll talk aboot it later, like.'

Before leaving for Al Amarah, Gray spoke via satellite

phone to the commander of the new infantry battalion at Abu Naji (the PWRR), Lieutenant Colonel Matt Maer. As Maer was battlegroup commander, he had to approve Gray's request to take a convoy into Al Amarah. Maer thought the situation in the city 'tense' but approved Gray's mission so long as he stayed on the western side of the river.

Roan cleared his head. He was in the second Land-Rover as the convoy stopped in traffic 100 metres from Al Amarah's main hospital. There had been no signs of insurgent activity since they had left Condor, but he grew nervous whenever Iraqi traffic boxed in his vehicle. Suddenly, without warning, the four ICDC wagons broke out, accelerating past Roan and George Lees. The Iraqis kept their eyes straight ahead as the Argylls looked on bemused. Then they turned left through a veil of dust and disappeared over a bridge towards the city centre.

'What the fuck's going on, like?' Roan could not get through on his mobile to the ICDC commanding officer. 'Why would they just shoot off like that? Do they know something we don't?'

They did. The ICDC casualties had been taken to a different hospital in an area of Al Amarah out of bounds to British forces. Roan called the Civil Military Cooperation house – a British aid facility in central Amarah. He spoke to a colour sergeant. 'Is there by chance another hospital in Al Amarah?' he asked.

'Yes, there's the Moqtada al-Sadr Hospital not too far away.'

'The Moqtada al-Sadr Hospital? I've never heard of it.'

'Well, it's not like a normal hospital. I think they've got some doctors there. It's pretty basic. It's run by his charity. Sounds pretty dodgy, I know.'

'Aye, well, maybe our ICDC guys are there.'

'Perhaps, but I've no idea. I think you'll find it's in one of the out-of-bounds boxes, though.'

Lees was a picture of frustration, with his hands on his hips in the roasting sun.

'George, there's another hospital belonging to Moqtada al-Sadr,' said Roan.

'Och, aye. I didnae know that.'

'Aye, but the CIMIC [Civil Military Cooperation] house guys reckon it's in an out-of-bounds area. Get the map out, will you?'

Lees spread the out-of-bounds map across the bonnet. The current threat level determined which areas were and were not passable. Other out-of-bounds boxes were added on an ad hoc basis as and when specific operations took place. 'Aye, boss, they're right. That Moqtada al-Sadr Hospital place is a no-go zone.'

'That's it, then, George.'

'The old Morale Dyson is no goin' tae be happy, though, is he?'

'No, but there's nothing he or anyone else can do about it. Just check with the Ops Room at Abu Naji, George. Just to be sure. Steve McQuitty will know.'

Gray's voice piped up on the PRR radio headsets: 'What's going on?'

'We were just checking the status of the other hospital, sir,' a voice replied.

'Boss,' Lees said to Roan. 'Aye, McQuitty says it's definitely in a box. All the routes to it are out of bounds as well.'

Gray was sweating by this time and marched to the front of the convoy. 'Sir, we've confirmed that with the Ops Room and with the CIMIC house,' Lees said.

'Let's go. This is a complete shambles,' Gray interrupted, stomping back to his vehicle. Lees could not believe his ears.

Gray would later insist that there was a misunderstanding

between the Ops Room, Roan and himself over whether or not they were granted permission to proceed into an out-of-bounds area. Gray claimed they were; Roan, who unlike his boss was in direct communications with the Ops Room, claimed that they were not.

The convoy of Land-Rovers drove up onto the bridge that marked the boundary. Roan's wagon was halfway across when he saw a gunman poke his head out from the top of a minaret. He was pointing a rocket-propelled grenade in their direction. 'Contact left! Contact left! Top of that tower,' Roan shouted, pointing to the target. 'One gunman, maybe two, armed with an RPG.'

'Can't see him,' Roan heard in his radio earpiece. As he looked back at the minaret, the second gunman opened fire with an AK47. The convoy was in his direct line of fire.

'Everyone follow me,' Roan shouted. He signalled to his driver to overtake George Lees and find cover. Below the bridge he saw another British Land-Rover parked at the side of the road. 'Who the hell does that belong to?' he thought. 'It's not one of ours.' Eight or nine British soldiers were strung out in a line, desperately trying to find cover against a low wall. Without assistance of the Argylls, they were in grave danger.

Roan ordered his men to adopt all-round defensive positions. He pressed his helmet against his head and checked he had a full magazine in his rifle. He ran across the open ground towards the stranded soldiers.

'Who's in charge?' He was directed towards a corporal who was watching enemy targets scurry between ambush positions. 'What's goin' on?'

'Who the fuck are you? We're PWRR. We were at the CIMIC house doing a recce as part of our handover. You know, get to know the place an' that.'

'What happened?'

'Got ambushed. We didn't know we'd gone into one of those out-of-bounds areas. Thank fuck you've arrived. They told me the quick-reaction force was going to be delayed. It's kicking off everywhere, apparently.'

'The QRF [quick-reaction force]? We're not part of that. We were just driving past when I saw the gunmen up there firing at you.'

'Glad to see you either way. We're TA guys, only just got here. Some of our lads went into that building over there. That's when we got shot at.'

'Which one?'

'That one.'

'That's the Moqtada al-Sadr mosque. No wonder youse guys got shot at.'

'Well, we won't be going there again. Will you lot be sticking around?'

'Yes, until reinforcements arrive. Better to leave in large numbers and head out of here in one packet, I reckon.'

George Lees guided other soldiers into more offensive positions. In the absence of his company commander Adam Griffiths, Lees had done his best to protect the commanding officer. Griffiths would be shocked to learn of Gray's actions. Because a quick-reaction force was en route from Abu Naji, Griffiths believed Gray should have kept a safe distance away. A dead commander was a useless commander. But Gray was only human and his adrenalin was pumping. To experience a contact was what infanteers of all ranks trained for throughout their careers. His priority was now the PWRR soldiers who were making their first visit to Al Amarah; the jundies were an irrelevance.

There was an exchange of fire between the Argylls and the insurgents. Neither Roan, Lees nor Gray knew it, but across the city locals were building roadblocks to trap the British forces. Hundreds of young men had gathered outside the mosque and were throwing stones and priming RPGs.

'We're getting fired on from all sides,' Roan said, speaking into his radio microphone. 'We've got to get the fuck out of here,' he told the TA corporal.

'Is it like this every day?'

'It's twinned with the Gaza Strip round here.' With RPGs incoming over their heads and the insurgents trying to outflank them, chaos ensued as the new battlegroup tried to comprehend the situation.

While everyone else scrambled for cover, Maer was conducting a recce in the adjacent street. Maer's voice came over the radio net: 'Get the fuck off the ground, get out of here.' Two Warrior armoured vehicles then arrived, providing further cover. The Argylls regrouped by their Land-Rovers. Al jumped into a wagon and asked Lees to carry out a quick headcount. The incoming fire intensified; the insurgents could see they were extracting.

'Just throw everyone into a wagon, George! Let's fucking go!' Roan shouted. It didn't matter who got in which vehicle or how many, as long as everyone made it out of Al Amarah.

Roan issued further instructions via radio: 'Everyone move now. Follow me. We are extracting immediately.' They sped back past the mosque and over the bridge, but the crowd was blocking the road. Roan's driver looked at him for orders. 'Just fuckin' charge!' They accelerated towards the mob, stones bouncing off the metal windscreen grille. The British knew that if the protestors could have stopped the convoy, they would have torn them limb from limb.

As they sped away from the scene, Roan recognised his driver. 'Shit, he's Gray's driver!' he thought. 'This is Gray's wagon! But where the fuck is Gray?'

'Where is he?' Roan asked.

'Who?'

'The CO! Where is he?'

'I dunno, boss. But just before we left I saw the adjutant [Justin Barry] jump out of the vehicle in a hurry.'

'What?' Roan glanced behind himself. Justin Barry had not climbed back onboard before Roan had given the order for the convoy to leave. 'So where is he, the adjutant?'

'I dunno, boss.' The driver might as well have shrugged and said nothing, for all he seemed to care.

'I don't believe it! We've left the adjutant and the CO behind!'

In a single day, Roan had had a barnstorming row with his commanding officer and had left him in a contact, surrounded by enemy. A radio check between Argyll call signs confirmed two people were missing: Justin Barry and Jonny Gray. This was an especially bad sign, as by custom Gray should have had a signaller with him in Al Amarah. As soon as they reached base, Roan went to the Ops Room, where the radio operators told him to wait while they put out an emergency call. The small-arms fire would be snapping over Gray and Barry's ears, the mob getting closer by the minute. Roan pictured the commanding officer and his adjutant arguing over who would get to shoot him, should they somehow escape.

'Roan, you fucker!' Gray cursed as he watched the Argyll Land-Rovers exit Al Amarah. The sight of his staff abandoning him would be his abiding memory of the day. Seeing his commanding officer stranded, Major Barry dived from the rear of the speeding Land-Rover, rolled across the tarmac and ran 100 metres under fire to be at Gray's side. Upon his arrival, Barry shouted, 'The adjutant never leaves the CO in the lurch!' Gray recorded later, 'I could have hugged him.'

Left to his own devices, Gray had linked up with Sergeant Mills of the PWRR. The pair had shaken hands in a very formal, English manner as RPGs and small-arms fire fizzed above their heads. Mills had given Gray a sit-rep, which included the news that the sergeant's Land-Rover had been hit. Gray had noted how cool Mills was, albeit after straying into an out-of-bounds area. Gray had then asked what Mills proposed to do. They could not retrieve the vehicle as it was under attack, but they could not abandon it either – it was carrying sensitive radio equipment.

'Let's get a Warrior to fire a couple of HE [high-explosive] rounds into the back to destroy it,' Mills suggested. Gray had agreed, adding that they should think about extracting as soon as possible afterwards. This plan had been dashed when they had come under attack from a third flank. The fighting had been intense.

It was to their collective relief several minutes later that they saw two Warriors speed towards them. The armoured vehicles did a 180-degree turn, and the heavy automatic rear doors opened. By the time they all squeezed on board, there must have been 11 people inside the cargo hold. The other passengers seemed very surprised to see a commanding officer get in. Gray and Mills exchanged 'high-fives' in their relief to have escaped alive.

The Warrior was driven by Private Johnson Beharry and commanded by Lieutenant Deane. The subaltern got a message in his ear. 'Boss, it's hard to breathe back here. Can we stop so some of us can get out?'

'No,' said Lieutenant Deane, 'we're still being shot at.'

'It is not me who is asking, boss.'

'Who is?'

'The CO of the Argylls, Lieutenant Colonel Gray.'

'Perhaps you could inform the colonel that in the interests of his safety he is going to have to grin and bear it until we're out of the contact area.'

The heat eventually became too much, and the mortar hatches were opened.

While suffering from heatstroke, Roan was relieved to hear Gray and Barry had been rescued. He was then asked to file a report of the Al Amarah incident. Why, he wondered, did battalion headquarters want an expanded memo when the commanding officer and adjutant had been on the ground? The fact was and would forever remain that Roan and Lees had their versions of events, Gray another.

The commanding officer later said, 'I will always maintain that when we drove over that bridge, we had permission to do so. As it transpired, we were subsequently able to assist with the extraction of a PWRR call sign which had requested urgent assistance. We then came under heavy small-arms and RPG fire from the mosque. There then started the "Battle of Yellow 3".

'The PWRR had sustained a casualty and my medic, Corporal Stewart, a TA soldier, rendered him first aid. We then fought a close-quarter battle for an hour or more, increasingly engaged from all directions as the mosque called the locals to arms. This was intense fighting, and other PWRR call signs answering the initial call for assistance became caught up in local skirmishes as they tried to close in on Yellow 3, including Matt Maer's own Rover Group.

'After some time and with Warrior support, we were able to extract to Camp Abu Naji. The camp was mortared extensively that night, but the next day I decided to make for Basra down Route 6. That journey was eventful [a rocket-propelled grenade was fired at Gray's wagon from the roof of the Office of Martyr Sadr in Basra – it missed]. On arrival in Basra we were locked down, and I was very sad not to be allowed to travel to SLB [Shaibah Logistics Base] to see Challis and Beeney before they were evacuated to the UK.'

10

Eight Ball

Kev and Col were flown back to Britain on a C-17 transport plane. Kev remembered lying in an army camp bed during the flight, with drips and tubes hanging out of him, and that the doctors would let neither him nor Col sleep. They carried out one test after another. When his family visited him in the military hospital in Birmingham, Kev learned that the army had sent two men in suits to his mother's house in Kent to tell Mrs Challis her son had been wounded. 'Suited and booted, they had been,' she recalled as she sat by her son's bedside. The problem was that not many people in suits visited Kev's mother. Not surprisingly, she had immediately assumed the worst, thinking her 20-year-old son had been killed. 'I am so glad you were only shot.'

'Couldn't they have just rung you first and told you I had been shot in the arm?' Kev replied. 'That would have made more sense, rather than scaring you witless.'

It felt like a miracle that he was alive – as though he had been given a second chance. Like Kelly, he was gutted not to be at Condor any more, as he had been enjoying himself. As he later recalled, 'I was having a great time until I was shot! It was a proper tour – the kind you join the army for. Northern Ireland and Bosnia were crap by comparison. But we had our own little camp at Condor, with no officers screaming and shouting at us . . . well, only Mr Passmore. He tried to be strict, but he was just like one of us, really, and liked a few pranks himself. I loved the competitions to see who could confiscate the biggest weapon, as well. We could get away with most things, but the Iraqis did not like us very much.'

There were benefits to being bedridden at the Centre for Defence Medicine, and Kev made a better patient than his platoon sergeant. He enjoyed the twice-daily bed baths given by the attractive nurses and did not mind everyone taking his photograph. He was getting accustomed to having an enormous hole in his arm, even if it was excruciatingly painful. He decided he would visit a colleague.

A call from James Passmore increased Kelly's desperation to return to Iraq. The telephone had rung as he stepped out of his house to visit the medical centre. 'Sergeant Kelly?'

He heard the trepidation in the caller's voice. 'Yeah, who is this?'

'Hello, mate. It's Lieutenant Passmore. I take it you heard about Challis and Beeney?' He spoke as if imparting a secret.

'Yes, the families' officer came around last night. But I didn't know who was injured.'

Images flashed inside Kelly's head as he imagined what had occurred. 'What happened?'

'We were on a routine patrol with the ICDC. We went to Al Kahla and around the back of Qalat Salih . . .' Passmore's voice lowered. Kelly pictured his solemn face. 'We entered the town and headed towards a roundabout. There was a large group of kids playing, and they all just ran off as we turned left . . .' Passmore's words died in his throat. 'As we headed north off the roundabout, we were fired on from both sides of the road . . . Beeney and Challis were on top cover on the last vehicle . . .' Passmore's voice trembled. Like a priest, Kelly heard his confession. 'They were shot

. . . We made our way out of town as fast as we could, getting mortared as we went . . . We got them back to Abu Naji for treatment. I am gutted about what happened . . . I can't tell you how much.'

'It's OK, it's OK. Things are going to be OK. They could be dead, but they're not. And I'll be back soon.'

Kelly wished he had been at Condor to dissuade Passmore from his actions. He was the self-appointed bearer of wise tidings, the man who would have steered them away from the ambush before it was too late. Over the following days Kelly set about piecing together what happened. With the benefit of hindsight, he concluded, 'I would not have gone on patrol that far from Condor. Not in soft skins and not passing Qalat Salih just when the Mahdi Army was starting its campaign and was openly patrolling the streets and setting up its own VCPs [Vehicle Checkpoints] . . . The street lights were off as they passed through certain areas – not a good sign. This happened a few times when I was there, going off and coming back on again – a sure combat indicator. The crowd of kids dispersed, and the street was empty – another combat indicator.' But he did not blame Passmore; he blamed himself for not being there. He was pleased for Rob Schwar that he had done the right thing. 'Yeah, he saved lives, stepping on the gas, bumping the ICDC pick-up out of the way. Good on 'im.' And Beeney. 'Shame about him. One of the best privates I ever met. Hope he'll be all right.'

Griffiths was working hard to ensure Kelly was cleared to return to theatre. He knew how much leading 6 Platoon meant to the sergeant, that Condor was more vulnerable for his absence and that he was going stir crazy at home. Apart from family, there was very little support for the wounded, and Griffiths considered the rear party insensitive towards what everyone was going through in Iraq. Kelly's return, even in bandages, would demonstrate to Griffiths' young Jocks that if something similar happened to them or they broke a limb accidentally, they could return to theatre as soon as it was medically feasible. It was highly dubious that he was physically ready for such an ordeal, but Griffiths wanted to 'show Kelly off'. Lesser non-commissioned officers would have been content to recuperate at home but not his 'attack dog'.

Back at Condor, Larks peered through screwed-up eyes across the plain. The horizon was drawn to a point of infinity, and, as always, the heat was almost visible. He propped his chin on his fists and scanned his arcs. Tiny ripples permeated the haze as if the ground was vibrating beneath the weight of the 50 degrees Celsius temperature. Enduring the sun was the biggest challenge of any daytime period on stag, and his limbs were weary. He glanced at his digital timepiece, the sort that still worked after being smashed against concrete, and wiped sweat from his forehead, as athletic a feat as he was to manage all afternoon. The army's dress recommendation 'sleeves up and down as per first and last light' had seldom seemed more academic. The sky was breathless. During the isolation that came with sangar duty, life seemed akin to that on a desert island, cut off from civilisation, as the Condorites were from the body of British troops. He could hear everything and nothing.

Larks struggled to come to terms with what life had thrown at him. Service in Iraq forbade the kind of irresponsible carousing normally available to a barely post-adolescent male. The recent 'Combined Services Entertainment' show staged at Abu Naji had been intended by the top brass to provide relief, yet a trio of shiny-haired, nubile female dancers parading before him and several hundred other sex-starved troops had only reminded them of what they missed most. The girls had sunbathed in bikinis all afternoon, and the soldiers had scurried from tent to tent seeking a better view – they had not seen attractive women for months.

Larks had seen *Apocalypse Now*; the Combined Services Entertainment evening was no less surreal than its cinematic equivalent. The zenith had been reached when the sound of gunfire in Al Amarah had eclipsed the music. The girls had danced in time with the beat, or had it been the AK47s? Everyone but the Jocks had been too drunk to notice the difference. The dancers had tossed back their glistening brunette locks; sober or pissed, it was torture when you had not had sex for months. Above them, the sky had burned with tracer.

Lieutenant Colonel Gray had upheld his prohibition order that night, denying the Jocks alcohol. If they had not felt sufficiently downgraded already, he had dug a tunnel for them to crawl below the private soldiers of other regiments. 'Two cans faer everyone else besides us? Thanks a bundle, Colonel Gray. We'll take a bullet for ye any day.'

Gray was familiar with their uncontrollable Scottish urges towards excess and the need to expurgate them: the 'ned' culture; the darkness in their collective psyche. Soldiering was a hard industry, one of the few remaining; self-destructive alcohol consumption went hand in glove with arduous labour.

However, any moral authority behind his edict would soon be lost. With socially catastrophic consequences, his coterie of officers would drink like neds themselves. However, this would be no illicit, moonlit session, sipping imported Buckie, but Gray's official dining-out ceremony.

Larks and the 6 Platoon lads had reverted to being PWRR soldiers for the evening in order to have a drink, while the Argyll hierarchy patrolled, keeping a sidelong glance for any surreptitious swigging. The more ingenious Jocks had filtered lager into empty cans of Pringles. Larks had watched the dancers move as if they wanted to wriggle themselves free of their clothes and had put down his drink. The sight of grinding female pelvises had defeated him: 'Sorry, guys. I'm fuckin' off to bed.'

'You what?' Izzy had been taken aback by Larks's comment. He knew Larks had an eye for the ladies.

'I can't take this, mate – it's torture. I'm trying to forget about women.'

'Forget about women? What do you mean?' Izzy had raised his voice above the music.

'I don't think it's right. I'd rather have a comedian. Lads get a sniff of a bird and that's it. They get a cock on their heads for 24 hours, or whatever. It makes them depressed about their own birds. I don't want to think about birds. It's not very nice, wanking in the Portaloos. We're living off copies of *Nuts* magazine here. I can't watch it.'

Everything he had wanted to forget that evening had now returned to him as he stagged-on. Closing his eyes, he saw the dancing girls again, cavorting with abandon. He was fed up with hand-jobs.

The sun was very high now, and in the shimmering heat the marker stones surrounding the minefields dwindled into the distance. His time on stag had a while to run. Suddenly, his whole body was taut with shock, and he felt a pain as sharp as a hornet's bite. Instinctively, he brought his hand up and dabbed at his hairline. He stared at his bloodied forefinger. He had been shot, but not by an Iraqi. Condorites took shots at whoever was on guard duty with an air rifle. Larks's head throbbed. His hearing weakened by dizziness, he just about recognised Goacher's voice. 'Oh, shit. I fink I shot 'im!'

Goacher's accomplice ran away, and he was left to placate Larks.

'Fucking hell, you prick! You could have blinded me!' Larks repeated the motion of dabbing his forehead, but his wound was too painful to hold his fingers against it for long. Goacher stood there, red-faced, saying nothing. 'Ah, fuck. Fuck, that hurts. The fucking pellet is embedded in me! You twat.' Larks swayed gingerly as he climbed down from the position.

'Yeah, all right, Larks, calm down,' Goacher eventually retorted. He thought the episode was comical.

'Fuck you, Goat Boy. Don't tell me to calm down. That was out of order.'

'All right, mate, I said. I wasn't aiming at you, right?'

'Well, you fucking hit me.'

'I was just trying to scare you.'

'I'd fucking shoot you if you'd hit me in the eye. I swear to God, I would.'

'It was an accident.'

Every vein in Larks's forehead stood out. He made it to the bottom of the steps. 'Accident? How far away were you? Look,' Larks pointed up at the defensive position, 'get someone up there, will you? I can hardly continue on stag, can I?'

Larks staggered off in search of Chris, the medic. Goacher followed guiltily, as he realised the implications of his actions. For starters, he was in trouble with Neneh and Hendy.

'I've been hit on the head with a pellet,' Larks announced. Few in the TV room paid attention except Chris. The cut and swelling were obvious, but the pellet was not. Chris turned Larks around and pushed him towards the Ops Room. Their curiosity aroused, the television watchers followed in procession. One of the Jocks offered Larks his sympathies: 'Hey, Larks, ya wee girl. If ye hadnae been so slow, he wouldnae've been able tae hit ye!'

'Yeah? You Jocks can get fucked.'

Chris paid the wound closer attention: 'Well . . .'

'Can you get it out?' Larks asked, wincing as Chris prodded the area.

'It's pretty deep inside there,' he replied, as if he was impressed by the firepower of the target rifle.

'Just cut it out. It hurts. It's throbbing. Can you get it out?'

'Well, I am not too sure. Let me have a closer look.' Chris combed Larks' hair aside with his fingers. 'Get down on one knee, will you?' He was getting agitated. 'No, I can't see properly. You'll have to lie down.'

Hendy walked into the Ops Room. 'Where's Goacher?' Hendy feared Griffiths would go berserk upon learning of the shooting. Commanders understood soldiers had to let off steam – but shooting one another in the head? Goacher should have aimed further off.

Neneh was more sanguine. 'Thank fuck Paul Kelly isn't here. He would explode.'

'Aye,' said Hendy, 'but if he has tae go tae Al Amarah, he'll have tae explain how he got shot. It's no gonnae look good, is it?' Hendy looked Chris squarely in the eye. 'What's the deal here?'

'I can't see it in there. It's lodged between his skull and his scalp.' Frustration crossed Hendy's face. 'You're going to have to take him to Abu Naji,' Chris told him.

This was the opposite of what Hendy wanted to hear. Condor was crashing down before his eyes. He could see every Condorite being summoned back to a life of order and scrutiny. They could bid farewell to strutting around naked, firing home-made mortars and letting rip with Iraqi weaponry. Every idle moment at Abu Naji would be spent filling sandbags. 'Can't ye dae it here?' Hendy implored.

'The pellet is hard to get at. He should really go to the medical centre. I don't have any anaesthetic.'

'You've got nae anaesthetic?' he replied, disbelievingly. But nobody at Condor was qualified to administer anaesthetic.

'I've requested it, but it hasn't arrived. The wound could get infected as well.'

'Faer fuck's sake.'

Hendy found Goacher quivering nearby. Almost on cue, everyone present stared at the pair. 'Do ye understand what ye've done?'

'I'm sorry, sergeant,' Goacher said meekly. 'I really am. It was just an accident. He moved.'

'Larks?'

'Yes, sergeant.'

'Couldn't ye see him shooting at ye?'

'No, sergeant, I was observing my arcs like a good soldier, wasn't I?' Larks retorted with an enthusiasm that belied his condition.

Hendy returned to Goacher. 'Ye know you're gonna get squared away faer this, don't ye?'

'I'll take it on the chin.'

'Ya wee prick, ye couldae blinded him,' added Neneh, not that he was in favour of formal action against Goacher: 'All that writing, getting statements. Then it goes up the hierarchy to the company commander, and he sits oan it faer a while. Waste of time.'

'OK, I can see it properly now,' Chris told Larks. 'Well, you can go to Abu Naji and get it sorted there, or we can try and wean it out here. Or, you can leave it for a couple of days and see if it just drops out.' The third option was left hanging in the air. 'If we cut it out,' he resumed, 'there is going to be a lot of blood, because your scalp is quite thick.'

'What are you going to do?' Neneh glared at Larks. 'I'm no sayin' ye cannae go tae Abu Naji, but we're gonnae be in trouble if ye do.'

'Look,' said Larks, 'I know I'll have to say how I got a

pellet in my head if I go there, and I don't want anyone to get in trouble for it. It was not on purpose. So just cut it out, yeah?'

'Good lad, Larks,' said Hendy. 'I'll hold your legs doon while he's operating on ye.'

'Aye, hold him doon, Hendy,' added Neneh.

''Ere, do you want some whisky while I do this?' Chris held up a tin of the Iraqi variety.

Larks smiled. He recalled characters in his favourite films using alcohol as anaesthetic. 'Nah, I hate whisky, and that Iraqi stuff is gopping. I won't have anything. How do you want me to do it, then? I can take a bit of pain.'

'OK, I've got to be able to work on your head, so I need you to lie down and put your head in my lap. Lie down on that bench.'

Chris poked at Larks's forehead with a scalpel as his patient bit into a wooden spatula. Larks felt the pellet scratch against his skull.

'Fuck!' he thought, his teeth digging into the bit clamped between his jaws. To his audience's amusement, his eyes watered.

'Larks, ya wee girl. Get oan with it!'

'What ye cryin' for, Larks?'

'Toy soldier!'

Like a boxer liberating his gum shield, Larks removed the spatula. 'Yeah, it's all right for you lot. You're not having a fucking scalpel put through your head.' He turned to Hendy. 'Can you get that lot out of here?'

'OK,' said Hendy, 'everyone out of the Ops Room. Let him suffer in private.'

Larks replaced the spatula and the operation continued. Chris was hesitant. He knew his actions caused his patient intense pain.

'Oh, fuck, he's missing it! He's pushing the pellet further

back,' Larks inwardly ranted. 'This is shit. Christ, he's cutting my head open. Aarghh!'

The operation was successful, and Hendy squared Goacher away. Afterwards, Wellsy could tell that Goacher was in need of company. His 6 Platoon mates reckoned Hendy had punished him severely for what had only been an accident. It was not as though they did not take pot shots at people with the air rifle.

'Don't worry, mate,' Wellsy said to Goacher, whose misery was showing. 'Larks is thick-skulled!'

The next day Hendy ensured the matter was laid to rest. He too liked Goacher, and Condor was a brighter place for his presence. Larks was given painkillers, but for the next week his head was too painful to wear a helmet. He only left Condor on driving duties.

Larks reckoned that the shooting brought him and Goacher closer. They had not talked or listened much to each other before, and neither had they much in common. Larks had these lady-killer eyes, while Goacher's suggested he smoked crack. He did not, but the whites looked more red than white.

One of Larks's first regular patrols after the pellet incident was with Izzy, Wellsy, Private Chris Dodd and Lance Corporal Frank Millerick. In the late afternoon they drove along Route 6. Doddsy was an infanteer first, but he was also the 6 Platoon combat medic (not to be confused with Chris, who belonged to the Royal Army Medical Corps). Doddsy had been seconded to the Argylls from the PWRR. He had volunteered to attend the Regimental Medical Assistant Class 3 course the previous year in order to escape Northern Ireland. Even then, his arm had to be twisted. 'I can get you three weeks out of the Province,' his sergeant major had begun.

'Yes, Dodd. I can get you on an RMA 3 course at Aldershot. There's a spare place. Yours if you want it.'

'Er, what is it, sir?' Doddsy furtively enquired.

'It's a medical course, the bottom rung.'

'Ah, I'm not really interested in that, sir.'

The regimental sergeant major was clearly keen that Dodd attend: 'It's three weeks out of Ireland, three weeks . . .'

Doddsy paused. 'OK, then, sir. Happy with that. I'll take it.'

The heat of the day had tempered to a relative cool as they approached Checkpoint Danny Boy, a junction synonymous with terrorist attacks. There were no road markings on the cracked tarmac. A strip of crusty, brown scrub divided the lanes. They passed a convoy of United States military hardware – Humvees, construction wagons, trucks and diggers on flat-bed lorries – all travelling south. American convoys were not such a rare sight, but this one was so long Wellsy could not help but gaze at it. Was that smoke he saw, drifting skywards? He craned his neck again. 'There's something not right back there,' he said, righting himself. 'That convoy is stationary for one thing.'

'Yeah, mate,' replied Izzy, 'but they've probably just had a blowout.'

As they drove on, both men silently calculated whether it was worth the drama to turn back. Their eventual decision was not based solely upon altruistic aspirations: curiosity about the Yanks' equipment, the opportunity to liberate spare kit and the prospect of delaying their return to Condor were factored into the equation.

The sun went down with guillotine-like speed and without night-vision aids they could not see the convoy. Because the US soldiers had night vision, they had switched off the lights on their vehicles.

'Where the fuck are they?' Wellsy asked, peering ahead.

'Fuck knows.'

'This is shite.'

''Ave a look through your Combat Weapon Sight,' said Larks.

'OK, I'll have to take it off my weapon first. Can't exactly see much through the windscreen with it.'

Wellsy's only option was to remove the night-sight and lean out of the window. A plume of noxious odours climbed unseen into the blackness. They were less than 30 metres from the rear US vehicle when Wellsy identified an American soldier. The Yank clambered hastily behind his machine-gun post.

'He thinks we're enemy!'

'Fucking stop or I'll open up!' The American clasped his hands behind the weapon, which was mounted onto the rear wagon. Wellsy saw him swivel around in his direction and cock the enormous gun.

'Fuck, he's going to panic,' Wellsy said. 'He's going to open up.' Wellsy leapt from the cabin and sprinted forwards, his arms waving frantically: 'We're British, we're British, don't shoot!'

'Hey, man.' The American looked up from beneath his helmet, which had a night-vision aid attached to its front rim. From his lack of insignia, Wellsy reckoned he was a private soldier. The Land-Rover eventually stopped ten metres from the Humvee.

'I thought you were more Iraqis coming at us in a taxi. We were ambushed in that town over there.' Words barely had time to fall from his mouth. 'We took some heavy incoming – RPGs, IEDs. Everything is really fucked up.' He looked serious and scared as he sniffed the acrid smoke given off by the burning vehicles. His hands shook, and it was a relief when he moved from behind his heavy machine gun.

'Any wounded?' Wellsy tried to sound calmer.

'Yeah,' he replied, 'we've got casualties.' He drew breath, seemingly for the first time. 'And fatalities.'

Wellsy was taken aback. If this guy was a representation of the US forces on this convoy, then they were a ragged crew. 'Look, where's your boss? Go and get him.'

The officer was just as drained and hollow-eyed as he pointed towards Al Amarah. But what had they been doing driving through the city when they could have circumnavigated it, Wellsy wondered? Nor could they have given prior notification of their intention to pass through the British-controlled city – as was required. They would have been unlikely to have received permission. The American convoy would have compromised the PWRR 'recce' teams staking out insurgent strongholds inside the city.

'Have you got medics?' Wellsy asked.

'No.'

'OK, hold on a sec.' Wellsy returned to the Land-Rovers, and Doddsy and Larks were called forward to provide assistance.

Two men sat motionless in the front of the Humvee. Both had been shot in the head. Successive flights of bullets had quickly entered the cabin before they could take cover. Larks tried not to look at their faces: he did not want to see them when he slept. He felt a hand on his shoulder as he climbed down from the cabin.

'Can you help my friends?' the American asked plaintively. 'Isn't there anything you can do?'

'No, I'm sorry, mate,' Larks gulped. 'They're dead.'

'Oh, my God.'

'Look,' Larks replied as the American began to mourn, 'let's concentrate on the rest of your guys, yeah? Where are they?'

'They're in the other vehicles . . .' he stuttered.

'Well, let's go through them, yeah?' Larks said, trying to

sound reassuring. 'See what condition they're in. OK?' Larks and Doddsy darted to each wagon in turn.

'Right, he's OK.'

'Next guy, wounded. You need to move him.'

'Larks?'

'Doddsy.'

'I want to centralise the casualties. If we can treat them all in one place, yeah, it'll save us bouncing around from wagon to wagon. They can come to us.'

'Yup, roger that, Doddsy.'

For all their shiny night-vision equipment, the Americans complained that they could not see anything and asked to use flares. 'You must be joking, mate,' said Wellsy. 'You're in a shit state here. The last thing you want is to let everyone know you're here. Trust me. I know the area – you don't want to go overt yet. You'll have everyone coming out of their villages wanting to see what's going on. That's what it's like here. If they get wind of broken-down vehicles and wounded soldiers, you're in big trouble. Do you even know where you are?'

The soldier provided his map. Having assumed that the Americans had 'Gucci everything', Wellsy was surprised to see Al Amarah drawn as a tiny speck. Only cities in the American-controlled sectors were precisely drawn, while there was no indication of the whereabouts of British military bases. 'You're driving blind, really, aren't you?'

'I guessed we'd just head south until we hit Basra . . .'

'Well, you're not going to make it, are you? It's bare from the Maysan Province down. You should have had a decent int-brief before driving through Al Amarah, especially with the PWRR tearing it up as they are. We'd escort you back to our camp, Camp Condor, but it's a bit small. It's just an outstation. There's only a few of us there, like. Just a couple of platoons.'

'Take 'em to Abu Naji,' somebody else suggested.

'Yeah,' Wellsy agreed, still clutching the map.

'Abu Naji . . . What's that?' The American thumbed his safety catch. It was a nervous twitch that made everybody jump. 'Some village?'

'No, mate, that's our battlegroup headquarters. Must be 1,000 blokes there. You went past it not even knowing it was there.'

'Man, he has the map,' the Yank snapped. He pointed at his colleague.

'It's not on the map. If it was, I would have said something about it.'

'What's the state of your vehicles?' Wellsy asked, interrupting their dispute.

'Been hit pretty bad. I think they collapsed one of the ambushes in the city and set another one up quickly once we reached the outside. Then we extracted to here. It was about five or six kilometres back that way. One of the low loaders and one of the Humvees . . . they are definitely out of commission.' Wellsy sighed, envisioning a night spent stagging-on. 'We've already blown them up,' the American continued.

'What?'

'Sure. We've got firing devices. It's what we do. That will be the big fire you saw when you came down.'

'Fucking hell, mate. It's a different world in your army, isn't it? If that was us, I tell you, we'd be here until the morning guarding those vehicles.'

Wellsy could not believe he and his mates were going to escort the Americans to Abu Naji. His section drove soft-skinned Land-Rovers, and they drove armoured Humvees. The roles should have been reversed. Just then there was a noise in the darkness, mocking them because it revealed so little of itself.

'Fucking shoot at it, man!' screamed one American.

'Whoa, whoa, you can't do that,' Wellsy interjected. 'It could be anything or anyone. It's probably just a goat or something.'

'Well, put a flare up!' he suggested.

'I've told you, no flares. Put a cordon of blokes out, all-around defence.'

'What?'

'You know, all-around defence?' Wellsy made a circling motion with his forefinger. The soldier just stared back vacantly.

The Americans aboard the flat-bed truck seemed an alienated group of souls. They were hunched down beside the casualties but not working to make them more comfortable. They were stunned, unable to rationalise the course of events. Doddsy's boots clattered against the wheel arch. He was brusque by inclination: 'OK, my name's Private Dodd, and this is Private Larkin. Now, what's the score?'

'Man, we just got hit from everywhere.' One of the Americans shook his head. 'Rockets, AKs . . .'

That was not what Doddsy had asked. 'What about him?' Doddsy pointed at a soldier who writhed in agony. His shattered fibula and tibia stood erect like stakes in a white picket fence.

'Oh, he's fucked.'

The injured American soldier was drifting into uncharted territories of pain, his mind turning inside and out. As all Condorites were equipped with phials of morphine, it seemed incredible the Americans had not been issued with the drug – perhaps they were likely to misuse it. Larks undid a pocket to remove his needle as Doddsy slapped on his plastic gloves. He crouched low beside the victim: 'What's your name?'

The American did not respond at first. But a rare moment

of clarity some seconds later produced an answer. His voice was weak, and his words scarcely met the air. Eventually, he revealed his rank. Doddsy's RMA 3 course had included the principles of triage; in particular the precedence of the silent casualty over the vocal casualty. Casualties were usually rendered mute because shock or bodily numbness masked grave injury. Doddsy pulled Larks towards him: 'Right, mate, I've got to look at the other guy now. So you stay with the sergeant. Just talk to him, and keep talking to him. Ask him whether his bird has got big tits or what his mum does for a living, yeah?'

'OK.'

'I don't care what you talk about, just so long as you talk to him. I've got to look at the other guy.' Doddsy's sense of urgency was palpable. Privately, he doubted the wounded officer would live to see the Blackhawk helicopter summoned from northern Iraq to extract him and the deceased.

Larks saw Airborne insignia on the sergeant's uniform: 'You've got wings, mate.' The American groaned in recognition. 'Look, mate. I'm Airborne, too. British Airborne. I've done P Company.'

The quiet man had been shot in the neck. Doddsy was relieved to see a cannula line in his arm. But rather than applying a spinal collar, his colleagues had taped his head to the stretcher. Adhesive strips were wrapped around his forehead. His head required greater support so Doddsy placed pads on either side of his face, ensuring optimum pressure on his skull without hampering his breathing. The victim reported that he was pain-free. Doddsy silently mouthed one word: 'paralysis'. He tore off the field dressing to assess the wound – the US dressing was thinner than the British-issue pad and had not compressed the wound sufficiently. The lump that protruded from his spine was firm to touch. Doddsy reckoned it was either a round or a piece of secondary fragmentation lodged in his vertebrae. That the American was unaware of Doddsy's prods confirmed his initial diagnosis. He threw away the US field dressings and applied two British ones, which he secured with tape.

'Doddsy?' The radio crackled into life. It was Izzy.

'Yup.'

'How are the casualties doing?'

'They need to be stabilised. They are in a very bad way.'

'OK. Well, just to let you know: the armour is on its way down from Abu Naji, then the Blackhawk will land. The pilot was chuntering about the pylons around here, even though the Chinooks just buzz around them. He wanted a grid reference as well.'

'I hope they're quick, mate. One of the casualties has got his eyes rolling, and he keeps trying to give up the fight. He's not flatlining it yet, but he ain't far off.'

'Roger that.'

An internal monologue played inside Doddsy's head: 'OK, what next? Do a further survey of his body. Check his airways, his breathing. Is he alert? Yes. Voice? Yes, I can hear it. Pain? No, he says he can't feel any. He's been shot in the neck. If he can't feel any pain, there is something seriously wrong. He hasn't got any breakages, bleeding or bruising, so do a pain test next. OK, better not tell him why, because then he'll know he's paralysed. Poor bloke.'

Doddsy gripped him all the way down his body and down both legs. 'Fucking hell, I'm squeezing him to fuck, and I'm not getting any response!' He pressed his fingers into the casualty's flesh as firmly as he could. Again, it did not register. 'You're fucked, mate. But I am not going to tell you that.'

'OK, mate,' Doddsy spoke aloud at last. He beckoned one

of the uninjured soldiers towards him. 'Keep his fluid levels topped up, yeah? He can't afford to run dry. As long as you do that, he should be all right. I've made him a bit more comfortable and secured his head. I've got to crack on with the other guy now, yeah?'

'Thanks, man.'

'Not a drama, mate.'

'You know,' said the uninjured American, smiling, 'you guys are amazing, man. You're not Special Forces, are you?'

Doddsy and Larks exchanged glances before simultaneously bursting into laughter. It was tempting to pass themselves off as SAS troopers. They certainly could have got away with it. 'Nah, mate. We're just regular British infantry,' said Larks, 'and he's just a basic medic, RMA 3.'

Doddsy shuffled away from the casualties to broadcast another sit-rep. He pushed the radio microphone closer to his mouth and formed a shield with his cupped hand: 'Izzy, mate. We need to get a shift on – these blokes are in serious rag.'

'OK, Doddsy. They're crashing out the QRF from Abu Naji, so we'll have some armour on the way up there. I don't know what's happening about the Blackhawk. Apparently, Abu Naji is under mortar attack as well. We might end up driving them up there – who knows? Just crack on, yeah?'

'Will do, mate.'

Larks was no medic, but he had at least administered the morphine correctly. 'I need a pen, mate,' he said to one of the Yanks.

'Sorry, man?'

'A pen, an indelible marker.'

'What's that for?'

'To write the date, time and group on his head. That's what you do when you've given 'em morphine.'

'OK, man, I'll ask Eight Ball.'

'Eight Ball?' Larks thought he was living in a Vietnam War film. 'Hey, Doddsy? You should hear this, mate. One of their blokes, this black geezer, they call 'im Eight Ball. Can you believe it? Fucking Eight Ball!'

They listened as the Americans shouted on their colleague: 'Hey, where's Eight Ball?'

'Tell Eight Ball the British want him.'

'Tell Eight Ball to bring his pen.'

'Yeah, man. Hey, Eight Ball!'

'Yeah?'

'The Brits need your marker pen.'

'There you go, buddy,' the Yank said to Larks, who wrote a capital 'M' on the patient's forehead. He was still laughing. He wondered how many of the Americans knew each other's complete names.

The sergeant who had suffered massive blood loss screamed. Doddsy cursed when he saw how badly the soldier's colleagues had attended to his wounds. 'You should have immobilised the injuries, you pricks,' he said inwardly. 'You can't just wrap tape around his legs and stick him to the stretcher!'

'OK, Larks?'

'Yes, mate.'

'Rip that shit off now,' he pointed to the dressings. 'Not much use just sitting on top of his wounds, are they?'

It was impossible for his eyes not to be drawn to the splintered bones: a grotesque but compelling sight. The soldier was lying on the stretcher in a half-inch-deep pool of blood, which seeped through the fabric and dripped onto the floor. Strangely, Doddsy did not feel any emotion. He was to discover how different it felt to treat your mates.

He again spoke to Izzy via PRR: 'What's the latest, mate? We have not got much time. This guy has got bilateral breaks of tib and fib. It's worse than a gunshot wound in terms of the amount of blood he's lost. There's not much more I can do for him *in situ*. We've got to get him to hospital or he's a goner.'

'Well, the latest on the extraction is the casualties are not going to be put on the Blackhawk now. The mortar threat is too high. They've got a lot of incoming at Abu Naji. We'll head up there with the casevacs [casualty evacuees]. They're sending an ambulance down from Abu Naji to RV [rendezvous] with us en route. The guys will be transferred onto it.'

Wellsy heard the conversation on the net and leant inside one of the Humvee cabins. 'Prepare to move,' he told the driver.

'No, I cannot do that.'

'What do you mean you can't do that?'

'All I do is drive. I do not tell anyone to move.'

'What? For fuck's sake! Just tell your boss what's happening. You've got a fucking mouth, haven't you?'

The severely wounded made it to the field hospital. Doddsy had saved their lives, but he would never see them again. His arms were bloodied up to the elbows, and adrenalin buzzed inside him. Goacher helped him pull off his plastic gloves. They burnt them, but as they watched the flames neither could find words to describe their feelings. It was a private ceremony, just the two of them.

Doddsy learned that one of the fatalities had just completed his one-year tour of duty and had begun his journey home. Had his commanders requested British assistance ahead of their passage through Maysan, his life would have been saved. This was not a tragedy, as such, just another day in Iraq.

The 80 US service personnel mingled with the Brits at Abu Naji as they awaited alternative transportation. They were a mixture of professional soldiers and reservists. Their number included a Vietnam War vet, whom Wellsy and Larks approached with awe. They hoped he would share Zen-like pearls of wisdom. 'Was it like the films?'

'I bet you've got some tales?' To their chagrin, he would only discuss R 'n' R in Thailand. Then the alarm went off to signal Abu Naji was under mortar attack.

Wellsy and Larks planned a raid on the US vehicles. In the middle of the night they stalked the silent convoy. They used their Combat Weapon Sights to see where they were going. But they had not counted on the Americans stagging-on through the small hours to prevent a stealthy operation by the under-equipped British. The next morning they scrounged 'Meals Ready to Eat' parcels. They grew tired of being told they were too young to be the soldiers who rescued the Americans. Things began to look up when a female US sergeant took a shine to Doddsy. He agreed to swap shirts even though he 'didn't think she was fit or anything'. He explained they had just 'cracked on' last night, as British soldiers did.

The United States Department of Defense listed the two fatalities as Staff Sergeant Oscar Vargas-Medina, 32, of Chicago, Illinois, and Specialist Ramon Ojeda, 22, of Romana, California. It also emerged that two US soldiers were left behind in Al Amarah at the time of the first ambush. They stole a taxi and drove out of the city. Their colleagues did not report their disappearance to the British.

Doddsy and Larks received Commander's Commendations. Doddsy's read:

Date: 2 May 2004. Call sign: Yankee 42. Location: Checkpoint Danny Boy.

The American medical support had been incapacitated by the attack, so the platoon commander decided to deploy his medics. Private Dodd was calm and professional, and without doubt prevented further deterioration of the casualties. The action was not offensive in nature, but at each stage he proved that he was the man for the job. He is most worthy of official recognition. Even more remarkable was the balanced and professional manner with which this man behaved, far in excess of what could be expected of one so young and relatively inexperienced.

11

Heavy Metal

Regulars at the Wetherspoon's pub in Canterbury divided into students, squaddies and sheepish-looking locals who wished neither of the other two communities had grown so populous.

Pale-skinned students wore beards and University of Kent Caving Club T-shirts, recording competitions against Aberystwyth, Reading and Keele. They drank bitter and looked vaguely ill. Squaddies huddled around the quiz machines. They wore tattoos and hair gel with their off-barracks uniforms of polished shoes and pressed jeans. They drank lager.

A father and son entered, or at least that was their assumed relationship, given their age difference. However, Paul Kelly and Kev Challis's bond was borne out of something rarer than biology. The private was staying at his platoon sergeant's house, where Kev chuckled watching Kelly bend down to remove imaginary crumbs from the lounge carpet; it seemed Kelly was as wary of Donna as Kev was of his host. They joined the throng queuing for drinks at the bar. Kev had a metal scaffold around his shoulder, Kelly bandages binding his wrist.

Kev had heard the rumours about Kelly's citation, and judging by his mood reckoned MC also stood for 'Miserable Cunt'. Kelly remained disappointed that his return to Iraq was being blocked. Kev switched off whenever Kelly brought the conversation back to Qalat Salih.

A frown spread across Kelly's dark features. He was stung by the indifference shown by those around them towards him and Kev. 'What is it, Paul?' Kev asked when they had finally been served and had taken seats in a corner.

Kelly fingered the rim of his glass of cider. 'You know, Kev, we should be able to come in here, and the bar should clear. Whoever they are serving, they should just stop, put their glasses down and come over to us and say, "Gents, for what you've done, you should have these on the house."'

Kev had not expected bugles, bells and welcoming cheers. He laughed. 'Paul, it's not like that. It's not going to be like that, either. People just don't care.'

'Well, they should.'

'Don't worry about it. I don't.'

'If they only knew what we've been through. They have not got a clue, anyone in here, what it's like to be shot.'

'Forget about it,' said Kev, downing his lager. 'Anyway, I'm hungry. Let's go to McDonald's.'

'McDonald's? I don't eat that shit – it's bad for you.'

'Come on. It tastes good, though.'

Angry Dad dutifully followed his son outside. There were no flags fluttering at McDonald's, either, or free hamburgers for those recently returned from the front.

The Mahdi Army uprising was met with three main thrusts into Al Amarah by the PWRR: operations Pimlico, Knightsbridge and Waterloo. The intensity of such clashes set back the beleaguered reconstruction programme. Fewer patrols were mounted from Condor, and ICDC training stalled.

It was said of the PWRR that, unlike their predecessors in Maysan, the 1st Battalion, the Light Infantry, they distrusted local people. The refusal to incorporate the ICDC into the security framework left the Argylls frustrated – what had happened to security-sector reform being the 'main effort' of the British brigade in Iraq? What was the point of the jundies receiving military training when they were not given proper tasks? For the benefit of the future security of the province, the ICDC had to be involved.

The role of a ground-holding infantry battalion such as the PWRR was to keep a lid on the uprising, but the view of the Argylls' commanders was that they went too far. The Condorites had been training the ICDC since January, but to what end?

James Dormer wrote to battalion headquarters pleading for the ICDC to be given an opportunity to put their training into practice:

> The soldiers are often keen and are quick to learn when given simple demonstrations. They are capable at present of performing low-level patrolling and VCPs. Their equipment and living conditions are primitive but acceptable. Where the ICDC is lacking at present is in direction throughout the organisation. The need for a clear mission for the ICDC is at the heart of this. The ICDC can develop the capacity to impose security on Maysan but needs strong leadership and clearly defined goals in order to do so.

The PWRR went on the offensive, targeting insurgents in the Kadem Al Muallimin suburb. Snatch teams carried photographs of suspects, but on dark nights bleary-eyed youths looked all too similar. Scores were lifted, the intention being to isolate 'tier-one personalities' at Abu Naji. British vehicles were ambushed during the extraction phase and Iraqi policemen taken hostage by the Mahdi Army. Matt Maer was told that the officers would be shot unless he agreed to their exchange for the suspects. With so many insurgents masquerading as policemen, it was impossible to verify whether the hostages were taken unwillingly or as participants in a ruse – nothing was what it seemed in Maysan Province.

The Mahdi Army also blockaded Al Amarah. With ammunition running low at the Civil Military Cooperation house, Maer opted to retake the city by force. This was the operation (Knightsbridge) on which Private Beharry won his Victoria Cross. The plan for Waterloo was to leave a heavily armed British force on one of the road junctions as bait. The chosen battleground offered clear arcs of fire for the Challenger II tanks and Warriors. There would also be US air support in the form of an AC130 Spectre gunship, an aircraft that bristled with awesome weaponry. This was no way to win a battle for hearts and minds.

Larks declared that his role to recce suspected insurgent positions in Al Amarah was the 'Gucciest' task of his tour. 'Cammed up' and weighed down with additional ammunition for two rifles and a heavy machine gun, he and Wellsy inserted at dusk. As they lay on a rooftop, Larks was distracted by a beam of light that reminded him of the Batman motif that shone over Gotham City. He followed the beam to its source: Wellsy's new watch. The lance corporal had bought a Traser, one of the glow-in-the-dark timepieces designed for divers and pilots. With hands and numbers filled with tritium gas, it was more powerful than other illuminated watches. 'Fucking hell, Wellsy! What the fuck is going on with your watch?'

Wellsy acknowledged Larks's accusation. Their mission was supposed to be strictly covert: 'Yeah, sorry about that, mate.'

'It's a bit of a giveaway, don't you think?'

'Fair one. It's a knock-off, actually, mate.'

'You what?'

'It ain't the real thing. Couldn't afford that. This one falls apart every time I put my bergen on and the straps brush against it.'

The pair had completed basic training together, and one of their instructors was now in the SAS. The corporal would be chuffed that his protégés had been given such an important task.

At this point a Danish armoured vehicle appeared. With the area crawling with insurgents, Wellsy feared that if they saw him and Larks they would open fire before asking questions. 'Go on, Larks!' he said. 'Get down there and tell them we're here. We don't want to get bumped. Take your machine gun with you.'

Getting 'bumped' or compromised was another no-no for an SAS patrol behind enemy lines. Larks and Wellsy did not want to disappoint their instructor. The drop was considerable, and Larks cracked open a glow stick to illuminate his landing area. Knowing the insurgents did not have glow sticks, he did not mind if the Danes saw it. He jumped off the ledge, and his boots thudded against the hard ground. He felt his ankle twist violently beneath him. Already within sight of them, he tried to disguise his pain. The ice-cool Danes were leaning casually against their Mercedes.

'British Forces, British Forces! Don't worry!' he shouted. Wellsy chuckled as he heard Larks cry. He sounded like a character from *Dad's Army*. 'Hello, er,' Larks stuttered as his ankle swelled. 'OK, me and,' he pointed at the roof, 'one other . . . are up there. We, er, British, yes? You Danes?'

An officer smiled flatly. He leant against the vehicle's chassis as if it was a parlour room mantelpiece: 'I beg your pardon for interfering with your operation. We will withdraw.'

Larks listened as the Dane continued in clear, precise English; it was like listening to James Dormer. He cursed himself for his stupidity: 'You spoke to them like a typical

Brit abroad, you twat.' Humbled by his own inarticulacy and awkward gait, he was anxious to bid the Danes a polite farewell: 'Sorry about that. You should be aware of the ops going on in the city. The threat state is high. I've got to get back up there . . .'

'The best of luck to you in what you are endeavouring to achieve.' The officer sounded as unflustered as before.

Larks put all his weight on his good leg and twisted to face the wall. He heard no human movement behind him so assumed the Danes were watching him. Larks considered himself a young man of physical prowess, but tonight he felt like the fat kid who was always picked last for playground football at school. His legs flexed, and he launched himself up the wall, leaping off his good leg. But his heels landed back in the sand. Even with fingers outstretched, he could not reach the ledge. He laughed and settled for throwing his weapon and webbing above him before making his ascent. So much for belonging to the best army in the world – he could not even climb up a wall. As he brushed himself down, he heard the Danes accelerate smoothly into the night.

'All right then, Larks?' asked Wellsy. 'How did that go?'

'Don't ask, mate.'

They were still on watch when US jets soared overhead. There was a spectacular fireworks display as suspected insurgent positions were destroyed. Dismembered bodies were discovered at daybreak; human beings ripped in two by cannon fire. From thousands of feet it had been impossible to tell bystanders from insurgents. This gave rise to insinuations of 'killing for killing's sake' and disquiet over British support for such a strategy. The PWRR had reverted to war fighting – a tactical error, it was later suggested, and a contributing factor to the malaise in southern Iraq several years later.

One officer commented, 'Almost overnight, with the

change of battlegroup from the 1st Battalion, the Light Infantry, to the 1st Battalion, the Princess of Wales's Royal Regiment, came trouble. This was expected, but it could have been handled differently, rather than with heavy metal. It was about understanding the culture, the people and the customs, not trying to conquer.

'It was far from a benign environment, but a different approach towards the insurgents and their leaders could have produced different results. The Light Infantry got out, got to know tribal leaders and established good relations with them, patrolled the border, mentored the police and had an excellent feel for the area. The PWRR did not, and immediately there was a detrimental impact.'

Another added, 'This is to take nothing away from Private Beharry, who deserved his Victoria Cross. But there is the issue of how we established the conditions in which a VC could be won. If you are resorting to battles of this size, it means you have failed on the ground to win the hearts and minds. There was a flurry of medals for this battlegroup, and one can't help thinking the army took the "Dunkirk option", i.e. when something goes wrong, throw a lot of gallantry awards at it as chaff. Had we forgotten what we were here for?

'We were not in Iraq to kill people. We were cutting down with heavy cannon fire the very people we claimed to have liberated. The scale of these contacts was enormous; scores of locals were being killed. Was it any wonder they objected to our presence and hence why we got bogged down in Iraq?'

Two days later the insurgents used their rudimentary weapons to strike back. A child threw a petrol bomb inside a Warrior armoured vehicle, setting Sergeant Adam Llewellyn's upper body and arms ablaze. His terrified colleagues poured water over him but watched in horror as it accelerated the burning process – the water was piping hot from being stored inside the vehicle. His best mate described Llewellyn's hands as 'raw flesh'.

Jonny Gray's dining-out took place on his last night in office. There could have been no more fitting venue than Saddam Hussein's palace in Basra. Gray was leaving to become the assistant director of the Future Army Structures Implementation Team.

Al Roan would have given his world to decline the dinner invitation, but it brooked no refusal. So he shared a soft-skinned Land-Rover to Basra with Adam Griffiths and a party of nurses who were on the first leg of their journey home. Like Gray, their tours were over. With British vehicles now in contacts on a daily basis, Griffiths' preference had been to make the journey by helicopter – he had intended to return with supplies for B Company – but none were available, so he had to drive.

En route from Abu Naji to Condor, Griffiths' Land-Rover triggered an Improvised Explosive Device. Mercifully, the device did not detonate as its makers intended, merely showering the wagon with mud and secondary fragmentation. The delay meant Griffiths and Roan were late.

At 1930 they were still stuck in thick traffic and inhaling toxic vapours from the sewer system – it was with heavy irony that Basra was dubbed the Venice of southern Iraq. The Mahdi Army was active there, and it was imperative that they avoided out-of-bounds boxes, regardless of the irony of straying into one that particular evening. Taking such precautions delayed them further.

Justin Barry eyed them up and down as they stood in the vast, dilapidated marble-and-tile lobby. 'You're late,' he said, his voice echoing around the hall. The new arrivals were exhausted and sweat-soaked. 'Hurry up and get changed as well.'

The party had begun some time before their arrival, and constant, raucous laughter was audible from the bar area. Later, when everyone present was drunk, the party-goers would ignore warnings to leave the building as mortars fell around them. They told the sober REMF who requested they don helmets and body armour to 'fuck off'. They could hear the blasts as they continued drinking. Gray described it as 'like a scene from *Carry On Up the Khyber*'.

Roan and Griffiths entered, the last of the invited guests, having travelled furthest to get there. Faces unseen for months were noticeably redder for sun and booze. They were all there, the Argylls' officer clique, washing away the dust of the war with red wine, having forbidden their junior soldiers from partaking in alcohol. Every soldier, regardless of rank, should have been entitled to escape this misconceived adventure by occasionally getting drunk.

The dining room was lined with old wood panelling and bathed in artificial light. Tables were laid and decorated with menu cards. Bagpipes were played. Gray took his place at the top table and sat with his back to an alcove.

Everyone else was dressed in desert combats, but Gray wore a thick grey shirt – others knew it as his 'Mad Mitch shirt'. While some judged Gray's choice a faux pas – they suggested he was inviting comparisons between himself and Mitchell – their sniggering was a little harsh. They might not have felt comfortable in grey shirts, but their commanding officer was entitled to wear what he liked to his dining-out. Commanding the Argyll and Sutherland Highlanders came with a responsibility to maintain the traditions of previous decades and centuries, however arcane they might seem. He was the custodian of a remarkable history. One of Gray's instructions to his regimental sergeant major before the battalion had deployed was that they should 'bring the silver'. As he later explained, 'This was what proper regiments do.'

The wearing of grey shirts was an honour bestowed on the 93rd Sutherland Highlanders by Queen Victoria after their campaign in India from 1857 to 1880. It would have constituted a dereliction of duty on Gray's part had he not venerated his predecessors' exploits. After all, this was the Argylls' first overseas tour since 1967.

As a successor to 'Mad Mitch' and Sir Colin Cameron of Balaklava and Indian Mutiny fame, the temptation to see action had proved too great for Gray in Al Amarah a fortnight before. For better or worse, getting a taste of it was what commanding officers of the Argyll and Sutherland Highlanders had always done, as demonstrated by Sir Colin's address to his men before the battle of Shah Najaf in 1857: 'I had no intention of employing you again today, but the Shah Najaf must be taken this evening. The artillery cannot drive the enemy out, so you must with the bayonet, and I will lead you myself.'

The wine filled most guests with a rosy sense of well-being, but not Roan. He realised why Gray and those at battalion headquarters misread the situation at Condor. James Dormer, Neneh, the Jocks and he lived in squalor, while the commanding officer and his acolytes were comfortably billeted. He shook his head in frustration.

Dinner was eaten, and there was much pipe smoking afterwards. Gray's presentation and speech followed. His eyes glinted keenly at the sight of the silver salver, pre-inscribed with his name and a letter 'X'.

'X' marked the spot where Gray hoped, quite reasonably, an honour might be added. He was to be disappointed when only a Queen's Commendation for Valuable Service came his way, and that was for his previous service in

Northern Ireland. He claimed later that it was a 'minor disappointment', but as a lieutenant colonel leading a battalion engaged in a project crucial to the British exit strategy it must have been saddening to receive no recognition. He was not alone: Brigadier David Rutherford-Jones and Brigadier Nick Carter, his fellow architects of the ICDC embedding project, gained no official acknowledgement. Gray thought those seeking to assist the locals towards securing their own provinces lost out to those who oversaw the killing of the same people.

'Yet again, my MBE eludes me,' he sighed. His tone failed to elicit any sympathy. 'I am,' he continued, 'the first commanding officer to take the battalion on operations outside Northern Ireland since Mad Mitch.' Again, he was on dangerous ground; to draw a parallel between himself and the hero of Aden was risky.

The party returned to the bar. Gray sidled up to a few captains and subalterns. 'So, Ollie, haven't you been in any enemy contacts so far on the tour?' Gray enquired of Captain Dobson. It sounded like a goad.

Dobson, who was by no means predisposed towards insubordinate outbursts, responded, 'Well, sir, perhaps that is because I have not driven into any out-of-bounds boxes.' A wave of unease crashed over those in earshot. Most young officers blanched with trepidation when mocked by commanders. Dobson's outburst was a glorious exception. Gray stared at the captain, 15 years or more his junior. Until that evening, his position had protected him from such verbal assaults. The officers had deferred to Gray; he was their commander and exercised control over their careers.

'Right, get me Steve McQuitty,' Gray said. A junior officer scuttled away in search of him.

A likeable fellow who seldom upset anyone, McQuitty

had been working in the battlegroup Ops Room on the day of the Al Amarah debacle. He knew he was in trouble the moment he heard Gray wanted to speak to him.

'What have you been saying about me?' The colonel's tone was hot with injured dignity.

'What do you mean, sir? I don't understand.' McQuitty sounded timid by comparison.

Gray leant forward: 'Dobson said I had driven into an out-of-bounds box. That must have come from you.'

'Well, sir, I don't know why, but you did drive into an out-of-bounds box. I did not make that up.' McQuitty spoke with conviction. In the twilight of his reign, Gray's junior officers were in revolt.

Gray cut McQuitty off. There had to be other conspirators besides him and Dobson. He spat his nemesis's name from his lips: 'Roan! Get me Roan!' Gray's tone could hardly have been more dramatic, and anger settled on his face. Those who had not previously taken much notice attempted to secure a vantage point. This was the only show in town, and there was no sanction against eavesdropping. Gray could not complain if people listened in – he was only their commanding officer for a few more hours. Officers shouldered each other aside to clear a path for Roan.

As the commanding officer glared at him, Roan was reminded of their confrontation at Condor. 'Right! What the fuck have you been saying about me, Roan? Your report on what happened in Al Amarah was crap!'

Al's recollections of the day were clear. 'Sir, it was my perspective on events, as requested by battalion headquarters.'

'It was not what happened,' Gray assailed him. The watching faces darted from Gray to Roan and back again. 'And you left me on the ground during a contact!'

'If there was anything left out, sir, you should have added to it.'

'Roan, this is all your fault!'

'No, sir, it is not. I did not drive into an out-of-bounds box.'

In his boozy state, Gray let loose a tempest of frustration: 'Roan, you are a cunt! I am sick to death of you and your ways! You are not a proper Argylls officer. You and I are finished. You hear me?'

Major Scott, Gray's second-in-command, took the view that the conversation should be terminated, his tone demonstrating that he was intent on restoring order: 'Sir, if I may . . .'

But Gray remained locked in resentment: 'Scott, fuck off!'

There was a hurried air about Scott. He had to act fast to avert social meltdown: 'I don't think we should be having this conversation, sir. You've been drinking.'

'I said fuck off, Scott. Roan, you can fuck off as well.'

Eventually, his voice tailed off. Scott gestured towards Roan, who moved towards the exit. The entertainment was over and random conversations restarted, but the audience awaited Gray's absence before regurgitating what they had witnessed. It had been quite a spectacle.

Outside in a muggy, moonlit night, Roan laughed to make light of the implausible drama. Scott caught up with him, a smile spreading across his face. 'Don't worry about it,' he said reassuringly, 'it's his last night.'

Roan would not grieve his passing. 'The king is dead, long live the king.'

Gray was furious, as he made clear to everyone within earshot. 'I am neither an idiot nor irresponsible! A number of things took place in quick succession. I am in no doubt our arrival saved the lives of the PWRR patrol. And Al Roan left me on the ground during that contact.'

The drinking continued in defiance of the mortars that rained down upon this British corner of Basra. It was what those belonging to a proper regiment did: smoked cigars, rowed, drank whisky and upheld the best social traditions of their officer brethren of decades and centuries past.

12

'Bad Faer Buckie'

Despite the mortaring of Saddam's palace, it was the playing of bagpipes into the wee hours that those not invited to Gray's dinner complained about the following morning. With formidable hangovers, Griffiths and Roan left Basra for Maysan.

Lieutenant Colonel Simon West, the Argylls' new commanding officer, had transferred from the Highlanders, a separate battalion within the soon-to-be-defunct Scottish division. As West's popularity preceded him, the Argylls were sanguine about the lack of a home-grown appointment. But there had been a disagreement behind the scenes as to when Gray would pass the baton. Gray had batted off Lieutenant Colonel West's attempt to assume control mid-tour, only for his appointment to the Future Army Structures Implementation Team in Whitehall to hasten his departure.

Gray was secretly planning his personal exit strategy from the army altogether. His new job was on a short-term contract, and he looked towards a future in the private security sector. As he later conceded, 'To everyone else, I appeared fully committed to the army and encouraged them to be also. Unfortunately, deception had to form part of my strategy.'

West, who looked almost obscenely wholesome beside his war-weary colleagues, faced two immediate challenges:

to make an accurate assessment of the varying capabilities of the ICDC; and to make the case for who or what should follow the Argylls. The disheartening prospect was that no infantry battalion was going to replace them. However mixed the results thus far, Gray had argued in favour of continued embedding, as it represented the most effective training method. The potential of this project looked set to be lost.

On his first visit to Condor, the youthful new commanding officer bounded into the Ops Room to greet his two subalterns, Passmore and Dormer. He delivered the customary 'keep up the good work and don't let the standards drop' speech before pulling a pot of mustard from inside his chest webbing. He placed the pot on the table in front of him and said something in schoolboy Latin. His facial expression suggested that he expected an answer, but the two Jameses could only stare at him blankly.

'Who wants it, then?' asked West, resorting to English.

'Er, thanks, sir,' replied James Dormer awkwardly.

West smiled again before leaving the office as briskly as he had entered.

'Mustard?' said James Passmore. 'How about some more fucking ammunition?'

Kelly listened to telephones ringing unanswered and chairs scraping across the floor of the medical centre. Tension induced by this background noise accelerated the speed with which he drummed his fingers on the reception desk. The staff there now knew him well; both parties had dispensed with 'nice to see you' conversational openers. He waited for a nurse to return – with bad news, he assumed. Seven weeks after his wounding, his file gathered dust in the in-tray of a senior officer from the Royal Army Medical Corps.

'Sergeant Kelly,' the nurse's return interrupted his

mental meanderings, 'whilst we still think you should be downgraded, the colonel from the RAMC says that if you can pass a few tests with the physiotherapist here, you can go back.'

The process of returning to Iraq had until this moment seemed akin to running up a descending escalator; everything was geared towards movement in the opposite direction. They had said no for so long, so why the U-turn? Kelly was not fit for service, but Griffiths' hustling on his behalf had paid off.

The door was ajar, and the physiotherapist's room was brighter and more airy than the corridor. They introduced themselves and shared an unflinching man-to-man handshake. Kelly felt reassured by the familiarity of the physiotherapist's Parachute Regiment T-shirt. Nothing about his demeanour constituted a threat. He seemed to be on Kelly's side.

'You don't know a colour sergeant in 2 Para called Glen, do you?' Kelly asked.

'Yeah, maybe. Why?'

Kelly sought to build on this bridge. 'Well, I was in a contact with him in Iraq. It was how I ended up back here. I didn't think I was going back.'

'Fuck it, mate, you are now!' The physiotherapist seemed to share Kelly's pleasure about this. Their conspiratorial laughter filled the room. 'Just get on that running machine for ten minutes. As long as you're not out of breath by the end of it, you're fine.'

They discussed Iraq and spoke with the same gruff informality of those with Airborne Forces experience. Eventually, physical stress tightened Kelly's voice, but he passed the test.

'Now,' the physiotherapist said, sounding a little more serious, 'I want you to get down on the floor, and when I say "go" you are to get back up again as soon as possible. OK?'

'Yup, not a drama.' This exercise would expose Kelly's inability to put weight on his bandaged left hand. Its deep wounds were reluctant to heal, so it *was* a drama. The patient was nervous.

'OK, Sergeant Kelly, when you're ready . . . Go!'

'I always get down like this,' he said self-consciously. He would not be able to return fire very quickly if he lowered himself onto his right side during a contact. But the physiotherapist was not even looking at him.

'Right, that's it,' he said, finally turning around. 'I'll recommend your return to Iraq.'

'Thanks.' Kelly was almost embarrassed. It seemed as though the test had been fixed.

He questioned himself as he walked home: 'Am I still up for it? Will I let people down? What will Donna think? How will the men react to my return?'

Kelly was correct in thinking that news of his return would divide opinion. 'I was pleased,' said one PWRR private, remembering the moment when he was told, 'even though I knew there would be changes. It was like when you were a kid and your dad comes back. It means you ain't "Barry Big Balls" any more.'

Neneh countered this view: 'Condor was running fine without Paul. He mustae been trying tae prove something tae himself, like. So I thought it was a mistake. MC? What did that stand for? Minor Casualty?'

'Haven't you given enough to the army?' Donna asked.

He acknowledged the truth in her statement: 'You're right, as usual. But this is not about the army.'

'Good, because what has the army ever done for you?'

He stayed on the rim of the conversation. 'Not much,' he conceded.

'Nothing.'

'But it's not about the army,' he said. 'I'm going back because of the blokes. They've kept me going. They need me.'

Kelly had convinced himself that soldiers' lives depended upon his return. He had also been angered by reports of Loz making the junior soldiers do press-ups. Loz was a mate of most of those he disciplined, but that did not stop Kelly complaining: 'You don't fuck the blokes around when at any time they could be attacked. At any time on patrol, one of them might not come back. We've already lost Challis and Beeney. And besides, only I am allowed to fuck the blokes around.' The truth was that Kelly's was a very brave and personal crusade.

'And what have they done? Tell me what they've done for you?' Donna persisted.

She knew her husband did more for 'the blokes' than they did for him. She had suffered for it when her husband had left her at a Sergeants' Mess function to visit Keegs in hospital after the latter had been on a boozing binge. Donna did not speak to him for three days.

His deep-set eyes averted her stern gaze. Donna was resentful towards the army for taking her husband away, yet 'the army' had done its best to persuade him to stay. She left the room knowing she was not going to change his mind.

Deprived of his platoon sergeant for company, Kev Challis spent afternoons staring into the bottom of a pint glass. He used lager to block out the pain and the flashbacks. Diagnosed with post-traumatic stress disorder and depression, his new army medical rating was 'F7': fit for the stores and making tea. He bumped into a few of the Jocks who had 'jacked' of their own accord. They puffed their chests out and claimed to be optimistic about returning to Iraq. 'Yeah, of course you are,' Kev thought. 'So why did you fuck off back here in the first place, then?'

Being shot had robbed him of his life's best soldiering experience. His only pleasure now was pulling birds. Recently returned to Canterbury on R 'n' R, Larks reckoned he would have the pick of them; surely they would favour him over a guy with half his upper body encased in a metal cage? Larks's ego deflated watching Kev flash his doe eyes. As Keegs had predicted, all the girls wanted to meet the wounded soldier.

On a beautiful early summer's morning, soldiers huddled in groups, checking watches and inhaling deeply on cigarettes, their last drags before the transit to RAF Brize Norton. As traffic jams were anticipated on the M2, M25 and M4, they had gathered at 0600. Dew glistened on the grass by their feet. They were to exchange this green and pleasant land for the featureless expanse of Maysan. Kelly stood alone, picking at his scabs of self-doubt. He was petrified, and it showed. No matter the notches on his barrel and medals on his chest, he felt he had to prove himself. His greatest motivation always came from within. 'Donna was right,' he muttered to himself, 'I should have stayed at home.'

Only one poor squaddie looked as ill at ease, the youth shuffling anxiously as if chewing gum was stuck to his boots. He wore the beret and insignia of the Royal Army Medical Corps. He told Kelly his destination was some camp in the middle of nowhere called 'Condor'.

'So, what have you been told about this place, then? What did you say it was called, again? Condor, was it?'

'Yeah, Condor, in Maysan, north of Basra. They're training the Iraqis up there, or something.'

'Really? 'Ave they 'ad much happen to 'em?'

'Yeah. I was told they had had a few contacts, like, they are good lads and the platoon sergeant was shot not so long ago. That's about it.'

The satisfaction of entrapment raised a smile. 'Right, right. I see. OK. So what training have you done for Iraq?'

'None.'

'None?' Kelly was shocked.

'I only completed my basic course a short time ago.'

Kelly wondered how this medic would have reacted when Smudger was blown out of his Land-Rover or when Challis and Beeney were shot. 'Thank God for Doddsy and his RMA 3 course' was all Kelly could think. 'Have you treated trauma victims?'

'I hope to get some training on the job.'

Kelly was fractious now. Did this kid really think Iraq was some finishing school for half-trained medics? 'Oh, you'll get that, all right.'

Kelly's parting comment was left to float in the morning air. He and the medic boarded the bus in silence, Kelly's offer of acquaintance withdrawn.

After no food or in-flight entertainment, he touched down in Basra the following morning in low mood. Tiles were missing on the floor and windows were smashed at the airport – the same ones that were damaged when he had first arrived in January. Warrior armoured vehicles escorted eight coaches to Shaibah Logistics Base, and shortly afterwards he boarded a Chinook bound for Abu Naji.

He undid the buckle of his harness, took a swig from a water bottle and tightened the straps on his kit bag. Through a porthole he gazed down at a landscape flattened into submission by the sun. Heat haze shimmered above Route 6. The sight of the highway plunged him back into the nightmare that he had insisted upon making a reality. But this was where he wanted to be. When the rear ramp descended, it was as if somebody had opened an oven door: Iraq had got hotter in his absence. The helicopter's undercarriage splayed momentarily, like a bird upon landing, and he coughed up a mouthful of aviation fuel as he crossed the threshold, taking short steps beneath the rapidly spinning rotor blades.

Infanteers standing beside the helicopter landing site recognised him among those who disembarked.

'Oh, shit.'

'It's him . . .'

'Is it? You sure?'

'Yeah, that Kelly fella. Got shot in Qalat Salih.'

'What the fuck's he's doing back here?'

'Christ knows.'

Kelly strolled indignantly towards the office of the man who had done most to resurrect his career. Adam Griffiths knew what a brave, proud man Kelly was. His thinking was that it was sometimes important to look after these types more than others. So he had badgered the system to allow Kelly to return. His actions had been partially self-serving. Griffiths told Kelly to run Condor as he had done prior to his departure.

If you did not like Kelly, or if Kelly did not like you, the gates of Condor must have seemed like a portcullis that had just slid down. Kelly jumped from the Land-Rover full of intent. Conscious that he was being watched, he feigned nonchalance and met low-level grunts of 'Hello, Paul' with a flat smile.

He said more to himself than to others. He was back. He felt he belonged and was free of the trepidation that had marked his journey. In his pocket was a pistol grip that he would screw onto his A2 in place of the conventional rifle grip: less painful for his left hand to wrap itself around.

When Kelly met up with Neneh again, it was only to

say goodbye. Kelly's return meant Neneh could go home to Scotland on leave. Neneh wound Kelly up, telling him his medal citation would have been better written up as an accident and emergency report.

Condor had other new arrivals that day: Royal Engineers tasked to build a more fortified camp gate. Having scarcely left the British headquarters in Basra before, they were nervous, while their status as reservists counted against them with their hosts. Territorial Army soldiers were too often dismissed when their skill levels deserved greater respect. This lot did the cause of 'STABs' (Stupid Territorial Army Bastards) no favours. When their time came to leave a week or so later, they found their shiny new gate was too small for their truck to pass through.

Richie Fieldman's 19th birthday fell on 10 May. Below a night sky lit by Iraqi tracer fire, he, Aldo and Smudger climbed onto the roof of their accommodation block for a private party. How else would any self-respecting Jock celebrate than with a heavy drinking session? They got 'steaming' drunk on the booze Richie's mother had posted from Clydebank. The code was that vodka arrived in lemonade bottles, Buckie in Coca-Cola bottles. They carried a stereo onto the roof and played hard-house CDs donated by a nightclub in Greenock. From his trouser pocket, Richie liberated the Iraqi whisky pinched from Hendy's room. Their heads bobbed in time with the music as their legs dangled beneath them. They were like school kids sharing a cigarette behind the bike sheds.

'Gees tha vodka, man!' said Aldo.

'Aye, come on,' echoed Smudger.

'I will, just keep the noise doon, eh? Gimme two ticks, I'll give ye tha Buckie in a minute, man. Hendy will square us away if we're caught.'

'Good on yer maw faer this Richie, no doubt,' said Aldo, raising a bottle.

'Aye, she's outdone herself this time,' her son replied.

Josephine Fieldman was looking out for the Jocks' welfare. After her son had mentioned there was a swimming pool at battalion headquarters, she posted him a paddling pool. Richie eyed visitors from battalion headquarters with envy. They had it easy down there.

Aldo questioned Richie about his Land-Rover: 'What's they mad markings on your door?'

'Ah, them. That's ma tally a road deaths, man.'

'Aye, right?'

'Aye, man. The livestock. I've got six sheep so far, a few dogs, two pigeons and a football. I draw wee pictures of 'em, like.'

'You're off your head, man. Tell us aboot that patrol wi Hendy and Passmore, the one ye came back from three hours late.'

Richie swallowed a gulletful of Buckie before waxing lyrical: 'OK, if ye insist. Well, it wis wi' a few of 6 and 7 Platoons, boys like Lee Gidalla an' that, and we wis oot in the middle a nowhere. I don't think any a us knew exactly where we wis, like. I'm drivin', right. There's no roads, just a wee track. I'm driving doon it, and it's givin' me the shittles right up maself. I think we mustae reached this mad settlement, nomads or something. There wis a herd a cattle, and just then these Iraqi tits started shootin' at us.'

'Did ye de-bus?' asked Aldo.

'Aye, man, we all jumped doon. It wis mental, right enough, when we wis all lying in this ditch with a load of incoming our way. The radio wis oan tha wagon, but I think it wis "Mad" Passmore who had tha satellite phone. He wis like, "Fuck, fuck, I cannae remember tha code number ye've tae press." So he goes tae Hendy, "What is it, like?" Hendy wis like, "You're tha boss – ye should know." We wis all laughin' faer a bit. Doormat had given it tae him, but Hendy had forgotten it. I couldnae remember it either.'

'Aye. But what happened next?'

'Well, we had tae get oot of there. We returned fire, but they kept shootin'. Then Hendy says tae me, "Richie, I want ye tae get up and run back over tae tha wagon and drive it back over here so we can bug oot." I couldnae believe what I wis hearin'. We wis under a lot a firin'. "Happy with that?" he adds, as if I would be.'

Richie stopped for a swig from the Coca-Cola bottle. He swayed sideways as the illicit brew kicked in. 'Watch ye don't fall off the roof,' said Aldo, 'and git oan with tha story, man.'

'Ma throat wis dry! Anyways, I says tae Hendy, "There's no fuckin' chance I'm getting up and runnin' over there. I'll get shot." Hendy's like, "Richie, they're shootin' too high – they'll never hit ye." I goes, "Oh, aye, then why do I see holes going through the canopy?" So Hendy gets up and walks forward, trying tae show it's safe. I swear this round only just missed him. He dives back doon ontae tha floor. "Too high?" I says tae him. "They wisnae warning shots."'

'And how d'ye get back tae Condor?'

'Did a few drills, fire and manoeuvring towards 'em. Gidalla and Passmore got us a bit more organised. We wis able tae peel outtae contact and remount soon after that. After a line of fire wis put doon, me and Hendy jumped through the passenger door. But we still had tha problem that nae one knew where we wis. We wis drivin' aroond in circles before we foond these friendly Iraqis. We had nae interpreters wi' us, and they were trying tae tell us where tae go. It wis totally dark the noo and am drivin' through this thick sand. We wis lookin' faer a river. Then we got close enough tae Condor tae use VHF comms. They wis about tae send the quick-reaction force oot tae look faer us. Hendy wis worryin' he wasnae gonnae make it back up tha road faer his R 'n' R!'

'Did ye use yer Arabic, Richie? I thought ye were tellin' me ye'd learnt it, no? I don't know why ye bother. I cannae hack it. Too much faer me,' Aldo added.

'I do speak a wee bit. I've been learning it faer weeks!' Richie's undisguised distrust of Iraqis had not deterred him from the language. This was a rare example of him using his natural intelligence. 'It gis ye a wee bit more control with the ICDC. They respect ye faer it, and they're more likely tae dae what ye tell 'em tae. I tell ye, those ICDC are fly, man, trying tae steal ma frequencies. You've gottae put maskin' tape over the radios so they cannae see which ones yer usin'. If they find that oot, we're fucked. They tell the insurgents enough as it is.'

Smudger asked Richie, 'Where were ye faer your last birthday, when you turned 18?'

'I think I wis oan exercise. Probably sleepin' in a shell scrape somewhere. That's the army for ye. I wouldae gone up Destiny's in Glasgow or doon the boully in Clydebank. Got so pished I wis unconcscious. Smudger, are ye still fruitbat about what happened in Qalat Salih?'

'Aye, a wee bit, maybe,' he replied. Smudger looked a lot younger than Richie and Aldo. 'I wis thinkin' of putting a picture of what wis left a ma Land-Rover in that magazine, what's it called, *Max Power*?'

'Aye, you should,' Aldo replied. 'That would be funny.'

'But I'm more fed up aboot the beasties – aw these mad insects ye get oot here. I won't miss them when am finally back up the road.'

Richie leant over the side of the roof. Feeling the vomit leave his stomach, his mouth opened like a fish. The sound of his puking met with Aldo and Smudger's derisive laughter. In the morning he had a hangover so bad he could barely hold his rifle.

The officers at Condor had been pushing for clearance to recce some of the insurgents' ambush positions on Route 6. Gidalla knew where they were, because his Land-Rover had been shot at from the same bunkers more than once. As the Argylls were only in Maysan to train ICDC forces, clearance was granted with some reluctance. A six-man team drawn from 6 and 7 Platoons and led by Hendy and Kelly would insert at last light. They would take additional ammunition and radios, including Tactical Satellite Communications (TACSAT). A back-up team would patrol Route 6 through the night in case they required rapid reinforcement. Should insurgents arrive to set up a new ambush, the Jocks would be allowed to return fire; under no circumstances could they initiate an engagement. The operation would begin on the evening of Friday, 14 May.

That morning Adam Griffiths was due to visit Condor. The battle for Route 6 was hotting up by the week, and this journey would be one of his first in the new 'Snatch' Land-Rovers. These had sufficient armour plating to stop a 7.62 mm round. Unlike the Warrior armoured vehicles used by the PWRR, they were defenceless against RPGs. The Snatches were less mobile for the additional weight they carried, and hotter. Crews made cups of tea from the bottled water they brought with them. Although they were not supposed to break the seal of the vehicle for security reasons, they habitually drove with one of the doors fractionally open to get a draught.

Griffiths' team, known as his 'Rover Group', made the journey from Abu Naji to Condor roughly once every three days. Today he planned to discuss the progress of the ICDC, which had been encouraging of late, with their senior officer Colonel Hikmet. Griffiths was adamant that the ICDC were capable of a great deal when mentored fully. He believed their detractors would do well to remember they were a fledging organisation in a corrupt society. It was little wonder to him some individuals played both sides.

Another mundane but essential task was to interview all the private soldiers and junior non-commissioned officers. These interviews fed into the compiling of their Confidential Reports, which were of paramount importance to those seeking promotion.

Among the party were Colour Sergeant John McNab, Griffiths' driver Corporal Hariwell and his admin clerk and jack of all trades, Corporal Tracey Garner. While Keegs flouted the ruling that he was not allowed to search female passengers or drivers when on Vehicle Checkpoint duty, bringing Tracey Garner on patrols was Griffiths' more tactful method of calling the Iraqis' bluff. As a woman, Tracey could search another woman and had found many pistols hidden beneath the full *burkha*.

With Majar al-Kabir remaining out of bounds and it not being sensible to pass through Qalat Salih unnecessarily after the siege of 5 March, Hariwell was limited to one route from Condor to Abu Naji: Route 6.

It was because Rover Group had been shot at so many times on the highway that Griffiths had been nicknamed 'Major Magneto'. About six weeks previously a crowd of locals had blocked Route 6 and thrown stones at Griffiths' Land-Rovers. They had even leaned inside the Land-Rovers in an attempt to pull British soldiers out. A few protesters had been bumped out of the way as the Argylls extracted. There had been no Iraqi Police Service officers at the nearest checkpoint to intervene, or join in. They had been replaced by shadowy figures dressed in black, members of the Mahdi Army. And two weeks before, the Argylls had caught a bomb-maker who had planted an Improvised Explosive Device on the highway.

13

Ambush

Al-Jazeera was the fly in the British ointment. An estimated 50 per cent of local households enjoyed access to satellite television, yet nobody watched Al-Jazeera more closely than the Coalition Forces. In Basra, brigade headquarters employed interpreters to monitor the station's output around the clock. Media watchers identified a pattern: a sketchy, often inflammatory report of a Coalition Forces engagement would first appear on Al-Jazeera, followed by a précis of the same incident, minus analysis or context, on Sky News. The BBC would run a slower-to-air but more in-depth package. Years of state-controlled media had dulled the Iraqis' critical faculties, yet US and UK heavy metal had made a greater contribution to the rise of the insurgency than any television channel.

To the chagrin of those committed to a more hearts-and-minds approach, hundreds of the very people the Allies claimed to have liberated had been killed. Earlier during the tour James Dormer had bought bananas and chatted to locals in Al Amarah. He had gone through the Northern Ireland-ingrained routine of 'five and twenties' – when each soldier drew imaginary radii around his position – without ever feeling endangered. Now the same streets were no-go zones to all British forces, unless cocooned in armoured vehicles and accompanied by Challenger tanks.

On the morning of 14 May, Al-Jazeera reported a US air

strike on the Imam Ali shrine in Najaf. British troops later claimed that this explosion was caused by unstable, rusted Iraqi weaponry.

Kelly awoke the same morning to the sound of men sleeping fitfully. He blinked, stared at his wounded hand and previewed the day's itinerary. The thought of that evening's reconnaissance operation excited him; Griffiths' visit did not. Kelly pictured 'sunbathing arse kissers' swarming around the company commander upon his arrival. Kelly recalled the phrase 'the Royal Family must think the whole world smells of fresh paint'.

With Hendy, Kelly oversaw the 'zeroing' of weapons. This entailed the tweaking of rifle sights according to each soldier's tendency to fire to the left or right, or above or below the target – there was usually a pattern to their inaccuracy. Both sergeants wanted to be sure that if their close observation team was engaged, it would win any firefight.

Kelly briefed the team: 'You're aware of this position, and we know it was used to attack Corporal Gidalla's Land-Rovers while I was away. This plan has been discussed with Major Griffiths, and we should have some sort of quick-reaction force cover from Camp Abu Naji should we encounter any resistance. We'll set up an OP [observation post] for a few nights, inserting after last light and extracting before first light. The teams will change around every night in line with the rotation system here at Camp Condor, but I will remain as OP commander. If the enemy are seen, we'll call in the QRF and let the Warrior armoured fighting vehicles deal with the threat.'

Kelly drew lines in the dirt to represent the Route 6 highway and the trenches used by the insurgents with a long, blunt-tipped stick: 'I'll now identify the location of the various insertion and extraction points, and the "actions on" on enemy "seen" and the "actions on" when in contact. The

OP position and the ambush site are on the eastern side of Route 6. To the west is a 1.5 km stretch of flat scrub, and further beyond that is Majar al-Kabir. It's dangerous territory. To the east of the OP position and the ambush site are two large U-shaped tank berms [short steep slopes in the ground used for tank exercises]. They sit side by side with a gap of approximately 20 metres between them. Behind is a long, high mound of earth. There are sandbags reinforcing this position as well.

'You'll also notice the large, oblong-shaped concrete building with no roof – an abandoned factory, or suchlike. Now, the Mahdi Army sit in the southern end of this building with binoculars and look out for passing CF [Coalition Forces] patrols. Sometimes an Improvised Explosive Device is triggered. This may be rudimentary, such as a few artillery shells strapped together, or may be more sophisticated. The enemy then follows up with medium and light machine-gun fire, rocket-propelled grenades, you name it. This usually results in a damaged vehicle, shaken soldiers and a very nervous drive back to Camp Abu Naji. The post-action intelligence reports suggest that after the contact the enemy retreat eastwards, where they have vehicles waiting, though this probably depends on the strength of the CF call signs they are confronted with. Hopefully, during the course of the OP, we will see where they come from and where they go.

'It is not our aim to stand and fight them. If we are contacted by them, we will be on our own for ten minutes at least while the QRF is crashed out. We all know it could be more like 30 minutes. Even so, I'm confident that even if we're outgunned and outmanned we can handle it. Agreed?' His audience nodded. 'Good. The first evening will be this evening. As I said, we will not be taking up our position until after dark.'

*   *   *

With Griffiths' arrival imminent, Passmore approached Kelly. Their relationship was strained. Since his return, Kelly had insisted upon leading every patrol leaving Condor, effectively reducing the lieutenant to the role of his operational second-in-command. Passmore was disturbed by Kelly's general behaviour. The sergeant carried a fluffy toy with him everywhere he went. 'Magic Monkey' was a present from his son Jack. Kelly reckoned, only half-jokingly, that Magic Monkey had saved his life before and would do so again: 'Until that day in Qalat Salih, I used to prop him on the dashboard. For some reason, I don't know why, I put him in my chest webbing that day. If I hadn't, he would have been blown up by that RPG, and so would I.'

The fluffy toy was employed as a weather vane on Vehicle Checkpoints. 'Magic Monkey says there's weapons in that car! Stop that car, that one!'

When others scoffed, he replied, 'Magic Monkey has never been wrong. When he has said there will be weapons in a car, there have always been weapons in a car.'

Passmore asked Kelly to ensure the battalion headquarters sign was taken down before Griffiths arrived. One of those timeless military traditions was to put up a sign with the distance to everyone's home town: London, Aldershot, Basingstoke, Canterbury, Bonnybridge, Shieldhill and Inveraray. Distances of over 6,000 km reminded everyone, if they needed reminding, how far removed they were from their ordinary lives. Kelly shook his head. 'Am I the only person with a sense of humour around here?'

Passmore was wary of Griffiths seeing the graffiti scribbled at the top of the post: 'BHQ [battalion headquarters] 30,000 feet and climbing!' Previously, Passmore had requested Kelly remove the sign only for him to put it back up again. 'OK,

OK,' said Kelly exasperatedly. 'I'll take it down. Jesus!' He laid it flat on the ground.

Griffiths and John McNab, the acting company sergeant major, alternated in terms of who drove the lead Land-Rover in their two-vehicle convoy. Both knew the second vehicle usually got hit; the first was an aiming marker for the insurgents. They reached Condor via Sparrowhawk, the smaller ICDC camp near Abu Naji. A new Iraqi commanding officer had been appointed there. He seemed more of a businessman than a soldier.

Somehow the battalion headquarters sign had found its way back. Griffiths laughed and asked to be photographed standing beside it. He was in a good mood; it was his wife's birthday that day.

Disappointed to hear Keegs had signed off from the army, Griffiths suggested he attend a promotion course. Keegs told Wellsy afterwards, 'It's true, mate. Nobody lifts a finger for you in the army until you tell 'em you're gonna leave. Then they can't do enough for you.'

Griffiths was unimpressed by the ICDC parade and told Colonel Hikmet so. His men had made improvements over recent weeks, proving themselves capable of planning and executing Vehicle Checkpoints on Route 6. Griffiths had hoped they would build upon this progress.

Public admonishment did not sit easily with Hikmet. He was a proud man and a member of the Malaki tribe, which offered him additional status. He had lost face. Al Roan and Brian Meldrum were left to soothe him. They promised to drink tea with him in his office, along with the army of flies.

McNab reminded Griffiths that they should head back before twilight. First and last light were the most dangerous times on Route 6: there was sufficient natural illumination for the insurgents to observe Coalition Forces targets and sufficient darkness to aid their extraction. Hikmet remained flustered when Griffiths said goodbye. 'Be careful,' he replied, quietly.

Griffiths was taken aback: 'Why?'

'Because Maysan is a difficult and dangerous place.'

They often discussed the threat level, and Griffiths attempted to dismiss what was at the least a disconcerting comment.

The Snatch drivers wrenched the steering columns hard over as they made to swing out of the ICDC compound: 'Look, sir. Up there.' McNab had spotted a recruit standing on a rooftop and holding a mobile phone to his ear. The Iraqi seemed conscious of being observed and shielded the phone in his hand.

'We've got to get going, colour,' Griffiths replied. 'I'll get somebody here to look into it.' It was rare to see a jundie with a mobile phone. They had little money and no status in their tribes. Phones were usually a luxury for tribal leaders.

'Sergeant Kelly?'

'Yes, sir.'

'Find out what that jundie up there is doing with a mobile phone, will you?'

The Snatches turned onto Route 6 and north towards their destination in Abu Naji. The passengers strapped on their body armour and tightened their helmets.

The next class on the ICDC schedule was physical training. Hendy and Corporal Brian Nicol could hardly be arsed to supervise the session. The recruits were in similarly idle moods. One brandished a document he claimed was his wife's death certificate: he wanted time off to mourn her passing. The roughened piece of paper was inspected by the interpreter. 'Yes, this is his wife's death certificate.

But it was exactly one year ago yesterday she died, not yesterday.'

'Right,' said Hendy angrily, 'get in line, now!'

'Let's just leave 'em tae it, Hendy,' Brian said. 'We can watch all this through our rifle sights, eh?'

'Aye, man. Good idea.'

There was a changing of the guard at Condor. Larks climbed the steps of the observation sangar. He found no joy at the top, only a machine gun. Wellsy began a shift in the Ops Room.

As the Griffiths convoy passed the Iraqi Police Service checkpoint near Qalat Salih, the officers shouted and made threatening gestures. They were not normally so openly hostile. Although he had no remit over the Iraqi Police Service, an implied task for Griffiths and other British officers was to report their behaviour at battlegroup level. He would flag this incident up on arrival at Abu Naji.

As they drove north, Route 6 curved right then left in sweeping bends that encouraged drivers to keep their speed up. Griffiths' men had an additional incentive to maintain momentum: acceleration in the Snatches was almost non-existent. The eastern side of the highway was noticeably greener than the western side, courtesy of the River Tigris. Two men stood beside a broken-down car by the roadside. It was shortly after 1630.

The Snatches came under fire from their left flank – it seemed the broken-down vehicle had been intended as a diversion. The Argylls counted ten gunmen. Their rocket-propelled grenade and AK47 fire started too high but quickly lowered. Rounds pinged into Griffiths' passenger door – accurate groupings at his thigh and stomach height. These would have shot through the skin of an unarmoured vehicle.

'Fuck!' screamed one of the top-cover soldiers. Instinctively, he ducked beneath the roof.

'Get back up there and return fire!' ordered Griffiths.

Tracey Garner was travelling in the cargo hold with the back door open. Coolly, she opened fire.

Griffiths wanted to warn other Coalition Force vehicles against straying into the same ambush. He attempted this first via the VHF and HF radios bolted onto the dashboard. But these were ineffectual unless the caller was in a static position. He resorted to his mobile: 'Kilo Zero [the Ops Room at Abu Naji], this is Yankee Zero Alpha. Contact. GR 123962, enemy small-arms and RPG fire. Have pushed 500 metres north and am observing.'

The other Snatches pulled over at the same distance. The passengers assessed the damage to the vehicles. 'Why today?' thought Griffiths. He knew it was a Friday, and the massive contact in Qalat Salih had also fallen on a Friday. But there was no obvious pattern of attacks on the Islamic holy day. The British would later discover that at that morning's prayers, the local imams had ordered their faithful to exact revenge for the US attacks on Najaf.

While some reports carried by Al-Jazeera were embellished, a real offensive was taking place in the holy city. US Special Forces wanted Moqtada al-Sadr dead. Officially, there was an arrest warrant out for al-Sadr in connection with the murder of Abdul Majid al-Khoei, a moderate Shiite cleric at the Imam Ali shrine, but were he to 'die resisting capture' it would save everyone the cost and inconvenience of a show trial. Saddam's was enough.

Pictures of Ayatollah Khomeini adorned the streets of Najaf. At a recent rally, the leader of the SCIRI had called for the creation of 'Shiastan': a Shiite-controlled governorate independent of Baghdad. Najaf was also Moqtada al-Sadr's base in southern Iraq and home to the operational headquarters of his Mahdi Army.

'Paul, you need to come in here,' shouted Wellsy to his sergeant. Kelly was reclining in a foldaway chair. His legs were stretched out before him, and his head was back – a position he intended to maintain for some time. 'Someone is having a contact close by.' Wellsy had heard only that a British call sign was in contact, not that it had extracted.

Kelly righted himself. It was like getting out of a bath tub. 'Contact?' he asked. 'Hobbsy.' Kelly signalled one of the privates. 'You'd better tell Dormer and Hendy, yeah?' The lad scuttled away. Passmore arrived and, soon after, so did James Dormer.

'Any more details, Wellsy?' Kelly asked.

'Just that a contact report came over the radio. A Coalition Forces call sign said they had been ambushed.'

'Whereabouts?'

'About three kilometres south of Danny Boy. The ambush came from the east of Route 6, and they were pinned down.'

All those apart from the Ops Room and guard duty personnel began scrambling for their kit. Hendy and Brian Nicol were doing push-ups when their platoon commander approached hurriedly. 'Stand to, stand to!' James shouted.

'What the fuck for?' Hendy was incredulous as James approached.

'There's a call sign under fire and pinned down on Route 6.'

'OK, James. I'll spread the word.'

Richie Fieldman was sunbathing and splashing oil over himself when everyone started running in different directions. He stood, pulled his trousers up and grabbed his webbing. Knowing he would be one of the drivers, he sprinted towards the Ops Room. 'Where's ma fuckin' keys?' he shouted. Richie was a fast driver. He claimed to have driven from Clydebank to Canterbury in five and a half hours.

The pandemonium attracted Larks's attention. He rose from slumber inside the lookout position. 'What's goin' on?' he shouted to one private below him.

'It's all kickin' off on Route 6, apparently. A British call sign is pinned down in contact.'

Larks's eyes darted left and then right in search of Baker, who was listed to relieve him from duty. Larks wanted to get on the quick-reaction force. 'Baker, Baker, get up here. Fuckin' relieve me, will you?'

Baker smiled as he pulled on his body armour. 'Fuck you, Larks. I'm off, mate!'

Larks was distraught. 'I'll never forgive you for this, Baker. Get the fuck up here!'

'You must be joking, mate. It ain't my time to go up there yet. Ha, ha.'

Larks could not believe it. He had missed the big one at Qalat Salih, and now something was rocking and he was not going to get on that. Tears welled in his eyes. 'Toy soldier' they had shouted after Goacher shot him. It was not his fault he was in the wrong place at the wrong time.

The Jocks howled with excitement as they mounted their wagons, experiencing the buzz every infanteer lived for. Larks watched his mates – Keegs, Doddsy, Jay Lawrence, Rob Schwar, Lee Gidalla, Private 'Trigger' Ashton, Tommo and Hobbs – as they mounted up. 'What have I done wrong?' Larks asked himself. 'Always the same names and never mine among them.'

Richie slammed shut his driver's door and propped his rifle beside him in the rack. He pressed together the Velcro pads that sealed his waistcoat of body armour, but they slid apart. For weeks he had intended to fix this.

Passmore, Kelly and Gidalla knew how difficult it would be for the various call signs to communicate as they sped up Route 6. They had wanted to get together with the 7 Platoon vehicle commanders for a 'snap O group' (conference) prior to departing Condor. But James, Hendy and Brian Nicol were already out of the gate.

'Fuck it, then,' said Kelly. 'We'll just have to get after them.'

Larks shook his head as the last of the Land-Rovers disappeared into the dust. He belonged to Loz Loseby's section. Their duty was to defend Condor. Also left behind were Al Roan, the Ops Room staff and the STAB Royal Engineers.

Griffiths gave instructions to Corporal Hariwell: 'Send a message to Condor on the HF radio. Inform them what has happened, and instruct them to place a roadblock south of Qalat Salih to prevent any Coalition Force convoys moving north. They are not, repeat not, to deploy in support.'

'Yes, sir.'

Griffiths and McNab stood by the roadside planning their next move, wondering if they would be ambushed again and by whom. Outside the urban environment of Al Amarah, this was the first time they had witnessed insurgents launch such a bold attack; they were usually more inclined to fire off a few rounds and then make a dash for it.

'Sir,' McNab pressed Griffiths, 'we're in greater jeopardy the longer we remain static here.' A sheen of sweat glistened on Griffiths' forehead as he considered the colour sergeant major's assessment. The sight of a rocket-propelled grenade spearing towards them made McNab's point. They ducked and hurriedly left the contact zone.

Griffiths updated the Abu Naji Ops Room: 'Kilo Zero, this is Yankee Zero Alpha. We are going to push north towards Danny Boy and Red 1, over.'

'Roger that, Yankee Zero Alpha. Out.'

The radio operator seemed preoccupied. He was. Unbeknown to Griffiths, ambushes had occurred in Al Amarah and gunmen were mustering in Majar al-Kabir. This would be by far the biggest concerted attack on British forces to date.

Griffiths' convoy reached a position just short of Danny Boy. They used their weapon sights to scan the ground. They saw the customary weight of traffic using the junction, travelling to and from Majar al-Kabir. There were some suspicious figures crowding around two flat-bed lorries.

As they advanced, somewhat uncertainly, McNab whispered into his radio microphone: 'Enemy left. Carrying RPGs and AKs.'

Griffiths turned to see 25 to 35 men now moving north along the bund line that ran parallel to the highway. The enemy were 50–100 metres north of Danny Boy and appeared to be setting up another ambush position. The Rover Group would have to run the gauntlet. Griffiths inwardly wished he had not distributed all the under-slung grenade launchers to his platoons; his Rover Group was entitled to adequate protection. Surprise was his only advantageous weapon. 'OK, let's go for it,' he shouted.

The Jocks on top cover fired accurately as Iraqi rockets speared in all directions. One found the rear axle of McNab's Snatch and exploded at the roadside. Griffiths opened his passenger door and fired ahead. This was the location where a few weeks ago his Land-Rover had been hit by an Improvised Explosive Device.

'John,' Griffiths called McNab on the PRR. 'On the left of us there's another ambush position, six enemy approximately and they're about 200 metres away. We'll have to fight through it.'

'Roger that, sir,' McNab replied calmly.

The insurgents made to flee at the last second, having primed their rocket. A loud explosion was followed by a billowing white cloud. The missile sped between Griffiths' and McNab's vehicles.

'Fuck!' One of the Rover Group came on the net. 'I don't know what the fuck that was, but it would have taken us out.'

Griffiths reported this latest instalment to the battlegroup Ops Room. His main concern remained the prevention of Coalition Forces call signs straying into any of the ambush positions. 'I'm worried,' he told his driver. 'The re-supply convoys have crap comms, and there are so many black spots around here. They won't know what they're about to drive into.'

Two miles south of Abu Naji was a prominent junction known to British forces as Red 1. Two Warriors and three Land-Rovers were parked by the roadside. These belonged to the PWRR quick-reaction force. The Snatches pulled up. On inspection, the damage to McNab's vehicle was worse than at first thought.

Griffiths spoke to Sergeant Dave Perfect, the Warrior commander. 'We've been in a lot of ambushes. I really need to talk to the battlegroup 2IC [second-in-command] and tell him what's happening.'

'Abu Naji is under mortar attack. You can't go any further towards Abu Naji than you are now.'

'We're heading to Abu Naji. Simple as that.'

Perfect consented. He was saving himself for what he feared would be an exhausting afternoon.

On arrival at Abu Naji, Griffiths was deflated to learn that two multiples had left Condor to come to his aid. He knew that they had little support and poor communications. There had been no need for them to deploy. Why had they not received his second message?

With Maysan Province in open revolt, there was heavy anxiety at Abu Naji. With remarkable speed, news of the attacks on British forces broke on Sky News. A dull explosion was then heard outside the Ops Room. A rocket fired from outside had failed to detonate; it could have taken out the entire command team. The wail of the mortar alert siren added to the sense of unease.

Colour Sergeant McNab later wrote a report that analysed the series of contacts that he and his officer commanding had survived:

At the forward edge of the first ambush site, a civilian vehicle appeared to have broken down, with two Iraqis outside the vehicle.

Comment: this may have been intended to distract the call sign from observation of the ambush area. Other than that, the first the call sign knew of the first ambush was SA [small-arms] and RPG fire from the west of Route 6. At the second ambush location, as the patrol had just been ambushed they were no doubt more alert, and the rear vehicle managed to identify the enemy prior to the initiation of the contact.

This was a complex and well-planned enemy action. They were well armed and had plenty of ammunition. This was clear from the heavy weight of fire directed at the call sign. Following this incident and subsequent offensive action by friendly forces, it appears the initial two ambushes were part of a complex ambush plan. It further appears that on both occasions the enemy were caught off-guard (more so in the second ambush) and were not yet in their correct locations.

It was assessed that the main killing area for the ambush was in the area around the Danny Boy checkpoint, with the first ambush as a cut-off, and the location where the possible Improvised Explosive Device was detonated as a further cut-off. As the enemy were positioned on the west side of Route 6, it was assessed that the ambush was designed to hit a call sign travelling from north to south, not in the direction the call sign in question was travelling. On both occasions, engagement ranges were extremely close at between 50–100 m. As both ambushes were suspected to be carried out at fairly short notice, it is difficult to assess if the enemy had a preferred vehicle to engage.

Capability gaps: as this unit was carrying out a unique task [an administration run to and from Camp Condor] they did not have the appropriate scaling of weapons and ammunitions for an incident such as this. The commander [Major Griffiths] assessed that 4x magazines were not sufficient. Had the enemy immobilised the vehicles, the call sign would have had to fight out of the ambush area with limited ammunition.

Recommend: possible movement in larger force levels (3x vehicle convoy) to give extra manpower on the ground. Use of air support for 'routine' observation of area may have deterred or detected.

14

Blocked Muzzle

If and when they saw the officer commanding's Snatches, Hendy suggested that they should halt and approach the ambush site on foot. James Dormer agreed. The Iraqi Police Service officers were dancing as they passed the checkpoint. The bush telegraph had spread news of the uprising.

The enemy were hiding in a derelict factory and bunkers dug into the eastern side of Route 6. They would begin their defence with a numerical advantage of two or three to one.

A flurry of RPGs welcomed the Argylls to the fray. One skidded across the road and showered Richie's wagon with shrapnel. To arrive at a contact in a vehicle sporting a canvas canopy was less than ideal. With his driver's-side front wheel slashed, he screeched to a halt a couple of hundred metres later.

The Jocks responded to Hendy and James's commands to de-bus. Being more experienced and 'nae English', Hendy was the man to whom they turned rather than their platoon commander. 'And get intae cover,' he added as rounds pinged off the tarmac.

'Aye, sergeant!'

'All-around defence!'

'RPG!' Missiles fizzed over their heads.

'You see that building 300 metres away?' Hendy asked.

'Aye, sergeant.'

'See the treeline?'

'Aye, sergeant.'

'There's people disappearing in there . . . Nae firin' unless ye have tae! Buddy up. In pairs, fire and manoeuvre towards the first point of cover. Go!'

James Dormer gazed along the extended line of perhaps a dozen Jocks nervously preparing to go over the top. He thought wistfully of Sandhurst and the smoothly organised platoons of 30 soldiers he was given in order to practise the directing of operations. James and Diesel Reid moved as a pair towards the enemy positions. 'There is no way I am going to survive this,' the young platoon commander thought.

The men in 6 Platoon stopped a few hundreds metres short of 7 Platoon. However, with no communication between the English and Scottish platoons since departing Condor, each was unaware of the other's exact whereabouts and intentions.

A rocket-propelled grenade missed the windscreen of Kelly's wagon by an arm's length. When he ordered his men to de-bus, a few remained huddled behind the wheel arch. 'Always get the hell away from the fucking wagon. It's the biggest target!'

Confusion contorted Rob Schwar's face. 'Where are they?'

'Who?' Keegs watched the incoming RPGs.

'The fuckin' Jocks.'

'Fuck knows,' Keegs replied, 'but there's loads of rag-heads.'

'Where's Griffiths? I thought we'd deployed because he was pinned down.'

'Dunno, mate. Somewhere over there, maybe?'

Two of the three Land-Rovers in which 6 Platoon had travelled were of the recently received Snatch variety. The soldiers formed an extended line parallel to Route 6 and divided into three fire teams led by Passmore, Kelly and Gidalla.

Gidalla addressed Rob and Keegs. 'I want you two to pair up and get yourselves across that road.' Rob nodded quickly. He could not wait. 'The guys on the Gimpys will cover you.'

'You hear that, Rob? Check your weapons pouches, we're off.' Keegs lifted his head, having 'squared away' his own personal admin. 'Rob? What the fuck?' They were supposed to cover each other's advance and dive to the floor every ten metres or so, but Rob was already running across the highway. So much for the buddy-buddy system. 'Fuckin' hell, Rob.'

Keegs wanted to put down a burst of fire as he advanced but heard the 'dead man's click'. Rather than getting into cover, he crouched, removed his magazine and pulled his cocking handle back and forth.

'Come on, Keegs. You're fuckin' jack,' shouted Rob, wondering why his mate was exposing himself.

Keegs arrived, knackered, but with his weapon fixed. 'Why did you fuck off like that?'

'Come on, mate. Just because you couldn't keep up.'

'I had a stoppage.'

'What were you doin' trying to fix it there?'

The furthest forward of the PWRR soldiers, they were joined by Trigger Ashton; his nickname preceded him.

Kelly directed operations behind them. 'Hobbs,' the sergeant shouted, 'get over here, now.' The kid was carrying an under-slung grenade launcher. It resembled a Hollywood movie prop. Alas, Hobbs was clueless as to how it worked. 'Hobbsy, I want one 40 milly round behind that sandbag position on the southern side of that concrete building, OK?'

Hobbs hesitated. 'Er, sergeant. Sergeant Kelly . . . Private Dodds gave me a broken UGL. It won't open properly.'

'What? What do you mean? Give it 'ere.' Kelly pulled it apart. 'There's nothing wrong with it, you mong. Get a round down.'

The dildo-shaped round slipped into the weapon easily enough but nothing much happened afterwards. Kelly grew impatient with Hobbs's fumbling. 'All right, Hobbsy. I know you don't know how to work it. You should have got refresher training on it. We'll do this the manual way instead. I can see where it's pointing now. I want you to turn it right a bit . . . right . . . a bit more . . . bit more. Stop. OK, come down a bit . . . just a bit. OK . . . Fire!' The shot was perfect. 'Good lad, well done. Now let's fucking get across the road.'

There were fatalities on the home side, and a corpse lay 50 metres in front of Keegs. For some inexplicable reason, he fired a burst into it. When he lifted himself above the bund line, enemy rounds whistled past his ears. Keegs felt like a centre-forward whose touch had deserted him when he needed it most. In the space of a few minutes he had attempted to fix a stoppage while in open ground, drilled rounds into a stiff and given the Iraqis free shots at him.

While Rob shot an Iraqi who popped his head up, Keegs's other strike partner had left his shooting boots at home. 'What you doing?' he asked Trigger.

'Firing at the enemy.'

'No, you're fucking not. They're nowhere near there.' Keegs grabbed Trigger's head with both hands and twisted it 90 degrees. 'There you go, mate. See 'em now?'

Behind them, Kelly was full of advice for 'Big' Wellsy as the private aimed his machine gun. 'When one of them sticks their head up, pick a section of ground just below the top of the trench and give it a good burst. The soil is loose. The Gimpy will just burst through that.'

Passmore and Kelly tasked soldiers to cordon off the Land-Rovers and cover rear arcs. 'Kill anyone who tries to drive any further up the highway than here.'

'Yes, Paul,' they replied nervously.

It was time for Kelly and Hobbs to advance. 'OK, Hobbsy, cover me now. I'm going across the road.'

'Yes, sergeant.'

Kelly was straddling the central reservation when the private shouted, 'Don't forget to zig-zag, sergeant.'

'Oh, yeah, good idea. Cheers, Hobbsy.'

He smiled. This contact was different to the siege at Qalat Salih. He liked being on the offensive. But on the frayed edge of his vision, Kelly eyed 'rocks' being hurled towards him: 'Grenade!'

Gidalla pulled him away from the immediate impact area, but shards of shrapnel sunk into Kelly's lower legs. Having promised Donna he would stay out of trouble, his first thought was how he would explain his latest wounds to her.

As Kelly grimaced, the Jocks were poised to outflank the insurgents. This entailed sending a fire team to clear the small buildings and the disused factory. Brian Nicol ordered Fishlips to advance; the Jock nodded compliantly. However, as he crested the bank of a dried-up river bed, he fell flat on his face as if on a hidden trip wire. His fall was seemingly unseen by the enemy but resulted in a blocked muzzle. He retreated.

'That way, ye fuckin' idiot! Towards tha enemy!'

There was despair in Fishlips's voice. 'I cannae, corporal. I've got a blocked muzzle.'

'You've got a pulled muscle? I don't give a fuck aboot your muscle! I'll pull your fucking head off. Git oan with it!'

'I've got a blocked muzzle.' Fishlips pointed at his weapon, caked in mud. From where Brian was positioned, Fishlips' run had presented no difficulties. 'The barrel's clogged up wi' shite, corporal.'

'Ah, faer fuck's sake. You're nae use tae anyone.'

While Brian left to join Hendy and Lance Corporal Billy Currie, Richie offered Fishlips his sympathies. 'How tha fuck d'ye do that? Ye only went forward two metres!'

Richie was thirsty. 'Ma mouth's like an Arab's sandal. Gis yer water bottle, Aldo.'

'Ye cannae drink that,' his mate replied, 'it's mingin'.'

As the Jocks drank pre-sealed bottled water at Condor, they had dispensed with the basic routine of cleaning out their army-issue black plastic water bottles carried 'on the man'.

'Fuck it, I'm so thirsty.' The rim was encrusted with sand. 'Urgh, Christ. This tastes like fucking sewage!'

'Told ye. Ha, ha.'

'An' it's boilin' hot.'

Despite some flank interference, Hendy, Brian and Billy Currie cleared the small buildings. They were engaged again when they reached the southern end of the factory, but not by Iraqis.

Hendy spoke to Passmore on the erratic Personal Role Radio system. 'Mr Passmore?'

'Hendy?'

'Stop firing at the southern end . . . Can you hear me? Acknowledge . . . Acknowledge. Over.' He tried again. 'I am at the southern end of the building. I am going to clear to the north. Over.' No response. 'Acknowledge . . . Acknowledge. Over. Fuck!'

Hendy and Brian knew they would just have to get on with it. With Billy in tow, they progressed bound by bound, each covering the advance of the man in front, along a long exterior wall. A turning into no-man's-land was getting closer; one of them would have to move around the blind corner. It fell into Billy's bound.

He gripped his rifle tightly and brushed the safety catch to reassure himself it was off. Sweat trickled down his forehead. When he turned the corner, he was confronted by a human figure. 'Don't shoot,' his voice of conscience screamed. Time slowed down.

Hendy judged from Billy's expression that he had encountered unfriendly forces, but why was he not shooting?

'Git doon, now!' Billy shouted. The Iraqi boy was already hunched in an upright foetal position, tears sliding gently down his rounded cheeks. With stringy arms, he clutched himself for reassurance. Disassembled rifle parts were scattered about him like toys on a nursery floor. 'Oan the fuckin' floor,' Billy repeated. Watery eyes pleaded for clemency.

Hendy scowled at the youth sitting in his 'pish and shite'. A bairn he might have been, but he was still a threat. He could even have been positioned there to lull them into a trap. In that respect, he was more dangerous for his innocence.

'Get a move on, Billy.'

'Aye, sergeant.'

'Take him prisoner. You've got plasti-cuffs.'

'Aye, sergeant,' Billy replied again, unsteadily.

'And put the AK back taegether and keep it with ye. We might need it if we run outtae ammunition.'

Hendy called Private Joe Connolly forward to guard the prisoner before updating James Dormer on the flow of battle. James could see the enemy driving south down Route 6 towards where some of his men were pinned down. 'The buildings are clear, but that's not the main enemy position,

James,' Hendy puffed. 'They're in a bunker in front of the factory. Six Platoon are putting a lot of suppressing fire over their heads, but it's a wee bit close tae us. I've tried, but I cannae get much comms with Mr Passmore on the PRRs.'

Connolly was riding a wave of adrenalin and getting rough with the prisoner. James grabbed the Jock by the shoulders and said, 'That fucking prisoner is your responsibility. Understand? He stays alive!'

'Aye, boss, nae dramas.'

James then removed his helmet and waved it above his head in an attempt to notify Passmore's men of his whereabouts relative to where they were firing. Watching from afar, Brian shouted, 'Git tha fuck doon, ya prick! Do ye want tae get yourself shot?' James turned towards him. 'Och, sorry, Mr Dormer. I wouldnae advise that, if I were you.'

'No, fair one, Corporal Nicol. Thanks.'

'It's risky,' added Hendy, 'but we'll have tae dae something to let 7 Platoon know where we are.'

James Passmore passed information from the Ops Room at Abu Naji on to his platoon sergeant. 'OK, everyone listen in,' said Kelly. 'We've only got to hold out for ten minutes. Suppress the enemy in that main trench. Keep them in there until the Warriors can run them over. The quick-reaction force is en route.'

A few minutes later Keegs saw what he thought was a little bird fly over the bund line. It was a home-made grenade hurled from the insurgents' main trench. A second missile exploded, sending up a heavy cloud of dust upon landing. But who was holding the cigarette lighter beneath Keegs's testicles? The burning sensation between his legs was unnerving. He rolled onto his back, placed his weapon by his side and stared at his crotch. Blood seeped through the tears in his trousers. He prodded his fingers through the two rips equidistant from the seam and felt his scrotum. Shrapnel had cut his sack open. 'Oh, fuck.'

'Man down!' The cry echoed across the battlefield. 'Man down!'

Keegs was inspecting his testicles when Doddsy arrived. 'Get your trousers down. What happened?'

'I think I caught some frag from that last grenade,' said Keegs, transfixed by the sight of two hanging white-coloured balls he had never seen before.

Doddsy pulled out a field dressing. 'I don't know how we're going to tie this in place. I think you'll just have to hold it!' Keegs screwed up his eyes. 'Do you want morphine?'

'Nah, mate, you're all right.'

Instinctively, Keegs wanted to be the hero and continue fighting, but when he tried to stand his legs buckled beneath him. Whether or not he received morphine, Keegs was out of the game.

Shrapnel from the same projectile had embedded in Jay Lawrence's hand, but his anger was roused more by Keegs's plight than his own. Gidalla only had to tell him once to advance towards the enemy position. He would relish shooting the one or two insurgents embedded there. His senses subsided in horror to find many times more, all armed with semi-automatic rifles and primed to shoot him. What followed became the stuff of Condor legend. Rounds aimed towards his stomach deflected off the gas block at the front of his rifle. He turned and dived back into the British bunker. Had Jay carried his weapon 'in the aim', as the shoulder-height position was known, he would have been killed.

'What the hell was he doing?' Kelly asked Gidalla. There had been a communications breakdown between the sergeant and corporal. A thumbs-up signal from Kelly had been interpreted as an indication to advance.

'You can fuck right off if you think I'm doing that again,' Jay told a smiling Kelly.

'Jay, you're a fucking nutter! Get back over here and keep some fuckin' heads down. Do you want to get yourself killed?'

Jay declined Doddsy's offer of medical assistance and pulled the piece of shrapnel from his hand. Adrenalin was a powerful painkiller.

'Give me a look,' Kelly said bluntly to Keegs.

'Fuck off, Paul. I am not showing you my nuts.'

'Look, get your tackle out so I can see how bad it is.' Keegs pulled down his blood-stained trousers to reveal a two-inch-long tear in his scrotum. 'Nice,' Kelly said, smiling.

'Don't matter, he doesn't use them anyway,' said another soldier. At such times, squaddie humour was distasteful and richly funny. 'You never pull any birds down Canterbury, so what you grumbling about?'

'You can all fuck off.'

Keegs smoked a fag and took some photographs. He realised that from afar it must have looked like he had jacked. He wanted to shout 'I'm not cuffin' it, lads'. He was anxious. 'Is that my limited sex life over?' he thought. Unless he kept perfectly still, the pain was excruciating.

Hendy arrived, having run across open ground. 'We made our way intae the concrete building,' he told Kelly. 'We've got one POW, and a lotae them have fled east. We are able tae fire into the back of their main position. I'm concerned about the friendly fire threat. I thought I'd tell ye what we're daeing.'

'Yup, crack on, Hendy,' said Kelly. 'Just be aware, too, that when you're firing into that position you'll be firing towards us, so keep your rounds low, yeah?'

Hendy was distracted by the sight of Doddsy's hand thrust

in Keegs's crotch. Had he disturbed a private ceremony? 'Shrapnel wound,' said Doddsy.

'I got it in the nuts, mate,' added Keegs.

Kelly passed Hendy's message along the 6 Platoon extended line. 'The Argylls will soon appear directly in front of us but behind the enemy. They are going to engage them from the rear. Do not fire at any other targets other than directly at the enemy position.'

The Argylls shot at 6 Platoon, who returned fire. 'Cease fire!' Kelly screamed as 5.56 mm rounds skimmed over the bund line. 'Where's the position? Where's the position? Stop firing! It's Hendy's blokes!'

'But they're shootin' at us,' said one of his privates.

'Shut up, you nob,' Kelly replied. He attached a helmet to the muzzle of his rifle and lifted it above him. The Jocks waved back.

Griffiths was stranded at Abu Naji when James Passmore rang him. 'We're in hard contact here and we're running low on ammunition. We've also sustained two casualties.'

'OK, James, hold tight. There are four Warriors on their way down to you. Call me on the satellite phone every five minutes, if you can.'

Griffiths told John McNab to 'sort some transport out'. He did not want to remain at headquarters a minute longer. He told Major Walch, the battlegroup second-in-command, 'I want to deploy south again, re-supply Passmore and get them out of the contact.'

'Sorry, Adam, I can't let you. I've already deployed four Warriors out on the ground, ostensibly to support Passmore. Allowing two lightly armoured vehicles isn't going to help. This is a confusing enough situation as it is.'

The relationship between B company and the battlegroup was already strained; 1 PWRR's seemed no more interested in the Argylls than they were in ICDC training. As the commander of a 150-strong company tasked with mentoring Iraqi forces, it was natural to consider such a view a slur. Griffiths' head was spinning. On reflection he would regard Walch's decision as the rational one but not yet.

The quick-reaction force was delayed due to heavy incoming fire on their journey south. The fields on the west of Route 6 were dotted with drainage ditches and pre-dug offensive positions, all of which were occupied. Running parallel to the highway was a six-feet-deep concrete ditch. Soldiers dismounted from the Warriors to engage in close-quarter fighting; others used the armoured vehicles' weapons systems. When they reached the ditches, they found three enemy dead and four POWs were taken. Their black uniforms were covered in dirt. Lance Corporal Muir attended to a wounded POW.

As one eyewitness later described, 'The man was lying on his front and had a large gash clearly visible on his right shoulder. The wound was about eight inches long, and his clothes were soaked in blood. When he was further examined, an entry wound was found on his front. A bullet had hit him in the chest and had torn a chunk out of him. He had what is known as a sucking chest wound, where each time the casualty breathes, air bypasses the throat and is sucked directly into or forced out of the wound. This causes bubbles of blood to emerge from the chest. Lance Corporal Muir continued his efforts to save the man for the next 45 minutes, whilst exposing himself to enemy fire. It was hopeless, and the man drowned in his own blood. But it demonstrated the professionalism and compassion of the British soldier.

'The prisoners were shifted into place face-down behind the sergeant major's wagon, where they were afforded some protection from the continual fire that was still coming from the militia men. The men were moved quite forcefully. There were few men on the ground, and the prisoners had to be controlled with the minimum number of guards. They used mine tape, shemaghs (sand-proof desert headdresses) and whatever was to hand to blindfold them, whilst their hands were bound with plasti-cuffs. Private Pritchard stood watch over them with orders to shove their heads back down into the ground if they tried to communicate.'

Another British witness added, 'We had used a mixture of weapons to suppress the enemy position: 30 mm Rarden cannon, chain gun and Minimi. The four POWs were stood there with their hands in the air and a pile of weapons at their feet. The look on their faces was one of defiance and shock. The POWs were just young men who obviously had strong beliefs in what they were trying to do. What did not make sense at the time was how ordinary these people seemed to be. They were just simple farm boys. We then gathered the enemy dead in and started to check for any vital signs of life, just to be sure.'

Help arrived for the Condorites from an unexpected source. Having been engaged by insurgents in Qalat Salih, members of the Household Cavalry approached from the south. The men from 6 Platoon flagged them down and an ammunition 're-plen' took place. Bandoliers of 5.56 mm rounds were broken up. Kelly cursed the fact that the LAW 94 rockets, which he reckoned would have finished off the contact in five minutes, had been withdrawn the previous day by the quartermaster.

Back at Condor, Al Roan was becoming increasingly nervous. He asked one of the TA Royal Engineers if he had ever fired an AK47. Roan thought this might be necessary as they had so few British weapons and NATO ammunition.

The answer was no. Roan was not sure the Royal Engineers understood the enormity of what was going on around them. He called everyone together for a briefing. 'We have to be prepared to take casualties from the firefight and defend Condor if needs be. Let's get our hands on all the weaponry and ammunition we can.'

James Dormer would have experienced no greater unfamiliarity with those he commanded had he joined the Gurkhas rather than the Argylls. The Jocks were a breed apart and did things their way.

Richie Fieldman saw stick-like figures moving furtively between bunkers. 'Mr Dormer, I can see tha enemy!'

'OK,' James replied. He and Richie were perched on the lip of the trench. James kept his head up. It was dangerous, but he wanted to be the first to break from cover and advance. 'We're going to get a couple of bounds forwards, so fire and manoeuvre up to the next dip in the ground.' The Iraqis fired over the Jocks' heads. 'Fieldman!'

'Boss.'

'Fieldman, put your head up and see where the enemy are.'

'Am I fuck gonnae dae that!' Richie switched from repetition to automatic fire on his rifle and held his weapon above his head. He let off a burst without taking aim. 'Hey, this is how we do it in a real war, sir!'

'Is it fuck, Fieldman,' James belatedly retorted. Rank did not necessarily translate into power on the battlefield.

The firefight continued until James had a stoppage. In his defence, he had crawled through numerous sand dunes. He gazed pensively at his weapon and prodded the round trapped in the chamber. It refused to budge. Seeing his plight, Richie rummaged in his trouser pocket for his 'racing spoon' (a knife, fork and spoon set for eating as fast as possible), unused since his breakfast but unwashed. 'Here, gie us the rifle, sir. This might shift it.'

'Thanks,' said James.

Richie jabbed at the trapped round but the spoon proved no use. 'This weapon is boggin',' Richie thought, although for once he kept his counsel. He remembered how Hendy ensured all the Jocks stripped, cleaned and reassembled their rifles daily. James looked after his weapon in his own time. Whereas generous clearance between working parts prevented an AK47 jamming, only a small amount of dirt would render an SA80 a blunt instrument.

'Can you get it out?' asked James, hopefully.

'It's no gonnae move.'

'OK, hang on to the gat for me.'

'I'll put it oan ma back, boss,' Richie replied, inwardly cursing his officer. Fortunately for James, Private Smullen, the Gimpy gunner, was carrying a spare rifle and magazines.

The sight of incoming mortars spread alarm across the PWRR's positions. 'Take cover! Get in that trench behind you,' Passmore implored.

'No.' Kelly's riposte was stern. 'If you're in the trench, you won't be able to move out of the way. They're going off above us – they're air-burst. We can't fire back either if we're ducking down.'

Griffiths could hear incoming shells when he called James Passmore. 'Try and consolidate and wait for the Warriors. Withdrawal is not an option, James. James?'

The line went dead.

15

Rest the Dead

Blinking sweat from his eyes, Hendy focused on the horseshoe-shaped trench 50 metres in front of him. How many Iraqis were hiding inside? Eight maybe? He could not tell. It was more the pity that he and Kelly had not assaulted this newly dug bunker when they had seen it a few days before. The grenades that had injured Kelly, Keegs and Jay had been thrown from there. The Iraqis had loosened the clay by night and day, a human chain of grubby hands scooping it up and piling it high in front of the bunker to form a protective verge. The position looked out onto the main road, so was an ideal ambush location.

The enemy, propped against the dusty slope with their rifles, were skinny and wizened, skin stretched tightly over knuckles and bones. They were also well armed, with ample ammunition. Kelly's 'ammo stat' fared poorly by comparison, and his section's machine gun was empty. His men had fired thousands of rounds, but still the insurgents held out. They had no military training but were imbued with an intractable belief in their cause.

'They're well dug in.' Hendy sounded a note of resignation as he shuffled stiffly around to face Brian.

'Aye, it's gottae be done, though. Us or them, like. Seeing as there's nae armour coming doon from Danny Boy.'

The knowledge that one blast from a Warrior's main arm

would destroy the position was frustrating. Warriors could be heard in the distance, every blast producing a dull thud and smoke, which merged with the cloudless blue sky. Fear raised the temperature, and with every minute spent mapping their approach, the wetter the nape of Hendy's neck became.

'This way, Bri.' Hendy motioned with his forefinger back towards the factory. He felt glad of the resumption of physical activity and hoped the act of moving, after being slumped in a defensive position, would clear his mind. He and Brian scuttled towards the nearest point of entry, their feet kicking up little dust clouds. In his mind's eye he replayed a scenario in which they made a clandestine approach only for the Iraqis to repel them, forcing him and Brian to retreat.

'What've ye got left, Bri?' he whispered, tapping his left hand against his magazine.

'Mag an' a half. You?'

'Aye, same. Not much.' Hendy coughed. 'OK, Brian. Through that gap where the window was. I'll lead.' A jutting of the chin signified Brian's compliance, whilst apprehension tightened his stomach. 'And peel out and get some rounds down.'

A successful assault would likely require all their rounds and more. Hendy's understated attitude registered with Brian; it was very Hendy to play down the whole thing. 'How many guys have you seen, Hendy?'

'At least two at this end of the trench. I know there's more further along, Bri. They're no the same guys as I saw before.'

Hendy and Brian scanned the open ground, their eyes darting rapidly but methodically from one patch of scrub to the next, preparing to creep up on the insurgents from behind. They paused. Any sense of time had evaporated in the heat, and they could only guess at how long they waited. The sound of incoming mortars stirred them.

The only matter occupying Hendy's mind over recent days had been his forthcoming R 'n' R period in Scotland. Now he could only perceive what was immediate. It was all or nothing. His mind stalled on whether he was going to see his wife and daughter again. 'On the count of three, rapid fire.'

Brian, who was to follow Hendy, nodded. A last instinctive brush of the safety catch confirmed it was flush. He advanced from cover, anxious any instability would compromise his aim.

Hendy's eyes were primed on the enemy position. As the first gunman came into view, he saw him kneel inside the trench and reload his weapon – unfortunate timing for the Iraqi. Around his feet were spent bullet cartridges and discarded magazines. Sweat ran down into the local fighter's eyes. He pulled up his T-shirt to wipe his face. 'Do not turn around now,' Hendy pleaded silently.

'One, two . . . three.'

Rounds fired into the Iraqi's midriff, thrusting him off balance. With his change-lever set to automatic, Hendy sprayed rounds from right to left. It took ten rounds to put him on the ground, where he writhed, eyes bulging, a tormented, dying man. There was no time for hesitation, as the gunman who had been hiding behind his bulky friend turned to confront Hendy. All Hendy noticed was that he was dressed in black and was skinny. Another burst of fire met him square on. He staggered then fell beside his comrade. Only when he stopped moving did the fire relent.

Hendy shuddered when he saw more gunmen at the far end of the trench; he needed to change magazines. Brian ran from behind him to engage them, while Hendy depressed the release catch on his rifle, sending the empty casing falling to the ground. Kelly now advanced towards the same trench and joined Brian's attack. His fire from point-blank range ensured there would be no rearguard action. All eight enemy were now dead, and the trench was littered with bloodied bodies.

'Position clear, Mr Passmore.' Hendy pushed the microphone of his Personal Role Radio closer to his lips.

'Roger that, Hendy.'

Keegs was left behind with Doddsy, while his mates did another pairs fire and manoeuvre towards the derelict factory. 'It's shit being back here,' he chuntered. He noticed Doddsy was carrying an AK47. 'What you doing with that?'

'I ran out of ammo.' Almost everyone had done so.

Doddsy gave Keegs a fireman's lift to the new harbour. The journey was excruciatingly painful. Keegs was so angry about being shot in the bollocks. 'All I want to do,' said Keegs, still protecting his testicles with a cupped hand, 'is go around that corner and give the POW a fucking kicking. But I can't even move to do that.'

His mates were throwing rocks at the Iraqi boy, who was kneeling down, tied and blindfolded with a sandbag. 'I'll kick him for you,' someone volunteered.

Most of the enemy had fled or been killed. No walking wounded could be seen. Kelly prodded a corpse disdainfully with the tip of his rifle. The flesh around his midriff resisted the muzzle, bending but not softening. It was a bit premature to be clearing bodies given that they did not know the area was free of enemy, but you did not always execute these procedures as per the order instructed at the army's Infantry Battle School in Brecon.

Hendy pushed the mouthpiece aside and turned to Kelly. 'Paul, let's get some sort of re-org going, eh?' Hendy was more anxious than he let on. If the enemy returned in greater strength, they would surely defeat him and his colleagues.

'Yup, Hendy, let's crack on. No time to waste. A condensed re-org, it'll have to be.'

'Get some sentries sorted as well. We need tae get all these enemy weapons made safe and collected. Yeah, Paul? Do an ammo stat, then get the fuck oot of 'ere. Bri, see how much ammo the blokes have got left and get 'em intae 180-degree arcs.'

'Aye, Hendy, fuck all. They're all on their last mags,' Brian replied. Hendy had feared as much but felt worse for hearing the news.

'OK, you get the southern flank sorted, Brian,' said Hendy. 'There's about three positions tae clear of enemy dead, so watch out faer booby traps. Get any other weapons off them. Then we'll bring the Land-Rovers around, and we'll dump 'em inside. Any more casualties other than Keegs, Paul?'

'Lawrence's hand got a bit of frag. I think Doddsy caught a little frag, and there's myself, but I don't count myself,' said Kelly. 'Mine's just a flesh wound. So just Keegs, and he's got Doddsy with him.'

'Aye, man. Keegs was shot in the nuts.'

'We've got one prisoner of war – the kid. He's going in one of the Warriors. Mr Passmore is sending a sit-rep to Abu Naji.'

Passmore had dodged the mortars and called Griffiths to report. 'Nine enemy dead. One prisoner of war. Enemy position clear.'

'Excellent, James. Very well done. Hopefully those Warriors will be with you very shortly.'

Griffiths passed on the news to a relieved Major Walch, who clenched his fist as if to celebrate a goal. James Dormer rang Griffiths to confirm the arrival of the Warriors. Griffiths passed on the instruction from Walch and Argyll battalion headquarters in Basra. All the enemy dead were to be collected and returned to battlegroup headquarters for identification.

Hendy and Kelly returned to the bunker they had cleared. Hendy shook his head as he recalled how they had unknowingly witnessed its preparation. Gazing down, it was obvious that it served no agricultural purpose and could not have formed part of any planting or ploughing system. What it could have been, as it was now, at least temporarily, was a mass grave for nightmarishly entangled corpses.

His eye was drawn to the largest body, belonging to a fat man in a white T-shirt. He was lying chest-down against the verge, his head turned to the right. His mouth and eyes were open as if he was staring. The closer Hendy got, the more gruesome the sight became. Between bulging, ulcerated lips the dead man's teeth appeared like melon pips. 'Just get on with it,' Hendy told himself. As he lay on top of the body, preparing to turn him over, Hendy swallowed hard. The smell was repulsive: a sickly, gut-wrenching aroma of blood rose from the dead man's suppurating pores. Grabbing him by his arms, Hendy then leant to one side, using his body weight to turn the corpse over with him.

'Fuck!' shouted Kelly. 'Grenade!' Hendy closed his eyes, hoping the fat Iraqi would shield him from the blast. 'You're OK,' Kelly smirked. 'The pin's still in!'

They cleared the other bodies, and Hendy returned to where James Dormer was waiting. The enemy dead were massed in one trench, their limbs entangled. But not all the inhabitants were dead. Two Iraqis scared the hell out of Kelly when they raised their rifles. They were both shot on sight. Kelly, being Kelly, emptied a magazine of 7.62 mm into them. The velocity of his rounds at such close quarters drilled through their bodies and into the ground. He cursed himself for not checking they were all dead. 'Rules of the post-battle re-org: do it exactly the same as on exercise. All-around defence out, search the dead, unload weapons and place in a pile, treat friendly casualties, treat any prisoners of war and keep them apart from our wounded, redistribute ammunition – well, there's none of it to redistribute; we're all fucked on that score – then clear the area. In other words, "Get the fuck out of here." Simple really.'

'Still alive?' James asked rhetorically.

'Just about,' Hendy replied.

'Thought you'd do it all by yourself?'

'Brian and I got eight, I reckon.' Kelly, had he heard this claim, would undoubtedly have disputed it.

'Good effort, mate,' said James, turning to see the Jocks passing around a plastic water bottle. To a man, they had been desperately thirsty. Although they were standing out of earshot, James knew what they were saying: that the water was the most refreshing they had ever drunk. James walked towards them and was handed a bottle, which he put to his lips. Water would never taste that good again.

James was comforted by the warm, familiar sound of the engine, which started first time. He heard Hobbs before he saw him, the hyperactive private babbling incoherently as he jumped onto the tailgate. Nothing compared to how Hobbs now felt – ecstatic to be alive. His senses were sharpened; these were uncharted territories of consciousness. 'Hey, boss. I thought we wis goners there! Tha' wis fuckin' mental, man!'

'Yes, Private Hobbs.' James smiled. He knew the Jock was not going to shut up. He was entitled to shout. It had been one hell of a day. Steering his vehicle towards the enemy collection points, James eyed the terrain nervously and thought it would test a proper 4x4 off-road vehicle. As the Land-Rover dropped down what seemed like a crevasse and up a mountainside, Hobbs was thrown off, landing heavily. James stared back at the empty space behind him. He braked and jumped from the cabin. He was reassured to hear Hobbs was well enough to swear at him.

'Fucking hell, boss! For fuck's sake! Ye nearly finished the job those bastards started.'

'Sorry, Private Hobbs. Got a bit carried away.'

Kelly split the men into pairs to carry out the final tasks. 'Unload the weapons that are not on the dead bodies. Stay switched on when you're handling the corpses. One of them had a grenade beneath it earlier. You and you will then unload the weapons and put them in a pile over there. You and you will be in charge of the ammunition, which is to be kept separate over there. The rest of you, for now, will be covering – we remain in all-around defence. Now get on with it. We haven't got much time. The enemy could return in greater strength, and it's still kicking off up the road.'

The aroma of flesh drifted on the late-afternoon breeze. Hauling the bodies back to Camp Abu Naji was a grotesque scenario, the living and the dead squeezed together onto the Land-Rovers.

'Watch out for booby traps,' Kelly ordered. 'I want any ammunition placed here and the bodies in a line here.' He pointed with a fingertip. 'OK, go. Let's get on with it.'

Kelly's soldiers shook in anticipation of their macabre task. 'His fuckin' arm's come off, Richie!'

'Aye, Aldo,' Richie replied. 'Am no' daein' this. They're covered in fuckin' blood, man!'

'Stinkin' Iraqis,' Aldo panted as the limb squirmed from his grasp. 'I cannae get a hold a him. This is fuckin' sick.'

This was the first time Richie had seen at first hand the explosive effects of rounds on soft tissue. The thought of picking up the bodies, embracing those whose last breaths they had extinguished, was literally sickening. They had not joined the army simply to kill people, let alone carry the corpses of those they had shot. These Iraqis had died holding their weapons. Rigor mortis locked their fingers around the rifle slings, while only the thinnest of fibre tissues prevented their legs and arms falling away from their torsos.

'Hey! Youse lot!' Hendy's voice silenced the cries. 'Jist git oan with it.' Running towards the Jocks, Hendy signalled his urgency with a clap of his hands. 'They're only dead bodies, and we've gottae get the fuck oot of here! Richie, git a fuckin' grip of yoursel' before I do! We're gonnae be fuckin' mortared again any minute.'

Hendy was more admired than feared, but the Jocks knew he would make good any threat of violence if required. At this moment, however, he sympathised: none of them were mentally prepared for this. The Royal Military Police edict about the returning of bodies also flashed through Hendy's mind. They had suggested months earlier that in order to counter any false accusations of unlawful shootings by British soldiers, bodies, if possible, should be recovered and returned to Abu Naji, from where repatriation would take place. In February it had seemed merely theoretical.

Richie and Aldo stumbled as they dragged the corpses towards the vehicles, leaving behind a stream of blood and entrails. At least one Iraqi had lost an eyeball.

James Dormer was getting fed up behind the wheel. Reversing the Land-Rover into position, he reproached himself for not commanding the post-battle operation, as a young officer should. 'A fucking Jock should be driving this wagon, not me,' he muttered angrily. 'I should be overseeing the re-org. Can somebody who's not a fucking platoon commander do this? I've got better things to do!'

James Passmore was sympathetic. 'I'm going to check on

the wounded,' he said as Dormer jumped down from the Land-Rover cabin. 'Have this.'

Dormer caught the satellite phone and called the Ops Room. 'We're going to pull back to Condor in figures ten.'

'No, the boss [Griffiths] wants you to come back here [Abu Naji],' said the radio operator. 'We'll sort you out up here.'

'No dramas.' James's voice belied his disappointment. Camp Condor was his and the Jocks' home. There were too many unfamiliar faces at Abu Naji; it was an alien environment by comparison. The camp was a babble of accents from across the United Kingdom, Scotland, the Caribbean and the Pacific. Condor was a Caledonian outpost at which the Jocks had installed trappings of home over the course of the tour and only reluctantly accepted the cohabitation agreement with the English members of 6 Platoon.

James found himself standing by one of the last corpses to be collected. Perhaps the Iraqi's skeletal structure had collapsed: he seemed too narrow, just a head on a stick. James saw how his flesh was skewered. Rounds had ripped through his insides and burst out at angles that seemed to defy physics. His body had been violated; natural arrangements of organs and bones had been altered, and his rifle was just out of range, as if he had died straining for it. He did not look intrinsically good or bad, just weak, just another victim – one of hundreds killed in clashes with British forces over the summer of 2004. Just a shrivelled shape in a pile of smelly clothes – nothing human at all.

James repeated flagrant untruths and other trite responses to himself, such as 'rather you than me, mate', as he bent down. He brought his face close enough to his victim for the cloying stink to enter uninvited into his mouth and nostrils. He was now alone with a man he or somebody he commanded had killed. Had such a scenario been described to him before he deployed to Iraq, he might have imagined it would lend itself to emotional reconciliation. The truth was that it felt too soon after the killing to provide for such. While fate had conspired to produce this meeting, it took place in an emotional vacuum, and James could adopt only the role of numb observer. Whatever had been required to keep the Iraqi alive was no longer there, and this absence of humanity compounded James's sense of detachment.

At least the dead man's shemagh offered something by which to remember him. The once pristine blue-and-white cloth tied loosely about his neck was now a watercolour palette of blood, guts and brains. 'This is my trophy of war,' James muttered, binding it to his webbing. If there was a deeper meaning to this act, beyond adherence to time-honoured tradition, he was unaware of it.

Without a backward glance he turned and stared fixedly towards Hendy and Kelly as they oversaw the loading of the corpses onto Land-Rovers. With his limp left hand, Kelly was spared carrying any enemy dead. In the background, the Warriors made their belated arrival.

Striding over the final tank gully, James saw a dark object lying on the ground. Six inches from his boot was an unexploded grenade. What to do now? Nothing. Just carry on walking without breaking stride. It had been a long enough day.

'Mr Dormer,' said Hendy, seeing his platoon commander, 'are we goin' back tae Condor or Abu Naji?'

'Abu Naji. Major Griffiths wants to debrief us.'

'OK. The Warrior drivers think they're takin' us back tae Condor. There's been a wee bit of a communication breakdown between England and Scotland.' Hendy smiled: the Warrior drivers were from down, not up, the road.

'So it seems, Hendy,' said James, reciprocating the expression. 'And not the last, no doubt.'

The state of Sergeant Perfect's Warrior told its own story.

The gears were broken – he could only travel in reverse – and the two main weapons, the 30 mm and the chain gun, were useless. Rammed into the hull of the vehicle was an unexploded rocket-propelled grenade.

The slurry of bodies aboard the Land-Rovers made Hendy's task of getting the fat Iraqi in the white T-shirt over the tailgate more exacting. The Jocks standing on the corpses laughed.

'Git that fat fucker up here, sergeant.'

'I thought all these bastards were supposed to be starvin'. Isnae that why we invaded?'

'No' that cunt. He wis niver a starvin' Iraqi.'

'Heh, you!' Hendy growled at a random Jock, his serious tone discordant after the banter. 'Get those bodies further back. I cannae get this fat bloke's head oot of the way to shut the tailgate.'

'Aye, sergeant.'

'No more pissin' aboot. Get that poncho spread oot over the bodies. I don't want any locals seeing what's beneath it.' Hendy used his boot to push against the forehead, but as he leant down to close the tailgate the head recoiled and the mouth fell open. 'Oh fuck!' Hendy dodged the frothy burst of blood and guts that shot from the dead man's mouth. The vile liquid seeped into the clay. Glancing at the hanging face, Hendy thought he was going to throw up as well. 'That is the sickest thing I've seen in my life,' he thought.

'Right, the rest of youse, mount up. Youse've all gottae get on there. And watch your arcs. I want all-around defence.'

Keegs and Doddsy mounted a Warrior. They sat alone in the darkness of the cargo hold until the heavy rear door swung open and the POW was thrown inside. The Iraqi had spent the last hour kneeling with a sandbag over his head and his hands bound behind his back. Every time British soldiers ran past him they had given him a kick. Keegs and Doddsy were told not to give him any water. More British soldiers climbed into the steaming hot wagon. Keegs's shirt clung to his back. Half-heartedly he continued to hold the field dressing Doddsy had given him against his testicles. He shook with pain.

'He smells like a fuckin' toilet – disgusting.' One of the privates pointed at the boy. Every time he pleaded for water he was kicked.

For the journey up to Danny Boy, Kelly stood in the cargo hold of one of the rear wagons. He cursed as his boots sank into the malleable human form below him. The first intention of his victim's afterlife seemed to be to deny him a comfortable firing position. The story was the same on every Land-Rover. The ponchos flapped wildly as the vehicles lurched forward to assume full speed, and the living passengers were catapulted forwards. The bulge of dead humans distended perilously from the tailgates.

It dawned on James that he had survived combat – and that there was no adrenalin rush to beat it. 'You can keep skydiving or bungee jumping,' he thought. Rationality would return soon enough, but for now he celebrated satisfying one of man's most primitive urges. Nothing else mattered. Looking about him, it seemed others felt the same. He shouted into the wind that the Jocks should 'watch their arcs'. The Jocks made a noise somewhere between speech and laughter, a kind of roar. When the Land-Rovers slowed again, James could hear them reliving the dramatic events. Craning his neck, he was soothed by a timeless sight: soldiers, previously exhausted and fearing imminent death, revived, having left the battlefield as victors. He shared their pride in their achievements.

Hendy sat with Robert Anderson, a young private soldier

regarded as one of the quietest Jocks. Winning the firefight had stripped him of his reticence. 'Did ye see the state of those bodies, sergeant?'

'Aye, I did.' Hendy smiled as he continued. 'You know, this is the most I've heard ye talk in all the time we've been here!'

'Are ye still goin' on R 'n' R next week, sergeant?'

'Aye, Anderson. I wasnae gonnae let them stop my R 'n' R. I'll be goin' back for a fortnight.' Hendy had a flashback to the moment before he stormed the trench, when death seemed more likely than going home.

Tears streamed down James's face as he looked northwards. Dabbing sand particles from his eyes, he saw more armoured vehicles parked by the side of Route 6. 'Surely with all those Warriors to shepherd us back to Abu Naji we're virtually home and dry,' he thought. He pressed his face further into the wind – the buffeting was like sticking his head inside a furnace – but was alarmed by what he saw. The Warriors were parked in line with the road to Majar al-Kabir.

'There's something going on at Danny Boy,' said the Jock standing in the top-cover position. 'Cannae quite make out what it is yet, but there's loads of smoke.'

The rumble of gunnery confirmed the resumption of an armoured battle. It dawned on James that he and his Jocks would have to fight through this position to reach Abu Naji. Peering through his rifle sight, he watched dozens of gunmen sprinting to join the battle. All about him cheers and laughs died on the Jocks' lips.

16

Self-therapy

'Incoming!' screamed a Jock. Hearing the unmistakable crack of small-arms fire, he returned the compliment.

'Pointless. We are too far away to hit anything, especially from a moving vehicle,' thought James.

'Oh, fuck, there's fucking dozens of them coming from Majar!' another cried.

'Get down.' James's command sent his Jocks deeper into the morass of corpses. And they all felt more exposed for the fact that this stretch of the highway was higher than the surrounding ground. It had been built on top of a swamp plain.

As they advanced north, the artillery battle at the Danny Boy junction was no longer a distant argument but an increasingly noisy dispute. Once in sight of the big guns, they felt their vehicles decelerate.

'What tha fuck?'

'Why are we stoppin'?'

The Warrior leading the vehicle column had braked in order to engage enemy targets. Those travelling in soft-top Land-Rovers were petrified. 'Fucking move!' a Jock cried. 'Come on, we're stuck here . . . We're gonnae get hit any moment.'

Diesel, a recidivist Jock perpetually involved in misdemeanours, seized the initiative. 'Where's he goin?' said one of his buddies as he jumped down and sprinted ahead.

'Oi, ya daft bastard, git back here!' Rounds pinged off the tarmac at Diesel's feet. 'He's a nutcase, man!'

Diesel kicked and banged against the lead Warrior's protective shell, attempting to attract the crew's attention. He was inches from taking a fatal shot. No non-commissioned officer would have sent him on such a dangerous mission.

'Move! Move! Yer fuckin' blockin' us in behind ye!' Diesel's words were to no avail. Argylls watching from behind felt helpless.

'We'll have to de-bus,' James said to Hendy. 'Call Diesel back.'

The command to de-bus was broadcast along the convoy. Seeing members of 7 Platoon hurriedly dismount, 6 Platoon followed suit. Enemy fire was inbound from both flanks. Confusion reigned over which side of Route 6 to take cover on. Everyone made it into the rows of ditches and joined the firefight. Notable hits included Gidalla's strike with an under-slung grenade launcher, which destroyed an enemy trench.

'Only fire at identifiable targets!' Kelly barked instructions. 'Save your rounds. Don't run dry.' This was the way he liked it: soldiers waiting under the trigger of his voice, until he delivered them into their futures. His men's lives were more within his compass than the enemy's.

The ground shuddered under the weight of fire from three Challenger tanks; the heavier the pounding, the more slowly the action seemed to take place. Enemy mortars glided across the sky.

There was a dreadful waste of life as Iraqis ran towards the British positions. A stringy youth gripping an AK47 stood no chance against a Challenger tank. Missions of heroic absurdity ended with the obliteration of bodies. Engagements such as this were sickening to observe at close range. Yet one soldier from Abu Naji later wrote how 'bodies littered the bund lines like a carpet of evil men for all good to step on'.

With their men almost out of rounds, Dormer and Passmore ordered their men to remount the wagons and make a dash for Abu Naji. As they drove, the music of falling mortars gradually drew quieter. This came as a great relief to James Dormer, as his replacement rifle had now broken.

With battlegroup headquarters only hundreds of metres away, Richie's Land-Rover broke down. He and James covered the remaining distance on foot. They crossed the finish line bewildered but exhilarated. Feelings of victory and relief were palpable for them both. Their faces were widened with grins. Before that afternoon the Condorites' combat experiences had been limited to short, spontaneous engagements with gunmen, be they insurgents or opportunist thieves. That day they had survived a bloody firefight, during which each boy soldier had had reason to fear for his life. It had been a prolonged clash, but they had no idea exactly how long it had lasted. As James put it, 'Time had little or no meaning when you were being shot at.'

His status as a casualty spared Keegs having to crouch on top of a corpse. Instead, he was hunched inside a Warrior with no forward gears and a chain gun jammed beyond repair. The crew fired rifles through the hatches. Keegs heard the 'proper loud bangs of the Challys' as they advanced north, slowly and in reverse.

'There's RPGs incoming,' one of the crew told him.

'It won't go through this, though, will it?'

'Nah, we should be all right. How are your balls?'

'Sore.'

The young POW, with a sandbag over his head, had still not learned his lesson about what happened when he asked for water.

Having driven backwards for 18 km, the Warrior reached the base, at which point its steering column broke. Crew and passengers dismounted to discover the unexploded rocket-propelled grenade warhead wedged into the vehicle's armour plating. The Warrior was then towed away, and the POW was taken to join the other captured Iraqis in the Guard Room. Among those detained was an Iraqi police officer.

Upon his arrival at the medical centre, Keegs was stripped naked – his trousers, leathery with blood, sat in a heap on the floor. Jay Lawrence had accompanied him. Keegs indicated that the chill layer of sweat and the cold floor inside the building 'did him no favours'. He was put on a drip and a cannula was inserted into a vein in his forearm. The doctors wanted to conduct tests; whether this was out of necessity or curiosity, Keegs did not know.

An anxious Adam Griffiths wanted to ensure his Jocks found hard cover – Abu Naji was braced for another mortar attack. The company sergeant major also asked Kelly how much ammunition remained. 'None, nothing, we have no ammo whatsoever – but we owe the Household Cav 450 rounds,' Kelly replied.

The air was fragrant with faeces and human flesh as the deceased were hauled from the Land-Rovers. The youth of the victims was apparent to all: these were boys, not men. But there were children on both sides of the conflict, only one side wore black, the other Disruptive Pattern Material. Richie, a teenager, stared as the arms of one corpse opened wide and its head tilted forwards. He looked at its face: one eye was screwed shut, the other gazed without focus. The dead man's mouth fell open. His face seemed composed of mismatching parts, with features imperfectly aligned, lips aslant and nose askew.

There were 20 bodies in all collected by the Argylls and

the soldiers who had deployed in support from Abu Naji. The Iraqis were formally pronounced dead, photographed and searched for items of intelligence value. Two were found to be carrying ICDC membership cards. The youngest was judged to be around 14 years old. They were taken to the makeshift morgue, where Padre Fran Myatt ensured they were treated with dignity. The mayor of Majar al-Kabir was told that the deceased would be ready for collection at 1500 the following day.

There was concern among some of those who had handled the corpses that they might contract hepatitis B, so they began a course of injections. There was no let up in Kelly's intensity. To exert his will, be it on the enemy or his soldiers, was his addiction. 'Put your kit down in a straight line here and stand behind it,' he ordered. 'Take your shirts off – drop your trousers to your ankles. You could have shrapnel embedded in you and not know about it. So buddy up and check each other. Corporal Gidalla, on me please. I want you to check the blokes over with me. Check under their arms, groin area, everywhere. If you find anything, let me know.'

The privates' voices were wearily obedient. They were desperate to strip off uniforms soiled with human body matter and excrement. The same clothes would have to be put back on after the shrapnel check. 'This is great,' said one Jock sardonically. 'My troosers are wet wi' sweat an' blood. There's nothing better than puttin' wet combats back on, eh? Are we gonnae get exchanges, sergeant?'

Hendy replied, 'I'll be going tae see the quartermaster later. Hopefully he'll squarc us away.'

Richie was asked to fetch a mop to wash blood from the wagons. Unfamiliar with the layout of buildings at Abu Naji, he burst into the regimental sergeant major's office. Hyperactive, he ignored the sign on the door. 'Have ye got ae mop?' he shouted. The regimental sergeant major paused contemptuously before inviting him to walk outside then come in again. 'Have ye got a mop . . . sir?'

'Get out of my office!' he roared. 'We don't keep the mops in here!'

'Nae bother.' Richie hightailed it outside. Telling his mates about it later brought some relief from the day's events. He explained that he had mistaken the regimental sergeant major for a 'fat, scruffy corporal'.

Maer asked Griffiths whether or not he thought Condor was safe, considering how few soldiers were located there and its distance from Abu Naji. It was decided a section of 24 soldiers commanded by Lieutenant Stuart Muirhead would be airlifted by Chinook.

On his visit to the medical centre, Griffiths was struck by how mentally shattered Jay Lawrence appeared. Griffiths addressed Keegs, placing a hand on his shoulder: 'You're in good hands.'

Keegs smiled gingerly. 'I ain't too worried about it, sir. But I'm a bit embarrassed, as everyone keeps pointing at my gonads.' Keegs would also be the main attraction at Shaibah field hospital. A Lynx helicopter was waiting to take him and Jay there.

Griffiths wanted his soldiers to escape any witch-hunt over the state of disrepair of the corpses. He instructed his platoon commanders to obtain witness statements. His men were on the point of exhaustion. Even if the threat status had permitted their return to Condor, Griffiths would have personally forbidden it. They were in no state to defend themselves en route or at their destination. That night, they would sleep in the briefing room.

Kelly and Hendy wanted their junior soldiers to engage in 'self-therapy', discussing everything they had seen and done, including incidents they chose not to document. If any of the privates had begun to cry, his friends would have followed. They had gone through so much together.

They yearned for Condor, their little island in the wilderness. If the enemy launched an attack there that night or on their eventual return, the small British party would be defeated by force of numbers. But they had lived with this unsettling reality for months; it no longer bothered them. The camp required its inhabitants to summon the frontier spirit. They liked it that way.

The sight of those Argylls based permanently at Abu Naji being forced to wear full uniforms and Tam O'Shanters reminded them of their own freedom. 'A fucking woolly hat when it is 130 degrees? Fuck that,' said James. For once his Jocks agreed with him.

As evening fell, the platoon commander penned his report:

Event Type: Ambush by enemy with RPGs and small arms. Fire support to suppress enemy. Clearance of enemy position. Further attack by enemy at a second position. Extraction and recovery. Engaged whilst Danny Boy was being attacked.

Light Level: Visibility good but light levels getting dim due to it being late in the afternoon.

Prior Intelligence – G2 Threat Assessment: Route 6 was used regularly by Coalition Forces as their main supply route from Al Amarah south to Basra and other CF locations. Attacks on this route were frequent. The unit knew that there were previously used firing positions, scrapes and tank ditches [along the route] and were thus considering mounting covert operations to monitor the area.

The day in question was a Friday, and although friendly forces were relaxed and not on a heightened state of alert, it was felt that the local populace would have been wound up/incited by religious fervour. There had been no specific planning for the event by friendly forces, as it was a reactionary [crisis management] to an unforeseen event. During the action, quick verbal orders were given. Vehicles were unarmoured, stripped-down Land-Rovers. All personnel were wearing combat body armour and helmets.

James was seething about the ICDC recruits, particularly their commanders:

Whilst driving to the scene, the first quick-reaction force convoy stopped an ICDC force of platoon-strength size and attempted to have them come along to lend support. This request was met with a complete refusal. Among the dead enemy from the incident, two had ICDC identification paperwork. A further two are believed to have had police paperwork.

The sequence of events can be broken down into separate actions as follows: driving through the killing area and stopping 300 metres ahead, then dismounting and providing fire support; fire and manoeuvre to 'close with' the enemy in the area of the long building; attempted assault by PWRR quick-reaction force of the enemy position; attack from and reaction to the second enemy force some 300 metres to the west; assault of the enemy position via window in long building; arrival of Warriors and extraction of all to Danny Boy; reaction of arriving in contact at Danny Boy; fire support and extraction from Danny Boy in contact.

Locating the enemy: On the first ambush the enemy was dressed in civilian clothing and shemaghs and carried small arms. The fact that they were (actively) present in the area of the contact made it obvious they were hostile. The hollow ditches and tank scrapes did offer good cover from fire and view. When the enemy broke cover to fire or move, they could be easily seen as they became silhouetted against the skyline or desert. There was little vegetation, with none of it being much above 0.5 metres in height. When the enemy fired, the crack and thump instantly drew attention to the firing point.

Enemy mentality: The enemy at all locations were fully prepared and ready to fight. One 'startled rabbit' with weapon dismantled did surrender at the end of the long building.

Capability gaps: This unit was carrying out a unique task [ICDC training] and as such they did not have the same scaling of weapons and ammunition as the ground holding units. The call sign had no Light Machine Gun, and smoke and hand grenades were not available. The first enemy position could have been assaulted with less risk to the platoon sergeant if high-explosive grenades had been available. The ability to project high explosives and smoke would have been a clear advantage. The commander considered that four magazines of ammunition for SA80 was not sufficient.

Mourners gathered outside Abu Naji for the repatriation. Emotions had been stirred by the discovery of more bodies and body parts on the surrounding plains. The victims had been ripped apart by gunfire and their bodies chewed by dogs. It was claimed by some that the bodies had been mutilated by the British and dumped outside the base. Allegations flew around that Iraqis had been captured alive, taken to Abu Naji, tortured and finally shot. After 30 years of Saddam's rule, people simply assumed that this was what would happen.

The bodies were handed to the Iraqis at the front gate and taken to local hospitals. Dr Adel Majid, the senior doctor in Majar al-Kabir, recorded evidence of 'torture'. In one case, the penis of Haider al Lami, a 21-year-old casual labourer, was recorded as being 'severed' and his genitalia 'mutilated'.

The doctor's judgement was backed by the influential provincial governor Abu Hatim. Hatim had once been Maysan's most powerful individual and had been courted assiduously by the British in 2003. For the first few months of the occupation he had ruled Al Amarah with the tacit approval of British military commanders. But he did not enjoy the same relationship with Lieutenant Colonel Maer as he had done with Lieutenant Colonel Tom Beckett, the commanding officer of the 1st Battalion, the Parachute

Regiment. Hatim revelled in the epithet the 'Lord of the Marshes' and was easily recognisable in flowing white robes. One tale, apocryphal or otherwise, had created his legend. It was said that under Saddam's reign, Hatim had disguised himself as a senior Iraqi Army officer visiting Basra from Baghdad and summoned the local commanders for a meeting. After admonishing them for their failure to quell sporadic uprisings against Ba'athist rule, he drew a revolver and shot them.

Hatim's power base had shrunk, and he saw the state of the bodies as an opportunity to gain favour by accusing the British of war crimes. The chief of police, with whom Hatim was engaged in a political dispute, rubbished his and the doctor's accusations. The following day Hatim and his associates had a confrontation with the police chief in Majar al-Kabir, which ended with the officer being shot dead. The gunman, a member of the provincial council of Maysan, was indicted by a local judge but never charged with murder. No action was taken against him by the British commander. Lieutenant Colonel Maer argued in favour of an Iraqi solution to an Iraqi problem. To have arrested him might have been perceived as a colonial response. To the dismay of dignitaries opposed to Abu Hatim, the 'murderer' continued to sit on the council.

On his return to Condor, James Dormer slept with fifteen AK47s and four crates of 7.62 mm ammunition beneath his bed. This and other countermeasures formed part of what was known as 'Operation Rorke's Drift'. Vulnerable they might have been, but it was great to be back home. To his friend Al Roan, James looked a different human being, emotionally spent.

The Royal Engineers, for their part, were glad to leave – once they had squeezed their truck through the new gate.

Condor had been an intimidating world compared to the one they inhabited in Basra. Nobody really cared what rank you were at Condor – a strange concept when you were visiting from brigade headquarters. They also disapproved of certain customs: corporals 'gripping' lance corporals who ignored orders, and lance corporals doing likewise to Jocks if they were physically capable of enforcing their will. The Condorites got along surprisingly well given the close confines of their camp. Discipline was informal. When disputes occurred, they were settled quickly and sharply.

Colonel Hikmet was still smarting from the dressing down he had received in front of his men. The psychological need to prevent negative judgement of character was inculcated during childhood and of paramount importance in Iraqi society. The Condorites were less sympathetic because the ICDC had refused to join the quick-reaction force two days earlier and because two of the gunmen had been carrying ICDC identification cards.

Keegs was offered a wheelchair to take him from the helicopter landing site into one of the wards at Shaibah. Doctors came running towards him from all directions. Surely there was not enough of him or his testicles to satisfy their collective curiosities? The nurses' voices were intended to soothe, but he only felt greater embarrassment.

One of the doctors asked him to lie on his front. 'I'm going to check for internal damage,' he said.

Before Keegs could consider how the doctor might do this, he felt a finger probe his rectum. 'Oh, God,' he groaned painfully. 'You could have lubricated it.' The doctor walked off, leaving Keegs to lie there feeling invaded and sore.

The morphine dose took about 15 seconds to hit home. The sensation began in his feet, and he felt like he was being lifted up. 'This is amazing,' he thought. 'Better than sex, any day.'

In surgery 18 stitches were sewn into his scrotum. Afterwards, he was given a bespoke pair of underpants crafted from bandages. The doctors were proud of their handiwork. Keegs felt self-conscious as never before. He was also worried that he might have lost the use of his reproductive organs but was too scared to ask the question.

A couple of days later, Larks sat in the accommodation block picturing Keegs having his scrotum sewn back together. He could not help but rummage through his mate's kit and spotted a 'Gucci-looking' GPS (Global Positioning System) navigation gadget. He smiled, thinking that he would 'look after' it. Wellsy walked in, looking furtive: he had his hands in his pockets and he was staring at the floor. Larks watched him scan the room as if he was checking the coast was clear before committing a crime. The room was poorly lit, so Wellsy did not spot Larks. Thinking he was unseen, Wellsy leant down to pilfer Keegs's secret cigarette stash from beneath his pillow.

'You bastard. Fancy nicking his fags!' Larks shouted from his bed, causing Wellsy to jump. 'You rat, Wellsy. How can you steal Keegs's ciggies?' he added, tucking the GPS beneath his sleeping bag.

It was late afternoon at Condor as the Jocks sat around in their off-duty uniforms of shorts and flip-flops. It was hot – very hot. In late May the temperature seemed to rise daily.

The Jock in the sentry sangar spotted it first. 'Come and have a look at this, boss.' Within half an hour it was visible across Condor.

'Something very strange is happening on the horizon,' thought James Dormer. Darkness appeared to be spreading across the whole of the province. Suddenly, bolts of lightning ripped the sky in two. In no time it was dark, and a gale brushed the radio antennae from the Ops Room roof.

'What the fuck is wrong with this country?' asked a confused Jock. That it would be hot and the sun would shine had been two reliable parts of their daily existence.

Everything that wasn't battened down was now flying around the compound. Millions of sand particles were swept up and stung the Condorites' skin as they ran for cover. Sheltering inside a building, James watched the destruction of the camp that he and his soldiers had spent months making their home. Then he was plunged into full darkness: the power supply had been cut. The storm ripped out the wooden window frames in the accommodation block and the square sheets of blue plastic that acted as windows were blown away like kites. The rain appeared to fall horizontally, as ridiculous as it seemed, and buildings were flooded. The Jocks were so wet they thought they were drowning. A tumbling sound brought everyone to the doorway to see two heavy plastic Portaloos barrelling across the car park. The earth could not swallow the water fast enough; it came up everywhere in pools.

'Fucking Iraq. Even the weather's trying to kill us,' shouted James.

The storm ended as quickly as it had begun. James and his Jocks looked at each other. 'Someone's got to clean the Portaloos,' James ventured. 'Any volunteers?'

17

Watering the Water Buffalo

The operational tempo slowed and excursions from Condor were fewer in number. There was more time for personal contemplation. James Dormer recalled a conversation with a former Iraqi Army officer now serving in the ICDC. The captain had described how he had ordered his tank battalion to pound the nearest marsh Arab settlement into the dust in retribution for killing one of his soldiers. James had initially considered this a brutal, disproportionate action. Now, having led his Jocks in action, he recognised the sentiment. If one of his privates had been killed, he would have had similarly vengeful feelings. For all James's affection towards his Jocks, he was no closer to being accepted into their kirk.

As a young officer at the Royal Military Academy, Sandhurst, James had been schooled in the British Army's intelligent, indirect approach to conflict, as had his former commanding officer Jonny Gray at Staff College. They, Al Roan and many others believed it was counter-productive to kill hundreds of the very people whose hearts and minds they had sought to win. Why had such an attritional campaign been waged in Iraq? The approach had run contrary to the establishment of conditions conducive to the British Army's exit strategy.

Gray, ensconced in an airy Whitehall office, pondered what could be read into who had and who had not been recommended for medals. Brigadiers David Rutherford-Jones and Nick Carter, the architects-in-chief of the ICDC embed programme, had been overlooked, yet those who had overseen a bloody and destructive campaign of war fighting had gained glory. Zealous commanders had seized on every opportunity to lead their men into action. This compromised the efforts of those working towards the reconstruction of Iraq and winning the support of local people.

Lieutenant Colonel Tom Beckett had chosen a different strategy after the murder of the six Red Caps in Majar al-Kabir. Instead of unleashing the onslaught his soldiers demanded, he had marched into the town and shaken hands with its leaders. Beckett deserved praise and official recognition for such a demonstration of moral courage. Instead, his men had chastised him with taunts of 'Chickenshit Beckett'. His leadership of the 1 Para battlegroup through the invasion phase of Operation Telic and after President Bush's proclamation of 'Mission Accomplished' had surely warranted a Distinguished Service Order. Instead, his name was scrubbed off the investitures list. Twelve months later, with the dust having turned a shade of crimson, Lieutenant Colonel Maer, the PWRR commander, won a Distinguished Service Order, and Military Crosses fell like confetti over Maysan.

Days of shifting moods followed nights of disturbing dreams. Passmore could not stop his hands from shaking, while convulsions of the mind brought tears. Earlier in the tour, pirate footage of Saddam's henchmen throwing grenades into pits filled with live prisoners had drawn a crowd. The Condorites had had their fill of combat; such snuff movies had lost potency and lay unwatched in the television room.

The ICDC recruits paid for the duplicity of their colleagues who had engaged their mentors on Danny Boy day: they had received their last demonstration of how to execute a section attack. And physical training plugged the gaps in the lessons timetable – the Iraqis hated physical training. But contempt was a two-way street: most recruits knew somebody who had been killed by the British.

Keegs walked back into Condor like John Wayne – his legs could scarcely have been further apart. His testicles were excruciatingly painful. He resumed his private competition with Wellsy.

'What did you think of being in a contact, then, Keegs?' Wellsy asked as the pair sat on Keegs's bed. Larks and Kelly loitered nearby.

'Well, it ain't like the films, is it? There's no plot line to follow. You might be leaving one of your mates behind any second, and that's fucking scary.'

'Yeah, you're right. But Danny Boy wasn't as bad as Qalat Salih, Keegs. No way.'

'Wellsy, I got fuckin' fragged in the nuts, mate. You never got a scratch on you.'

'Let's ask Paul. He was at both . . . Paul, which contact was worse?'

'Qalat Salih, definitely.'

'Why?'

'I never thought I was gonna die at Danny Boy. I don't know why. Even when the grenade exploded in front of me, I knew I was going to live. I thought I was a goner at Qalat Salih.'

'I'm not 'avin' that, Wellsy. You ain't been shot. I 'ave. And I was at Al Kahla. End of story.'

When only the two of them were present, Larks persuaded Keegs to discuss a sensitive subject.

''Ere, Larks,' Keegs said, lowering his voice. 'Don't say nothing to no one, like, but . . . and I'm telling you this in confidence, as it goes . . . but I've got a bit of a thing. A bit of a problem.'

'Yeah, what problem?'

'Well, it was what they did to me, like, when I was in the hospital. Something I didn't think they was going to do, and I didn't like it.'

'Go on.' Larks was salivating.

'This is in confidence, mate.'

'Sure, of course it is, Keegs. You know that.'

'When I was in the doctor's, they had to check that I didn't have any more shrapnel inside of me, like, so this doctor stuck 'is fingers up my arse.'

'Really? Oh, that's bad, mate. That is bad.'

'But I don't want you saying nothing to anyone, like.'

'Nah, of course not, mate, of course not.'

Keegs shuffled towards the door as discomfort spread across his face. It was to be etched there for weeks. Larks waited a minute before shouting. 'Oi, Wellsy! You'll never believe this. All the doctors stuck their fingers up Keegs's arse!'

Wellsy brought his video camera when he and Larks joined a patrol of deserted marshland. As their section commander, Izzy got to play with it first. 'Here's Mr Frank Millerick,' said the corporal, pointing the camera at the lance corporal, 'driving the Land-Rover that has survived more RPG attacks than Saddam Hussein's had . . .'

'I'm looking incredibly cool here!' Frank stuffed his PRR radio into one of his front pockets.

'Larks. Look in, look in the front, son.'

Izzy panned behind him. 'What am I looking for, mate?'

'Over here. Look at me, son . . .'

'Hello.'

'We've got Larks in the back there. Where's fucking . . . ?'

Larks feigned dropping his trousers.

'Hurray. Nice arse.'

'What about Jay Lawrence?'

'Jay "Lorenzo" Lawrence? There he is, yeah.'

A thin smile spread across Jay's lips, but he did not reply. Having returned to Condor with Keegs, he was a ghostly presence. Unsurprising for a man who knew he should by rights be dead.

'We're going to go now,' said Larks.

'Where are we going today, Frank?' Izzy asked.

'Some minefield somewhere!'

'Steve,' Larks questioned Izzy, 'is it just us patrolling today?'

'Yeah.'

'Mate, come on me, then.'

'OK, this is our patrol state,' said Larks, gripping the roll bar as the wagon accelerated. 'Weather – I reckon it's about 28 degrees, wind is moderate, visibility is good, ragheads are recced. If I don't make it back from this, Jay Lawrence can have my porn stash. Steve [Izzy] can have my three grand in the bank . . .'

'Cheers, mate.'

'And Loseby gets fuck all.'

'What was that? Loseby gets fuck all?' queried Izzy.

'Yeah. Ha, ha.'

Izzy turned the camera on himself. 'OK, you're probably thinking "ugly bastard" – Wellsy, you can stop laughing, and all. I would just like to say then, er, obviously Frank is driving so it is getting a bit scary at the moment.'

'I don't know where I'm going or nothing – just randomly.'

'You don't, do you?'

'Nah.'

'Oh, yeah, go right there, Frank. Go right.'

'Where are we going?'

'Where are we going? We're going to "Al Fartus", Frank. Nice little town. I would quite like to live there one day. It would go well with me. Have you seen this?'

'What?'

'The bombed-out building here . . . Hold on, here we go.'

'What's this?'

An empty four-storey building stood at the roadside.

'Yeah, you can see this building from camp . . . Obviously, this is Bainsy's house before he moved out during the war,' Izzy continued. The basement was filled to the ceiling with putrid water. 'It's under renovation. Nice little swimming pool there in the garage. Needs a couple of windows, though.'

'Are we in the property market? It's out of my price range,' a voice said, interrupting Izzy.

'Yeah, some patio furniture. Bainsy would be all right here.'

'Nice drive, look.'

'Ideal location.'

'Yeah, the road's missing, that's all.'

'Yeah, I could see why Bainsy lived there, like. It's nice.'

'Right, this is us on patrol,' said Larks, assuming the narrator's role a few minutes later. 'Looks like the middle of bloody Africa. Camp Condor is over there. And there is that dodgy little town that we reckon is mortaring us every now and again.'

'Bloody bastards,' said Jay.

'I'll zoom in here. There's Wellsy, and that,' Larks said, zooming the camera in on the rear Land-Rover, 'coming in for a bit of the action. There's Trigger doing top cover.'

Trigger was looking elsewhere. 'Observing his arcs as usual!' Larks said sarcastically. 'Wellsy is driving. I don't know who's in the commander's seat. There's some cattle – nice – some locals, some more bloody palm trees and our illustrious leader, Mr Izzard.'

'Is that what you want to call him?'

Frank brought the Land-Rover to a standstill beside a natural pool. Izzy jumped down from the wagon and adopted David Bellamy's voice and mannerisms. The likeness was uncanny. 'What we have got here is the local habitat. We've been through some greenery, and found some snakes and some scorpions. What we want is water buffalo. We really want water buffalo because they are around this area somewhere . . . Wait . . . Look right . . . Water buffalo.' Snouts broke the surface, and two private soldiers urinated on the animals' heads. 'That's it, lads, water the buffalo. Water them up, yeah. 'Ave a drink, lads, yeah. There you go. Help yourselves, yeah!

'What's that there? There's a Trigger there, and you don't get many of them around. Now the water buffalo seem to be walking this way. And there's no way I'm fucking getting in their way!'

As the water buffalo approached, everyone retreated to the Land-Rovers. The huge creatures looked confused, as if they had mistaken golden showers for rainfall. 'And that was us, as you saw, watering the water buffalo!'

'Awesome, mate.'

Filming resumed as Wellsy revved up his wagon. 'You ready? Go on then. OK, good to go. I bet you can't get in the air, though. This is Lance Corporal Wells driving over a bump.' Wellsy accelerated as he crested the hill. Lessons from Larks had improved his driving.

'Better than Butlins, isn't it?' said Goacher, smiling inanely.

'Goacher doesn't get out much,' said Larks. Wellsy stopped the Land-Rover and de-bussed. 'There you go,' Larks continued, 'proof for the RMPs: Lance Corporal Wells getting out of the driving seat whilst drunk [Larks was joking].'

'Hello, lads. We've just travelled all the way down there . . . all the rough terrain and that, because we should have been on that track there. Corporal Izzard – soon to be Lance Corporal Izzard – was doing the map reading.'

The further they drove, the less certain they were of their whereabouts. 'She'll be coming around the mountain when she comes.' The Land-Rover shook as it tackled the rough, bone-dry terrain. 'Stop, stop, stop. We are in the middle of nowhere. Possibilities of a minefield – don't give a fuck.'

'It's not a track. The river there is the track we were going through.'

'But you know halfway down there'll be a cut along it.'

'Frank Millerick looking quite impressed. There's the driver Private Wells. Or should I say Lance Corporal Wells, soon to be Private Wells. Trigger, shit state. Trigger? Any words, mate? Any last words? Goacher?'

'I love you, Mum.'

'She don't love you, though.'

'We're gonna get eaten if the dark comes up,' said Frank. The light was fading.

'Thank you very much, Lance Corporal Millerick, non-commissioned officer in the British Army.'

'Corporal Izzard over there, commander of the team, what are your comments at this point?' asked Jay.

'We'll have to turn around. Obviously we followed the water buffalo tracks, and the herd must have hibernated west, or something like that. So what we need to do . . .'

'He's just trying to butter it up, like, but we're fucked.'

'Larks, optimistic as ever.'

'I'm an optimist, mate, but we're fucked, gents.'

They drove back along the six-feet-wide track. There was a steep drop on both sides. Baker taught Wellsy to use the high- and low-ratio gear setting on his vehicle. 'Try again. It's in, yeah?' Baker asked Wellsy. The pair were alone in the Land-Rover cabin with the camera perched on the dashboard.

'Nah, is it fuck.' Wellsy continued fumbling with the gear stick.

'That's it,' said Baker. 'It should clunk. You should feel it.'

'Take the handbrake off,' Wellsy replied, as if that would make a difference. Baker was more concerned with the gears.

'Up, that's low ratio. Now yank it all the way down to the bottom.'

It worked at last. Wellsy was pleased with himself. 'See, Bakes? I'm the driver, Baker. Don't look at me, look away. Bakes, I'm gonna bitch-slap you in a minute.'

The engine groaned its disapproval at Wellsy's driving. Eventually they made it back to Condor.

Not long after, Larks gave Wellsy another driving lesson, but this time closer to home and on more agreeable terrain. Frank Millerick joined them on the airfield and filmed the event for his DVD. Wellsy attempted a few handbrake turns with Larks instructing him from the front passenger seat. The Land-Rover had no roof and just one roll bar above the cargo hold. It had been stripped down to combat the heat.

Wellsy was driving at 40 mph when Larks shouted, 'Right, when I say, I want you to turn hard right, and I'll pull the handbrake with both hands. OK?'

'Yeah, OK.'

'Now!'

Larks pulled the handbrake. Frank, standing behind them, panned the camera around to capture the trail of burning rubber on the runway. The Land-Rover tipped onto its passenger-side wheels before crashing over. Frank kept hold of the camera as centrifugal force catapulted him across the cargo hold. The picture then went fuzzy.

After such a dramatic sound, the silence was complete. A few seconds later Wellsy untangled his body from Larks and trod on his head as he pulled himself up through the driver's-side door onto what was now the highest point of the vehicle. Larks remained squashed against the ground. His elbow had smashed through his door window and all the kit and weapons had fallen on top of him. As the wheels spun, so the implications of the accident became apparent. They paced around the Land-Rover, wondering how to solve the problem.

Frank broke the silence. 'We're going to have to think, lads. We're fucked if we can't get it back over.'

'I know,' said Larks. 'Let's slash one of the tyres and make it look like we had a blow-out.'

'Well, unless anyone can come up with anything better,' Wellsy replied, fearing he might lose his single stripe.

'We'll stab it. What else can we do?' Larks insisted.

'OK, then,' Wellsy consented. Air whistled from the tyre. It no longer seemed a viable solution. 'That was fucking stupid, wasn't it?' said Wellsy.

'Why?'

'Well, you can still see the skid mark all the way down the runway. It wouldn't have made that if it had blown out, would it?'

Battery acid seeped down the side of the wagon, eroding the paintwork. Wellsy only made things look worse when he attempted to clean it off.

'Well, we're gonna have to get help then, aren't we?' said Larks. 'One of us is going to have to go back to Condor and get another Land-Rover out here with a tow rope.'

'Fucking hell. It's six miles back to camp the safe way or two miles through the fucking minefield.'

'OK,' said Larks. 'I've done a few weird things in my time, but this would really be it. I'll go across the minefield. We haven't got time to run six miles. Kelly or the boss is gonna notice we've gone and there's a vehicle missing.'

'Go on then, mate.' Wellsy sounded supportive. 'Fucking hell, we're flapping here. We're gonna get in big trouble. Get a couple of blokes to help us, but don't tell anyone you don't have to.'

Larks dodged his way through the unexploded cluster bombs. He reckoned he got past the gate without being spotted by the Jock on sentry duty and commandeered Goacher, who, having shot him in the head, owed him a favour. Bainsy came too, and they returned to the airfield. The overturned Land-Rover was righted and towed back to camp, where the slashed wheel was replaced. Only Izzy noticed something was awry. 'You flipped that Land-Rover over, didn't you?' he asked.

'Nah,' said Larks. 'What you talking about?'

'Yeah, something's definitely happened to that Land-Rover. It's the battery acid.'

'What battery acid?'

'I can see battery acid has leaked down the side of the wagon.' Izzy crouched and pointed towards the area of corroded paintwork. 'It's a tell-tale sign.'

'How the fuck did you know that?'

'You forget I used to be a mechanic, then? Before I joined the army?'

'Oh, shit.'

'When you roll a Land-Rover, the battery acid from behind the seats rolls down.'

'Fuck,' said Larks, acknowledging he had been rumbled. 'The only other damage was my elbow going through the window, and we just took that out. I'm quite impressed that you knew that, mate.'

'Don't worry. Your secret is safe.'

'Yeah, cheers for that, mate. You'll keep it to yourself, yeah?'

Frankie included his footage of the incident on his DVD. One day he left his laptop with the disc inside in the Ops Room. Kelly played the DVD and, in Larks's words, 'went mental'. Mr Passmore also 'went mental'.

Kelly was a bit of a grouch these days: he sensed there were powers within Condor plotting against him. His behaviour was too erratic for most to stomach. Richie Fieldman acted as his driver on a rare two-vehicle patrol. The Jock watched uncomfortably as Kelly fiddled with the lucky mascot he had plucked from his chest webbing. 'Magic Monkey makes me lucky,' said Kelly. 'I always get some action when I've got Magic Monkey with me.'

'Is that right, sergeant?' Richie replied, sensing that he was disturbing some private ceremony. He kept his eyes on the traffic.

'Come on, Magic Monkey.' Kelly stroked the toy. 'Which car is carrying weapons today?'

Richie's superstitions were more traditionally expressed. He was a Roman Catholic, albeit non-practising, and had brought a Bible to Iraq. Richie had no truck with the 'Auld Firm', or with sectarian in-fighting, but growing up amidst such tensions had served him well in Northern Ireland. He had trodden a thin line when the Argylls policed the Holy Cross school dispute. When he parked his Land-Rover to face the Protestants, the Catholics had accused him of bias.

Just then, a local vehicle veered across the road, seemingly to escape the British patrol. As Richie swerved, Kelly wedged Magic Monkey between the dashboard and windscreen. 'Get after them,' Kelly commanded. 'They're bound to have weapons.' He was correct – or Magic Monkey was.

Richie swung his Land-Rover across the dual carriageway and accelerated. When he drew level with his quarry, Kelly gestured aggressively for the Iraqis to pull over. Instead, they took a sharp turning onto a dirt track.

'Come on, Richie! Don't let 'em get away!'

'I'll get tha bastards.'

Richie kept his gears low and his revs high. Kelly glanced at the dashboard. He did not register immediately but something was different. Suddenly, a look of horror flashed across his face. 'Stop the fucking wagon!'

'What?' Richie was agog. 'We're in tha middle of a car chase!'

'Magic Monkey! Magic Monkey!'

'You what?'

'I can't find Magic Monkey!' Kelly visualised the toy spinning through the open passenger window. 'Fuck!' He pawed desperately below him as Richie decelerated. The Iraqis made off into the distance, and the second Land-Rover sped past in pursuit of the suspects. 'Monkey? Monkey? Oh, thank God!' Kelly sat upright. He clutched Magic Monkey with the joy of a tramp who had found a bag of chips.

Two official piss-ups were arranged: one for the Jocks and one, a few days later, for the PW Ha Has. Funds were relieved from the ICDC building programme and additional supplies of alcohol were acquired from the usual Iraqi sources. The Jocks hoped their party would prove more of a morale booster than the recent swimming trip arranged by James Dormer. They had driven across country to reach the secluded pool, following a bearing based on a set of GPS coordinates. James had paid off the locals with a slab of Coca-Colas and some bottled water – they had smiled and shuffled away. The

Jocks had dived into the pool from the bonnets of the Land-Rovers. Everyone was happy until they saw the lumps of human excrement floating past their heads. The Iraqis used the pool as a toilet. There was a mass scramble to get to the shore.

On the evening of the Jocks' party benches were carried outside from the briefing room and food was laid out. No one had observed the dry-tour ruling, but weight loss and dehydration had reduced everyone's alcohol tolerance levels. The atmosphere was cordial and a few non-Jocks arrived, including Kelly and Passmore. Neneh was also there, having recently returned from leave.

Later, nobody could remember what was said to enrage Kelly, but he suddenly stopped laughing at everyone's jokes. For a man no taller than five feet ten inches he could be very intimidating. Passmore tried to placate him, but Kelly was adamant that he was going to tell everyone what he thought of them. His emotional dam had burst. If anyone at Condor had post-traumatic stress disorder, it was him.

His black, forbidding eyes bore into the soldiers, while above him tendrils of cloud provided a gothic backdrop to his outburst. 'You Argylls, you don't know shit! You've been through fuck all compared to 6 Platoon. My platoon has been at the two biggest contacts, and we had Kev and Col wounded at Al Kahla and Keegs and Jay wounded at Danny Boy. We're the best platoon in B Company, and everyone knows it. We've had it the hardest!'

While some of the older non-commissioned officers sought to calm Kelly, the Jocks muttered behind his back. 'He's a fuckin' mad warmonger! It's drivin' me off ma nut listenin' tae that shite.'

'Aye, can we no just have a few bevvies without him givin' it that big 'un?'

'He's talkin' a load a pish. The warmonger has lost his

melon. He's got an MC. Well, if he deserved one, then Hendy shouldae got one after Danny Boy.'

'Aye, man.'

Kelly's rant was wordless to them now, just a noise. He went off to beat his brains elsewhere while the Jocks resumed drinking.

Doddsy was on sangar duty armed with a machine gun. An ammunition belt extended from the weapon. He heard a thumping noise below him and looked over to see Kelly. 'Just let a fucking burst off into the front gate!' Kelly said.

'Nah, I can't do that, Paul. Do you know what I mean?' Doddsy spoke gently.

'Yeah, you can! What do you think would happen if you did?'

'Er, I don't know.'

'Nothing, nothing would happen.'

'No, Paul.'

'Do you think anyone would come running? Do you think anyone would have a go?'

'Paul, you're pissed. Go to bed.'

'Am I?'

They chatted and gradually Kelly calmed down. He and Doddsy hugged each other. Doddsy did not think anything more of what had happened. He just thought Kelly was 'fucking him around' to see what he would do – a test of sorts. By not conceding ground, he had passed.

The next morning, a severely hungover Brian Meldrum was put on a fluids drip to hydrate his body. Everybody laughed and took photographs.

Meanwhile, Al Roan drove to Abu Naji to discuss Kelly's future with Griffiths. 'I think he's a danger to himself, Adam. I'd like you to remove him from Condor, for his own good. He is not stable. You just don't know what he's going to do next. The camp needs to get back to some sort of normality before his actions get somebody hurt. I've got no gripes with him personally – we sort of get on – but for his own mental welfare something has to be done.'

Griffiths agreed to act but wanted to spare Kelly the humiliation of being marched out of the camp. He had heard a few disturbing tales. Kelly had apparently threatened some Iraqi interpreters, saying that if any more of his soldiers were wounded he would find out which village the culprits lived in and 'get even'. Although a great admirer of Kelly's courage and dedication, Griffiths could not tolerate a platoon sergeant saying things like 'Let's kill' prior to a patrol.

Griffiths devised a plan to spare Kelly's blushes. He told the doctor to summon Kelly for a check-up. He was to tell him that he had to leave Iraq because his open wounds would only heal if he returned to Britain.

18

Cutting Loose

Passmore came running into the gymnasium. Through their drunken stupors, the men could see he was perturbed. 'There's a tent on fire, you'd better put it out,' he said.

The 6 Platoon lads were having too much fun. 'Yeah, whatever, Mr Passmore. I don't give a fuck.'

He had been drinking with the boys earlier but condemned their setting fire to camp property. The fact that they had ignored his request was not a sign of disrespect. On Danny Boy day he had not asked anything of his soldiers he was not prepared to do himself. He too had 'closed' with the enemy. Throughout the tour he had struck a balance between leadership and compassion. That evening he swayed towards the latter.

Keegs had been on duty in the Ops Room on the night of the Jocks' piss-up, and now he wanted to cut loose. Music blasted from his stereo system: a power ballad by Queen. He and Wellsy were adamant that they were not going to listen to Horsehead's 'MOBO' (Music of Black Origin). Keegs sat with his legs tucked up in front of him so he could squeeze into the ice box. Wellsy and Doddsy threw 1 kg weights at him like frisbees. He thrust one of the gym mats in front of himself as a shield.

Having justified his return on the grounds that his boys required discipline, Kelly was an enthusiastic participant in their carousing. He shared their sense of abandon and was beyond caring what the senior Argylls thought. So what if they disapproved of his return and mocked his inability to cut up his own food? He had led his boys through another firefight – even if Rob Schwar had had to change magazines for him.

This was a special evening for Rob. For weeks after the ambush in Al Kahla he had been immune to reassurances that his driving had saved Kev's and Col's lives. He told himself that it was his fault for driving into the village when he had sensed an enemy presence. That night he stripped himself of his guilt – and most of his clothes.

Kelly threw a weights bench and the ice box through the window. The next thing everyone noticed was petrol poured over the floor; this was set alight. They all danced amidst the flames. Nobody was going to tell them what they could and could not do. Month by month they had been wound tighter and tighter – such an explosion was inevitable. Life was hard enough in Maysan when you belonged there. They knew they did not. From the first day to the last, their mission had been predicated on uncertain 'truths': that it was safe to train the ICDC and that such a force could one day stabilise the province. They needed more than Jonny Gray or Adam Griffiths to convince them that this was possible. But that night their spirits were joyous and carefree. The future of Iraq could not have been further from their minds.

'Fuckin' hell,' said Keegs, wiping perspiration from his brow. 'It's too fuckin' hot in 'ere. Let's go outside.'

They set fire to a pile of tents that had UNHCR stamped on them and belonged to the United Nations High Commission for Refugees. The tents had sat unused at Condor for weeks. The blaze made the sweat glisten on their arms and faces; they looked like members of a tribe on a desert island. More platoon members came stealing out of the night to cheer as the flames rose. Somebody made a token effort to extinguish the fire, throwing a cup of water. It splashed one of his mates and a water fight ensued. The fire was still alive, and so were they. They had become a single throbbing organism.

'I don't give a fuck about anything tonight,' one said.

'Yeah,' another agreed. 'This is the best piss-up I've ever been to.'

'It's like anything we could ever have wanted to get away with, we could do it tonight. No one is going to stop us, are they?'

'Fuck it. The Jocks can clear all this up in the morning. We squared away their shit after the other night.' The Jocks would have a lot to do: chunks of wall were missing in the gymnasium and there were burn marks on the mats.

'I can't believe we're just standing here watching tents burn!'

'Yeah, but we're gonna burn the camp down if we're not careful. How the fuck did this get so wild?' Nobody knew.

Having broken away from the throng, Keegs and Wellsy pulled open the doors of the chef's cooled containers and ransacked the shelves. They escaped with cold pies, sausage rolls and pickled onions. They ate a few onions, but it was more amusing to suck them and spit them back into the jar.

Reality returned at dawn when the Jocks stood over the still drunken PW Ha Has and eyed them angrily.

'Aren't you goin' to clear up our shit?' one asked.

'No fuckin' way, pal. Ye went too far.'

At lunch Keegs and Wellsy sniggered uncontrollably when onions were served. The warmth of their breath had barely had a chance to cool.

On Griffiths' request, Kelly visited the doctor. The doctor lost his nerve and blurted out the officer commanding's plan. In a furious mood Kelly looked up his company commander.

Why had Griffiths campaigned for Kelly's return only now to force his dismissal?

They sat opposite each other on benches, their faces partially averted. The tension was palpable. Griffiths insisted it had been with the best of intentions that he had roped the doctor into his plan. 'I used him, Sergeant Kelly, because I wanted to save you face – to protect you. I know how difficult life is with your wounds, even though you never admit it. But I think you should return to the UK now.'

'You must be joking,' Kelly snapped. 'I'm not leaving. My hand is fine, and so is my head.'

'We've both achieved what we wanted. You've come back and proved you could overcome your injuries – and that's fantastic – and I've been able to show lesser men what a commitment one of my platoon sergeants was prepared to make.'

'This is crap. I don't accept that. I can't believe what you're doing.'

Kelly's eyes glowered as Griffiths went on. 'Sergeant Kelly,' – there was no easy way of saying this – 'I just don't think you're right in the head.'

'I am fine,' Kelly replied perfunctorily, as if he had heard it said before. 'I know what I'm like. But I am OK. I am not leaving Condor or any other camp until my blokes are finished.'

'There have been a lot of complaints about you.'

'So? I'm telling you. I am not leaving my blokes.'

'You can't go around saying things like "let's kill".'

Kelly had wanted the Iraqis to know that they could not 'fuck' with his blokes. He had issued threats – threats that he thought were justified. He scratched the solid mass of his chin and thought, 'Yeah, a pat on the back *is* just a recce for the knife.'

No matter where Griffiths aimed a jab or a verbal uppercut,

his blows struck the same high-gloved shield. 'I am not leaving my blokes,' Kelly repeated, again and again. The Royal Military Police would have to drag him out through the gate. He would have liked to have seen them try.

Griffiths would have been similarly disappointed if his own boss had gone behind his back. And as much as he thought that Kelly should be placed out of harm's way, he would remain at Condor. Kelly's private soldiers would also have disapproved had the B Company hierarchy's plan succeeded. No matter his pettiness, obsessive nature and temper, they had begun the tour together and wanted to end it with him.

A football match was arranged between B Company and the ICDC to coincide with the completion of the training programme. Captain McQuitty captained the Jocks. Al Roan volunteered to referee the contest, which took place at Camp Sparrowhawk, near Abu Naji, on the morning of Saturday, 19 June. The more skilful and aggressive jundies won by three unanswered goals. A note on Keegs's brutal tackling found its way into the match report.

There was frantic activity on the touchline when an Iraqi arrived with Viagra for sale. Richie and Neneh topped up their supplies. They were happy shoppers so long as the price and thrill were right. Taking Viagra was something harmless and amusing to do – if not a bit pointless, too. Selling it for profit back home? Well, that was just common sense.

B Company received the order to collapse the ICDC training mission. The Condorites packed up and headed to Abu Naji. Time spent at Abu Naji meant the wearing of uniforms, saluting everyone and no more 'Hesco surfing'. Hesco was the trade name for the metal sheeting shaped and filled with sand used to form protective barriers. The Jocks had attached spare sheets of Hesco by rope to a Land-Rover and been swept along at high speed. There had been minor injuries and several cases of skin-chafing.

The Condorites bade farewell to the camp that had given them their identity and united them as soldiers and friends – within their respective platoons. The invisible Hadrian's Wall between the English and Jocks had proved insurmountable. It was strange that they boarded the Land-Rovers so gingerly, having looked forward to the day when they would leave. The tour that had seemed to extend inexorably onwards was drawing to a close. Until that day it had seemed as though the calendars in their heads had pages that could not be turned. They would not miss this broken land, but would yearn for the comradeship and humour they had shared there.

Nobody wanted to leave anything behind for the 'sand chogies', so they burned everything they could not carry. James Dormer pinched the Scrabble set.

Keegs said the recruits had only signed up for the 'money and the bum sex' and claimed to have seen two jundies 'at it' one night behind an accommodation block. A fortune had been spent equipping and training them, but their own quartermaster, an Iraqi, knew their habits too well to issue them with new uniforms, fearing that these would be sold. James had paid their expenses from a $500 petty-cash float. When this was spent, he received another $500. Few questions were asked, and he accepted that the Iraqis took advantage. The ICDC was a 'fit for purpose' organisation that inevitably encouraged petty corruption. When they had asked him for $200 to buy desks, he handed over $100, knowing that the furniture cost a fraction of their requested sum. The toss was not worth arguing and, as James conceded, 'we're stealing their oil anyway'. More money had also been spent on the jundies' accommodation than the Condorites'. Their billets had been rebuilt with new doors, windows, toilet blocks, air conditioning and fans.

James suspected corruption at a higher level:

I bought fans, slabs of soft drinks, booze and electric lights, and a regular ice delivery was established. Great pillars of ice arrived on the back of a pick-up every morning and were smashed and distributed in buckets, helmets, armfuls, however people could carry it. By the end of the tour, the guy had stopped asking for receipts. I don't feel a shred of guilt about that. The big fraud happened when senior people were sent to negotiate building contracts or vehicles purchases. The Arab way of 'backsheesh' was eagerly adopted by many. With Kuwaiti car dealers offering such deals as 'buy 15 pick-ups from me and get a Landcruiser free', 'off the books' deals were hard to resist. A cut on major building contracts to whoever awarded it was just standard practice. I can't say for certain but too many people who should have known better went along with it.

The Condorites watched the jundies sprint triumphantly towards their accommodation. It was as if this moment had been long awaited. 'Ha, ha. If they knew there was fuck all there for 'em,' said one departing Condorite, as the Land-Rovers accelerated away, reducing the jundies to smaller and smaller figures until they faded into the dust. The recruits scooped up sand bags and pieces of wood. They must have been poor, the Condorites thought.

Al Roan and Larks shared the journey to battlegroup headquarters. 'Boss, I hope we don't get contacted on this wagon. I packed this thing. Look what we are standing on!'

Al saw the four butane tanks Larks was referring to. He looked back up at Larks and burst into laughter.

The Jocks were given lots of 'bullshit' tasks to keep them

out of mischief at Abu Naji; 'sandbagging' was a favourite of the hierarchy. As something of a protest, Hendy filled them in while in the buff.

A few days later Griffiths decided that the Condorites should lead the B Company withdrawal to Shaibah Logistics Base. Al and James Passmore agreed half-jokingly that he was 'trying to get rid of us'.

Under cover of darkness, 6 and 7 Platoons left Abu Naji. Al Roan had dismissed the Viagra tablet as a placebo – it had taken several hours to work its deviant magic – but he noticed his erection when he settled into the front passenger seat of his Land-Rover. He pulled the map across his lap. His driver, Tracey Garner, kept her eyes on the road. He giggled like a schoolboy; his member was unusually big. George Lees's preposterous claim to have maintained a hard-on for 16 hours had persuaded Al to sacrifice his Viagra virginity. As the Land-Rovers rolled out through the front gate, he tried to concentrate on navigation and recalling the names of obscure Scottish football teams. It proved to be a futile bid to persuade his penis to shrink.

Standard operating procedures for patrols were observed, with soldiers armed and standing in top-cover positions. At around 0300, when they turned onto the highway, everything in their fields of vision moved more slowly because of a lack of sleep. They faced a long and dangerous journey south. So tired were they that a bleary-eyed dream sequence seemed to be unfolding. Home felt closer; they could almost hear the pipers serenading their arrival at RAF Brize Norton.

The headlights of the front wagon bore yellow holes into the blackness. They passed the turning to Condor. They would take home a sense of ownership of their little plot of Iraq. Further on, the top-cover soldiers signalled a broken-down vehicle ahead. As they drew closer, they saw a mini-van. The passengers, two of whom were armed, seemed anxious to secure the attention of the passing convoy. British soldiers de-bussed and disarmed the gunmen. Larks and others were ushered with some urgency towards the mini-van.

As none of the Iraqis spoke English, and the Condorites travelled without an interpreter, there was a limit to what could be mutually understood. Fortunately, the meaning of the words 'Ali Babas' was universal.

Al and Tracey remained in the Land-Rover. Her attention was drawn to his crotch. 'Sir, have you got a hard-on?'

Al smiled. 'Yeah, all right, don't go on about it.'

'I'm impressed,' said Tracey. 'You waited until your last day before taking Viagra!'

Larks returned from the mini-van. Its windows had been shattered by gunfire and the upholstery scorched by bullet marks. 'Sir, whoever's robbed 'em has fucked off into the desert, but they've got a wounded baby in their van. She's caught a ricochet in the head. Looks pretty nasty. She's losing blood – she's in a really bad way.'

'Right. Let's get Private Dodd up there.'

'Yeah, she needs Doddsy. I've had a decent look at her. I don't think she's got long.'

'Doddsy!' one soldier shouted.

'Medic!' shouted another.

The child was an affecting sight: one soldier vomited by the roadside. The stark reality of the situation tempered Al's compassion. To save her life would involve transporting her to the nearest hospital – which was in everyone's least favourite town. The risk involved in undertaking an excursion into Qalat Salih seemingly outweighed the slight chance of saving the baby's life. The darkness would lift in a couple of hours' time, while the locals would very likely assume the British soldiers were the culprits.

Al had been spared the fighting at Qalat Salih and

Danny Boy. His jaunt into Al Amarah aside, he was a self-confessed 'red arse' who had sat behind a desk while his mates were ambushed – not that he had chosen to do so. Who was he to order those who had survived such bloody engagements to risk their lives again? Many of them were emotionally spent. Countless times the locals had attempted to kill them. What did he and his men owe the community? If this little girl died, she would just be another statistic: another day in Iraq, another innocent life lost. Her passing would be easy enough to reconcile. Who outside of her family would mourn her death?

The answer lay with his men. They needed her to live so that their individual healing processes could begin. They wanted a memory that would provide hope – if only false hope – that their efforts to make southern Iraq a better place had not been in vain.

Gazing at the Iraqi child, Kelly had a vivid reminder of his daughter Abbygail. Doddsy found him leaning against the vehicle with his head in his hands. Asked if he was OK, Kelly forced himself to say that he was.

The hysterical woman running towards Doddsy could only be the child's mother. The pitch of her voice was sharpened by distress. She screamed as Doddsy uncoiled her tight, bony fingers from his shirt. He addressed his mates: 'Lads, you've got to get a grip of her. I can't treat the kid with her goin' on like that.'

The infant was passed from her father's arms into Doddsy's lap. Her faint cry quickened his heartbeat. He combed aside the shock of black hair, matted by perspiration and blood, that had fallen across her face. Life was draining from her. His trained hands found the indentation left by the round. Her head was so small that he tore a field dressing in half before pressing it against the thumb-tip-sized wound. Doddsy felt the eyes of the world staring at him. 'I don't need this,' he thought. 'I really don't need this. Not on my last night.'

'Doddsy, how bad is she?' someone asked.

His lips trembled. 'Mate, it's pretty simple. The round must have bounced around in here and slowed down. If it hadn't, it would have taken her head off. She's slipping in and out of consciousness. If she doesn't get to hospital soon, she'll die.'

'Fuck. What can you do for her?'

'It's tricky getting a line into her. Her veins are just so small, and the venflon needles are too big.'

'It's either Qalat Salih or she's "panners",' Al Roan said. Passmore, Kelly and Gidalla looked confused because his expression was derived from Scottish rhyming slang: pan bread, dead. Sharing his sentiment at least, they nodded. Al was against putting his soldiers' lives at risk for the sake of one Iraqi child. But, at the same time, he knew he could not live with himself if they just left her to die. There was no thought for their own safety; Passmore, Kelly and Gidalla were already planning the order of march into Qalat Salih. Al was struck by their humanity. He considered his war-weary soldiers a credit to the British Army.

The Condorites approached the town in two Land-Rovers. Doddsy and the junior Royal Army Medical Corps medic stayed in the mini-van.

'Fuck!'

'What is it, Doddsy?' The other medic was the youth Kelly had briefly befriended in Canterbury when he had been injured.

'This is a fucking nightmare. I can't get a cannula into her when we're bumping around. Are we doin' the Dakar Rally or something? I've had to wrap a tourniquet around her arm a few times just to get a vein. Then every time I get one, it just fucking collapses.'

'Keep tryin', mate.'

'She does this thing where when she's conscious she flicks her arm away from me when I put the needle anywhere near her. At least I know she's alive then. She comes around for a bit, then she goes . . .'

It was the worst feeling in the world: holding this little girl with her black hair and soft skin as she teetered on the threshold of existence. Another heat-hazed day was about to dawn. Doddsy doubted she would live to see it. Her eyes held his whenever she fleetingly opened them. They were dark brown, like chocolate.

A passenger in one of the Land-Rovers, Wellsy's hands fastened around his weapon. Chill feelings revisited him: he had hoped not to see this town again. His tour was to end where it had begun, here in this bandit town. They stopped and formed a cordon around the entrance to the hospital.

The seconds lengthened as Wellsy crouched beside the wagon, scanning the rooftops. He knew them well enough to point to where he had got his kill. This was not a memory he revisited with any sense of triumph, not that morning. He and the other sentries glanced nervously around. Any noise given off by their movements might arouse the natives. It was still dark – but only just.

Doddsy felt the moist, warm blood on his hands as he passed the child to the doctor. He was reluctant to leave her. How was he to cope with not knowing her fate? He felt bitterness deep inside. How could the Iraqis call a couple of fluid racks, two steel beds and one basically proficient medical professional a hospital? There was not a sterilised surface in sight, and the staff looked as if they had never seen a white coat. The doctor unravelled Doddsy's bandages to reveal the baby's wounds for himself. She was motionless and silent.

'We've got to go now,' Kelly said, pointing to the door.

Doddsy's eyes flashed from the girl to James Passmore standing in the doorway. He was as anxious as Kelly to leave.

'What? No, no, we can't,' Doddsy pleaded. 'We can't leave her here!'

'Come on, we have not got any choice,' said Kelly, his sympathy laced with self-preservation. 'It's too dangerous around here.'

'We can't fuckin' leave her, Paul!' Doddsy said, raising his voice. 'There's fuck all here! They haven't got anything!'

'Just give them your medical kit, then – any spares.'

Doddsy shook out the contents of his 'med bag' and combed through the bandages, tapes, field dressings, needles and fluid bags. 'Christ,' he thought, 'I bet he's never seen kit like this.' He pushed the items across the bed. The doctor picked a few up, inspected them and put them back down again.

Kelly guided Doddsy outside by his arm. They reached Shaibah and then Britain some days later. Every time he closed his eyes, Doddsy saw her face.

19

Route 6 Revisited

James Dormer was decommissioned in mid 2006. As a civilian eyeing a career in private banking in the City, he recalled with some admiration how the Iranian security services had bought off several of the 'tier-one personalities' in Maysan: tribal leaders, police and legal figures. This was a tactic he believed the British should have adopted: 'If we had spent a couple of million pounds judiciously and quickly, we could have saved a lot of blood and treasure in the long run.'

Looking back, it was particularly disheartening for James to witness the breakdown of relations with the locals, as the heavy-handed tactics of Coalition Forces and poor planning came into play. 'At the beginning we did the Northern Ireland routine of soft-hats on, shaking hands with people and going into shops,' he recalled, 'but I remember spending one evening on a road checkpoint as part of the cordon operation around Al Amarah.

'A Challenger tank came speeding past followed by 15 Warrior armoured vehicles and then another tank bringing up the rear. The noise was thunderous as they headed into the city. Then, overhead, a US Spectre gunship arrived. There was this incredible pounding as it delivered its ordnance. It was an incredible sight, but walking down the streets with people and shaking hands simply isn't going to work once you have done something like that – there's no rowing back. So none of us were surprised by the complete breakdown in relations.

'I would not go as far with blaming the PWRR battlegroup,

because before they arrived you had the Light Infantry rinsing villages and being very aggressive. The very bloody battle of Qalat Salih happened on their watch. As it all went sour, we did not have enough men on the ground, engineers in particular, to accelerate the process of reconstruction. We failed to persuade the local people to take our side. What was in it for them? Very little. Improvements were not occurring fast enough. There were insufficient infanteers on the ground to protect the engineers as well. The upshot was that relations broke down completely, and it became increasingly difficult to make progress with the ICDC. They did not want to take sides and blamed the British for the increased bloodshed.'

Members of 6 Platoon who had been seconded to the Argylls at Condor rejoined the PWRR. Those rejoining the 2nd Battalion (2 PWRR) had the worst of it, as the unit had yet to deploy to Iraq. One soldier, who preferred to remain anonymous, said, 'If anyone wanted to know anything about it, they would ask you questions, like "Did you kill anyone?" and "Was it shit?" You did not want to talk about it, you just wanted to go away and get drunk. The senior NCOs were the worst – those that had been in for 20 years and never seen any firefights. Miserable bastards. They had a look of disgust in their eyes, as if to say, "Why wasn't it me who was out there getting that?" If I had waited that long, I would have felt the same, but they did not have to make us suffer for it.'

Paul Kelly suggested to the 2 PWRR Sergeants' Mess that he talk the non-commisioned officers through the major firefights as a 'lessons learned' session. But his Military Cross and mood swings had made him a pariah. 'They didn't want to know,' Kelly explained. 'The enemy did not always do what we anticipated they would. I tried telling them that.'

The old warrior sensed his army career was drawing to

a close. He deployed again with 2 PWRR to Iraq but was confined to the storeroom.

'It saddened us the way the PWRR treated Paul,' said one of his privates. 'We had a whip-round to buy him a leaving present, but the other NCOs did not want to know. He was our dad in Iraq, and I don't think we would all have made it home if he was not as strong as he was.'

Kelly and his family at least had the pleasure of receiving his gallantry medal from Her Majesty the Queen at Buckingham Palace. Posing for photographers with Jack in his arms, he looked almost content. Griffiths and Gray had done Kelly proud with his citation:

Military Cross citation for Sergeant Paul Kelly (period covered 18 January to 10 March 2004)

Sergeant Kelly is the platoon sergeant of the platoon from the Princess of Wales's Royal Regiment (PWRR) attached to the 1st Battalion, the Argyll and Sutherland Highlanders. In January 2004 Sergeant Kelly found himself as the platoon sergeant of a platoon of Argylls and PWRR soldiers based at the isolated Camp Condor in the south of the notoriously lawless Maysan Province. Twice during his abridged tour he found himself commanding Argylls in the most demanding, dangerous, chaotic and life-threatening situations. His conspicuous gallantry and exemplary leadership when under heavy and sustained fire, and latterly when wounded, displayed all the hallmarks of a brave and inspirational leader.

On 11 February 2004 Sergeant Kelly was tasked to conduct a joint vehicle patrol with some soldiers of the local Iraqi Civil Defence Corps (ICDC) company. At approximately 1825 the patrol stopped on the main road in the area of previous hijackings. Stones had been placed across the road. Sergeant Kelly walked to the front ICDC vehicle to assess the situation. As he reached the vehicle, a heavy weight of automatic fire was received from the west. Sergeant Kelly took cover and under heavy incoming fire issued clear and decisive orders to his men, who all engaged the enemy whilst firing illumination flares and 40 mm grenades to win the firefight. Several hundred rounds were fired by the patrol in this engagement to suppress the enemy. As the firefight was being won, and with little regard for his own safety, Sergeant Kelly seized the initiative and led a rapid and decisive charge towards one of the enemy positions. Together with some of his men, he there apprehended two armed bandits. Subsequently, they received long jail sentences from the local judge, who conveyed his appreciation to Sergeant Kelly and his men for their brave action in apprehending the gang and starting to bring peace to the area.

On 5 March 2004 a Light Infantry patrol in the village of Qalat Salih requested assistance in making a number of arrests following a shooting incident. At 1330 Sergeant Kelly deployed into the village with a patrol. Sometime after arriving, the situation exploded into a crescendo of violence, with local tribesmen engaging Coalition Forces with machine guns, rocket-propelled grenades (RPG) and small arms. Sergeant Kelly was shot through the hand in this initial action, and his Land Rover was destroyed by 2 RPGs, wounding an Argylls soldier. Despite being in severe pain, Sergeant Kelly rallied his men in the confusion of this initial engagement and set up a strong-point in a building. There, he and his men fought an exhaustive close-quarter battle for over five hours. The enemy repeatedly attacked the position from three sides with intensive and unusually accurate light and heavy machine-gun fire, RPGs, grenades and satchel charges of explosives. Sergeant Kelly soon expended all his six magazines of ammunition and his 40 mm grenades. He then switched to using a captured AK47 semi-automatic rifle and a 9 mm pistol. Firing with his good arm, he hit and killed several enemy combatants during this period. He also organised his men into shifts of firing, ammunition re-supply and looking after the five casualties. He proved to be an inspiration to all those around him throughout this chaotic and adrenalin-charged battle. Once armoured reinforcements arrived, Sergeant Kelly was extracted to safety and was then moved by helicopter to the Field Hospital at Shaibah Logistics Base, where he refused treatment until word was received that there were no more casualties in his platoon.

He then underwent emergency surgery. He was subsequently evacuated to the UK for further surgery and recuperation.

Sergeant Kelly's first act of gallantry and exemplary leadership under heavy fire resulted in the arrest of two members of a violent gang, probably responsible for numerous murders, rapes and vehicle hijackings in the area. His second act of gallantry, whilst wounded in one of the biggest engagements of the campaign, was truly inspirational to those around him. His remarkable leadership, selfless commitment and conspicuous gallantry are most worthy of the highest official recognition.

Jay Lawrence, by contrast, received no recognition for his actions on Danny Boy day. This disappointed some, given that he had single-handedly stormed a position. Nor did Major Jim 'Danger' Faux after the siege of Qalat Salih. This perhaps suggested that somebody, somewhere, blamed him.

The worst aspect of battalion life for the ex-Condorites was going on exercise, as one junior soldier explained: 'Blank firing just didn't do it for me any more. Live ranges were just boring after two-way ranges. It's sick, but I used to get excited about exercises – it was always better than doing shit around camp. Getting dirty – getting amongst it. But it was different after Iraq. For the first 48 hours in the field I was still buzzing, because I was out on the ground doing something. But then you would realise that it was not going to be as good, that it was going to be another buckshee exercise, firing blank rounds at targets that don't do anything. And then, if it was live, which was rare, it was just not the same feeling. Nothing was going to happen. I knew I was going to fire at the same wooden target for about two miles with someone saying "You can't fire there because you are too close to your mate" or "You can't fire there because it's out of arcs", and then you would post your grenade into a pre-determined position which was really, really obviously sited and then everything would stop. What would happen after that? Nothing. It was end-ex and we would all go home for tea and medals. It just seemed like a waste of time.

'You could not really be taught again how to do a section attack or clear a position once you had done it for real in Iraq – tuition was pointless. Soldiers snapped. You could not tell them after the firefights they had been in what was and what was not a stable firing position.'

Kev Challis served half of a 12-month sentence after pleading guilty to attempting to supply cocaine. The judge at his trial suggested his battalion could have done more to help him. He received counselling for post-traumatic stress disorder and used his stint in the glasshouse as an opportunity to reassess his life. He had experienced a lot for a 22 year old. He signed off from the army but remained close to many Condorites.

Having both signed off, Wellsy left Keegs to nurse his still-sore testicles when he deployed to Afghanistan as a reservist in November 2006. He was army barmy after all. Keegs worked on the docks in Gravesend.

Paul Kelly joined the likes of Neneh and Hendy on the private security circuit in Afghanistan. He joked that once he had paid off his mortgage, he would get a job pushing trolleys at his local supermarket. At least people hoped he was joking. The customers of the Canterbury branch of Asda might not be ready for him.

ACKNOWLEDGEMENTS

I wish to thank all the soldiers who contributed to *Condor Blues*, as well as my family, friends and those who assisted editorially, Jonathan Mantle and Paul Murphy in particular. I am also grateful to Andrew Lownie and Bill Campbell.

I hope this book was as entertaining as it was informative and that I captured the humour and the courage of the leading characters. For obvious reasons I cannot thank you all by name, but special mention should go to James Dormer, Hendy, Al Roan, Neneh, Keegs, Kev and Wellsy. I hope I have presented an accurate and reflective account of your tour.

I am also indebted to Jonny Gray for his aerial overview of Iraq as a British commander plunged into such a demanding situation.

I offer my last and deepest expression of gratitude to Paul Kelly.